FRAUD

The Strategy Behind The Bush Lies
And Why The Media Didn't Tell You

PAUL WALDMAN

SOURCEBOOKS, INC.
NAPERVILLE, ILLINOIS

This publication is designed to provide accurate and authoritative information
in regard to the subject matter covered. It is sold with the understanding that
the publisher is not engaged in rendering legal, accounting, or other professional
service. If legal advice or other expert assistance is required, the services of a
competent professional person should be sought.—*From a Declaration of
Principles Jointly Adopted by a Committee of the American Bar Association and a
Committee of Publishers and Associations*

Published by Sourcebooks, Inc.
P.O. Box 4410, Naperville, Illinois 60567-4410
(630) 961-3900
FAX: (630) 961-2168
www.sourcebooks.com

Library of Congress Cataloging-in-Publication Data

Waldman, Paul.
Fraud: the strategy behind the Bush lies and why the media didn't tell you /
by Paul Waldman.
p. cm.
Includes index.
ISBN 1-4022-0252-0 (alk. paper)
1. United States—Politics and government—2001–. 2. Mass
media—Political aspects—United States. 3. Bush, George W. (George
Walker), 1946– I. Title.
E901 .W35 2004
973.931—dc22

2003023239

Printed and bound in the United States of America.
QW 10 9 8 7 6 5 4 3 2 1

For Jem

Contents

"Whenever the people are well-informed,
they can be trusted with their own government."
—*Thomas Jefferson*

"Democracy is a device that insures
we shall be governed no better than we deserve."
—*George Bernard Shaw*

"If you tell a lie big enough and keep repeating it,
people will eventually come to believe it. The
lie can be maintained only for such time as
the State can shield the people from the
political, economic and military consequences of the lie. It thus becomes
vitally important for the State to use
all of its powers to repress dissent,
for the truth is the mortal enemy
of the lie, and thus by extension,
the truth is the greatest enemy of
the State"
—Joseph Goebbels—

Introduction

The unfortunate truth is this: George W. Bush is a fraud.

From the moment he arrived on the national scene, George W. Bush has been telling us how honest he is, and for just as long—despite the ever-mounting evidence for the opposite conclusion—most Americans, even many of those who oppose him politically, have agreed. He may be unqualified and of questionable competence, and he may have a retrograde agenda, but at least he's honest. However, this belief is entirely false. As Thomas Paine wrote, "a long habit of not thinking a thing *wrong* gives it a superficial appearance of being *right*, and raises at first a formidable outcry in defense of custom."[1] Bush's supporters will no doubt raise such an outcry at the assertion that Bush is fundamentally dishonest, but as you will see, the facts speak for themselves.

What Bush and his advisers have perpetrated is nothing short of a fraud—and an epic one at that—that started when they began planning his ascension to the White House in the early 1990s and continues to the present day. The fraud involves the propagation of a set of central lies about Bush, each carefully crafted and spoken with a numbing repetition. He and his compatriots have known from the beginning that if the lies are asserted often enough, they will stand despite being refuted on a continual basis by Bush's actions. They have said that George W. Bush is an ordinary guy, that he believes in American values, that he loves freedom and democracy, that he is compassionate, that he brings Democrats and

---

[1] Thomas Paine, *Common Sense*, p. 3.

Republicans together, and above all, that he is a man of great character and integrity. Each of these contentions is demonstrably untrue, but each has nonetheless been often accepted by the press and largely accepted by the American people, including a healthy portion of those who voted against Bush in 2000 and plan to do so again in 2004.

Contrary to what he seems to never tire of assuring us, George W. Bush is not a man of integrity; in fact, he ranks among the most dishonest presidents in American history. For this president, lying is only sometimes done ad hoc, as a reaction to an unexpected question or a discomforting criticism. But most often it is the essence of his political strategy, the key to every major policy move. Whether the topic is taxes or Social Security, the environment or education, Medicare or foreign wars, the aggressive deception of the American people is the foundation on which each Bush policy is built. He consistently deceives the American people by masking his agenda in a carefully constructed cloud of misleading rhetoric, pleasing pictures, disingenuous displays of emotions unfelt, and outright lies.

We have seen in recent years how anger at political opponents can all too easily devolve into the belief that those one opposes are not merely wrong but positively evil. I make no such claim about George W. Bush. While he has a multitude of shortcomings as a president and a person, Bush is not evil. He believes, as all of us do, that he's trying to do the right thing. He often lies, but that does not mean that he is incapable of telling the truth. His policies are often ill-considered and detrimental to the goals he claims to espouse, but this does not mean that he does not occasionally make a good decision or two. So why would he choose this path of deception?

At some point, George W. Bush took a good long look at who he was and what he wanted for the country and decided that the American people would never buy it if he gave it to them straight. He came to understand that they would never elect to the highest office in the land a man of such limited skills who had been given so much and accomplished so little, whose claim to power rested solely on his last name, who was so plainly hostile to the values on which their nation was founded. They would never assent to a reactionary agenda whose every element was opposed by a majority of Americans. They would never knowingly elect someone whose most passionate convictions lay in enhancing the wealth of the wealthy and the power of the powerful.

So Bush and his political machine made their decision: the American people would have to be lied to. They would construct a persona that would be everything Bush was not. They would take the same old Republican agenda and cloak it in comforting catch-phrases and pleasing visuals, presenting to the public a false image of sympathy. And they would repeat this message endlessly.

The project isn't an easy one, and it requires sustained effort and plenty of money. How do you convince working people that unions are a threat to them? Or that making sure everyone has medical coverage is a bad idea? Or that the only way to respond to a poor economy is to give the largest tax cuts to the wealthiest among us? Or that investment income should be taxed at a lower rate than wage income, money people actually work for? Or that working people are a "special interest," while corporations are not? Or that a man who has a former president for a father and a former senator for a grandfather, whose entire life has been graced by wealth and privilege, is just an ordinary guy? It is hard to do so by being honest. The only way to pull off such a feat is to build lie upon lie, always keeping the media and the people deceived and off-balance.

During the Clinton impeachment, Republicans argued that one could not separate the private man from the public official, that if Clinton committed adultery and wouldn't admit it, then he was unfit to remain in office. A lie about one's personal life, they said, was just as consequential as a lie about a policy matter. Democrats countered that the two could be separate; while none defended

Clinton's personal integrity, they argued that it was irrelevant to evaluating his performance as president. Republicans tried to convince the country that what a president did with the powers of his office was less important than whom he was sleeping with, an argument the American people sensibly rejected.

We might consider Bill Clinton a dishonest person but a relatively honest politician. His ideological proclamations were a fair summary of the policies he actually ended up pursuing, and even his opponents would have a hard time finding a lie he told on a significant policy matter. George W. Bush, on the other hand, is just the opposite: someone who may well be honest in his personal life but is *not* when it comes to public policy, the things that actually affect the American people.

On this, the evidence is clear: George W. Bush is a profoundly dishonest politician. He has lied to the American people about matters large and small, but mostly large. Whether he is honest in his personal life we don't know, although I have no reason to doubt that he is faithful to his wife and loyal to his friends. Bush does not appear to have given us any reason to invade his bedroom. But when he lies to us about policy, telling us he wants what we want in order to achieve exactly the opposite, it is a profound betrayal of his office and our trust.

"Disagree with me, fine," begged Bush during the 2000 campaign, "but do not challenge my integrity."[2] Bush's integrity is precisely the issue.

EXECUTING THE FRAUD

The fact that most people consider George W. Bush to be so honest represents both a remarkable feat of political dexterity on his part and a dramatic failure on the part of the journalists on whom Americans rely. When Gary Hart was confronted with rumors of infidelity during his 1988 campaign for the White House, he challenged reporters to follow him around to see if the rumors were true. Unfortunately for

---

[2] Campaign advertisement, 2000 South Carolina primary.

Hart, one newspaper took him up on the offer.[3] Bush issued a similar challenge, asserting again and again that the very reason for his candidacy was that he was a man of honesty and integrity, so different from the man then sitting in the White House. But while reporters were consumed with the question of whether he was smart enough to occupy the Oval Office, they largely ignored the far more important question of whether Bush is in fact a man of integrity. Instead, many simply accepted his assurances as fact and continue to do so to this day.

The notion that Bush isn't too smart is key to how the Bush machine has manipulated the media, and thereby the American people, into ignoring his dishonesty. The one area where Bush has received plenty of criticism from neutral observers, sometimes even devolving into ridicule, is that of his lack of felicity with his mother tongue. Bush has been lampooned a great deal for his malapropisms, and there is no doubt they are amusing. But they also serve to distract us by leading us to view Bush as merely a comic figure. Although he may sometimes say foolish things, Bush is no fool. He is a shrewd political strategist who has managed again and again to compile political victories while maintaining the impression that he is possessed of minimal skills and thus each deft move, no matter how small, should be hailed as an extraordinary accomplishment.

The image of Bush as an amiable dunce started as a liability, eventually turned into an asset, and quickly became a strategy. Nicholas Lemann reported this clever remark from the Bush campaign bus in New Hampshire: "'I haven't unleashed my great line yet, which is that my mother taught me not to be a know-it-all.' (Pause for a perfect beat, quick innocent glance around the room.) 'I didn't let her down.'"[4] Even while calling attention to the artifice and calculation behind his words, Bush offers a little insouciant smile that says, "Is this a great act, or what?" We are all supposed to laugh along with him.

---

[3] Hart challenged them this way: "Follow me around. I don't care. I'm serious. If anybody wants to put a tail on me, go ahead. They'd be very bored." The *Miami Herald* then staked out his house, whereupon they saw a young woman named Donna Rice entering and leaving the house. "Newspaper Reports Weekend Guest at Hart's Townhouse," Associated Press, May 3, 1987.

[4] Nicholas Lemann, "The Redemption." *New Yorker*, January 31, 2000.

Bush and his people realized that reporters had decided that Bush was incapable of lying, because if he said something untrue it must have been that he made a mistake or was too dumb to know what the truth was. "The story line is Bush isn't smart enough and Gore isn't straight enough," said Cokie Roberts during the 2000 campaign by way of explaining the post-debate coverage that savaged Gore and let Bush off the hook for the multiple lies he had told. "In Bush's case, you know he's just misstating as opposed to it playing into a story line about him being a serial exaggerator."[5] It didn't "feel" like a lie. Since Roberts "knew" that when Bush said something untrue "he's just misstating" as opposed to intentionally lying, she and her colleagues felt the need neither to correct the misinformation nor inform citizens that Bush had lied to them. The cascade of falsehoods issued from the White House once Bush took office did nothing to change reporters' minds.

There may be no fraud on the people and the press that Bush carried out more shamelessly and with greater success than his war on Iraq. From the shifting justifications Bush offered for launching the war (first it was an imminent Iraqi invasion of the US with its arsenal of weapons of mass destruction, then Saddam Hussein's supposed relationship with al-Qaeda, then the freedom of the Iraqi people) to the fabricated evidence offered as "proof" of fictitious Iraqi nuclear weapons to the absurd notion, offered repeatedly, that the president had not made up his mind to invade until the last minute, the White House looked Americans in the eye and lied to them again and again. They knew that once the bullets started flying, Americans would heed the instruction to "support the troops" by supporting the president, and any who raised questions could be quickly quieted with accusations of insufficient patriotism.

But more than anything else, Bush knew he could play the media like a violin. To paraphrase the apocryphal quote attributed to William Randolph Hearst, the White House supplied both the pictures and the war, and the press went along as they were told,

---

[5] Howard Kurtz, "Bush Team Devised Truth Trap That's Tripping Gore," *Washington Post*, October 16, 2000, p. A11.

offering paeans to the heroic commander in chief. Once the fighting was over, the American taxpayers even chipped in a million or so dollars (exactly how much it cost, the administration refused to say) to produce footage for Bush 2004 campaign commercials. On May 1, 2003, Bush was flown out to the aircraft carrier *Abraham Lincoln* to deliver a perfunctory speech declaring victory and situating Iraq firmly within the war on terrorism. The real point of the trip was the staging of Bush landing on the carrier in an S3B Viking naval aircraft, then hopping out in his dashing flight suit (the landing would later be commemorated with the sale of a Bush action figure). The networks complied by not only showing the event live but replaying shots of Bush in the flight suit again and again. All noted that Bush was a real pilot, since he had flown in the National Guard; few were so rude as to mention that he got his safe spot in the Guard through family connections and that he was AWOL from the Guard for more than a year. Later, the White House would distribute ID tags for reporters to wear featuring a shot of Bush in the flight suit.[6]

The administration told reporters that it was necessary for Bush to take a plane to the carrier instead of flying on the Marine One helicopter because the carrier would be hundreds of miles out at sea, out of the helicopter's range. This turned out to be a lie; in fact, the carrier was only thirty-nine miles from San Diego when Bush landed. But had he taken the helicopter, there would have been no reason for him to don the flight suit, and the photos of him hanging out with the sailors wouldn't have been quite as good. Of course, the carrier's position was shifted to avoid having the California coast visible to the cameras so the deception could proceed.[7] After the administration finally owned up to the fact they had lied to the press, that same press predictably failed to find the courage to write that the administration had lied to them and through them to the American people. Instead, the *New York Times* headline read, "White House Clarifies Bush's

---

[6] Howard Kurtz, "The Reportage Report," *Washington Post*, September 8, 2003, p. C1.
[7] Scott Lindlaw, "Accommodating TV-Friendly Presidential Visit Caused a Few Changes in Navy Carrier's Routine," Associated Press, May 2, 2003.

Carrier Landing,"[8] an act of editorial spinelessness so pathetic it must have been greeted with howls of triumphant laughter in the West Wing.

The lengthy string of lies on which support for the Iraq war was built was only the latest case in a history of deception that dates from the beginning of George W. Bush's emergence into public life. In order to understand all of the Bush fraud we have to examine its history as well as its present incarnation. And part of Bush's genius is that he seems to imbue the journalists who are supposed to act as watchdogs with a kind of collective amnesia, as context is banished and nearly every story seems to play out exactly as he would want. Like Obi-wan Kenobi calmly saying, "These aren't the droids you're looking for," Bush and his machine seem to have only to assert a reality as they would like it to be, and reporters accept and repeat it as truth. Bush can portray a tax cut for the wealthy as a "jobs program," describe his attempts to dismantle Medicare as a move to "strengthen" it, or launch a war with a series of shifting and blatantly disingenuous rationales, all while being described as a man of admirable forthrightness. Lies go by unexposed, administration-wide incompetence and failure is ignored, stunning hypocrisy is praised as astute politics, and the fraud of the Bush presidency continues apace.

THE BUSH MACHINE IN ACTION

The operation of the Bush fraud is implemented by a large, complex, and highly competent political machine situated within the White House and the Republican National Committee. While the Clinton administration was criticized for engaging in the "permanent campaign," Bush's may be the most political administration in history. Of course, there's nothing inherently wrong with being political. What is irksome is Bush and his administration's endless insistence that they never consider the political implications of anything, that neither Bush nor anyone who works for him cares about polls, that anyone who criticizes them is being "partisan"—something they would

---

[8] Richard Stevenson, "White House Clarifies Bush's Carrier Landing," *New York Times*, May 7, 2003.

never stoop to. As former White House Press Secretary Ari Fleischer said just after Bush took office, "The president's actions and his words are supported by all but the most partisan Americans."[9]

So even the most blatantly political moves are presented with assurances that politics never entered anyone's mind. For instance, six days before the 2002 midterm elections, the White House staged a "radio day," in which fifty mostly conservative radio hosts were brought to the White House lawn and set up under a tent with recording equipment to interview senior administration staffers and cabinet secretaries, who took time away from their duties to speak to Oliver North and Sean Hannity, among others. "I just don't see a political component to it at all," said a White House spokesman.[10]

In that same election campaign, more than three hundred administration officials were dispatched to close House and Senate races around the country; at least some were told by the White House that they "needed to show their Republican credentials"—in other words, prove their loyalty (and hold on to their jobs) by taking vacation time to work for Republican candidates.[11] Cabinet secretaries and high-ranking officials from virtually every department traveled the country holding public events promoting government programs, each of which just happened to prominently feature a Republican candidate engaged in a close race (all paid for by taxpayers). In 2002 Bush raised $142 million for Republican candidates, obliterating the fundraising records Bill Clinton had set when he came under such harsh criticism for a seemingly endless quest for money.

John DiIulio, who served as the head of Bush's effort to direct federal money to religious groups, said after leaving the White House, "There is no precedent in any modern White House for what is going on in this one: a complete lack of a policy apparatus. What you've got is everything—and I mean everything—

[9] Mike Allen, "Bush on Stage: Deft or Just Lacking Depth?" *Washington Post*, February 19, 2001, p. A8.
[10] Jennifer Loven, "White House Welcomes Radio Hosts," Associated Press, October 30, 2002.
[11] Mike Allen, "Bush Enlists Government in GOP Campaign," *Washington Post*, October 24, 2002, p. A8.

being run by the political arm."[12] (DiIulio's experience shows what happens to you if you cross Bush's White House, even if you've already left. The next day, administration spokesman Ari Fleischer said DiIulio's charges were "baseless and groundless." A few hours later, DiIulio himself obediently apologized to the White House and recanted, saying his previous comments were "groundless and baseless."[13]) The most influential person in the Bush White House is not a policy advisor, not even the vice president or the chief of staff, but Karl Rove, the political consultant who engineered Bush's rise to power.

In the same *Esquire* article for which DiIulio made his comments, reporter Ron Suskind spoke to a number of White House officials who agreed to talk off the record. "You have to understand, this administration is further to the right than much of the public understands," said one. "The view of many people [in the White House] is that the best government can do is simply do no harm, that it never is an agent for positive change. If that's your position, why bother to understand what programs actually do?" Another official Suskind described as "an honored member of the political Right with a flawless conservative pedigree" told him, "There has been no domestic policy" in the Bush White House. "Not even a pretense of it." He went on, "We got into the White House and forfeited the game. You're supposed to stand for something...to generate sound ideas, support them with real evidence, and present them to Congress and the people. We didn't do any of that. We just danced this way and that on minute political calculations and whatever was needed for a few paragraphs of a speech."[14]

The result of this dance is a reasonably high level of public approval and a shockingly low level of actual accomplishment. There is little doubt that the Bush administration is extraordinarily good at keeping

---

[12] Allen, "Ex-Official Blasts White House," *Washington Post*, December 2, 2002, p. A7.
[13] Dana Milbank, "DiIulio Saga Highlights Primacy Placed on Secrecy," *Washington Post*, December 10, 2002, p. A27.
[14] Ron Suskind, "Why Are These Men Laughing?" *Esquire*, January 2003.

people in line, extraordinarily good at message discipline, extraordinarily good at handling scandals—in short, extraordinarily good at politics. But they are extraordinarily bad at policy. They have won a series of political victories while failing to accomplish anything that might actually improve Americans' lives. George W. Bush has run the country like he ran his oil companies—into the ground. Virtually everything he has done has been a failure. Economy? Worst job-creation record since the Depression. Federal budget? From the largest surpluses in American history to the largest deficits in American history. Health care? Nothing done about the forty million Americans without health insurance. Patient's Bill of Rights? Nothing. War on terrorism? Osama Bin Laden still at large; Afghanistan returned to chaos; anthrax attacker uncaught; and American ports, chemical plants, and nuclear facilities still desperately vulnerable.

I would not attempt to catalogue every reprehensible thing George W. Bush's administration has done in its brief time in power, since such an effort would require a book whose length would tax the patience of Evelyn Wood herself. When congressional Democrats decided to assemble a list of Bush administration actions that had harmed the environment in its first two years it stretched for thirty-two feet.[15] Examine the websites of groups opposed to the Bush agenda and you will find lengthy lists of Bush horrors committed against working people, women, the environment, and on and on. But simply knowing what Bush has done will lead us nowhere unless we understand how and why he has accomplished these deeds. These elements form the foundation of the Bush presidency, a campaign to manipulate the media and mislead the American people about George W. Bush, the person and the president.

EXPOSING THE FRAUD

Those who raise questions about the ambitions and motives of the current administration will with utter predictability have their patriotism questioned by Bush's supporters. They contend, explicitly and

---

[15] Mark Sherman, "Senate Democrats Rap White House Environmental Policies," Associated Press, January 16, 2003.

implicitly, that the measure of one's love for America is the vigor with which one waves the flag—and the degree to which one assents to anything and everything the president wants to do. But anyone can wave the flag. True American patriotism is far more difficult. It requires of citizens everything that Bush wants us to cast off as unnecessary: being informed, asking questions, engaging in active citizenship, and believing not that America is perfect but that America can always be better.

When we look back on our history, whom do we see as the true patriots? Is it those who proclaimed their love of America in the loudest voice, or those who stood up for freedom and in the process nudged America closer to its ideals? Who was the greater patriot, J. Edgar Hoover or the man he believed was a communist, Martin Luther King Jr.? One demanded an unquestioning obedience to government and sought to enforce it by keeping citizens under surveillance, blackmailing officials, and treating all dissent as subversion. The other defied unjust laws and cast a light on his country's failings. Who did more for America?

The personal and national triumphalism Bush propagates in both foreign and domestic affairs is antidemocratic because it assumes that America—and by extension the government—has a moral perfection that makes its actions unquestionably right. America has been blessed by God, they say, and so too has Bush been chosen by God to lead it. Bush and his underlings continually argue not merely that Bush is right but that no reasonable person could disagree with Bush; doing so is *prima facie* evidence of bad motives.

The American system, in contrast, assumes the eternal *imperfection* of the political order, that no leader or policy is beyond question and criticism and debate. It assumes a constant reexamination and evolution through the input of the citizenry. That is what we call democracy. Those who charge people with treason or lack of patriotism whenever they criticize Bush's actions fail to understand that demanding unthinking obedience to the president is itself the most un-American of acts. Americans are not a people bound by place of birth or even shared history; we are bound by a set of principles, none higher than the idea that no government is above questioning and criticism. As Lyndon Johnson said, "It is the common failing of total-itarian regimes that they cannot really understand the nature of our democracy. They mistake dissent for disloyalty."

The Bush White House has hidden its motives and actions in complex bills and simplistic rhetoric aimed at misleading the media and the public. It is therefore incumbent upon us—our patriotic duty, in fact—to periodically glance back at what he has said and done, to jog our memories and shake away the cobwebs obstructing our vision. As Bush himself said, "A lot of times in the rhetoric, peo-ple forget the facts."[16] But the problem is not so much that people forget the facts but that Bush's rhetoric is constructed with the intention that people will ignore the facts or never learn them at all. Ignorance, inattentiveness, and indifference are Bush's greatest polit-ical allies. He nurtures them and depends on them, for without them he would be lost. Only by wading through the rhetoric to find the facts, identifying and understanding the lies, and examining both the forest and the trees, can we see this president and this pres-idency for what they truly are.

---

[16] Speech to the Hispanic Chamber of Commerce, Washington, D.C., March 19, 2001.

1.

Just a Good Old Boy, Never Meanin' No Harm

Constructing the Myth of "Dubya"

Before a press conference in August 2002 at the Bush estate in Crawford, Texas, workers brought in hay bales to cover up the propane tanks sitting in camera view, the better to give the impression that the president was a real old-time rancher. But what is the truth? Bush had purchased the spread just before the 2000 campaign.[1] The hay-bale tableau was in many ways a perfect metaphor for the persona of George W. Bush himself: artifice intended not only to conceal reality, but to give the impression that Bush is "real," a simulation of authenticity itself.

The popular perception is that George W. Bush is just a "regular guy"—unpretentious, friendly, likes country music and peanut butter and jelly sandwiches, not some high-fallutin' know-it-all who thinks he's better 'n other folks. But this image is a persona. This first step of the fraud was carefully constructed over the years to deal with one of the key difficulties facing members of the Bush dynasty. After all, we are talking about a man afforded advantages available to literally but a few dozen Americans, who walked on a path paved with the priceless cobblestones of influence and wealth, who earned so little in life but was given so much. When Bush's father was defeated in 1992 in large part because of his perceived inability to

[1] Adam Nagourney and Thom Shanker, "A 'Patient' Bush Says He'll Weigh All Iraq Options," *New York Times*, August 22, 2002, p. A1.

understand the struggles of ordinary people, the son's advisers understood that a man with George W.'s particular combination of experience and skills could hardly be presented to the public as a model of empathy. So as the scion of the Bush dynasty was prepared for his entry into public life, he was burnished with a down-home gloss, and a new man was created. The creation of this persona came off virtually without a hitch.

So who is George W. Bush? To hear him tell it, he's a real Texas cowboy with big boots, big belt buckles, and a big ranch. He doesn't speak too well, but he says what he means and means what he says. Unlike them other politicians, Bush said in 1999, "I've never lived in Washington in my life."[2] (This, by the way, was a lie; in 1987 Bush moved his family to Washington, D.C., for a year and a half so he could work on his father's campaign.[3])

While some of the details may be phony and some may be false, the package comes off very convincingly. And the continuing success of Bush's regular-guy routine is what makes it less likely that reporters will question its veracity. Though they strike a cynical pose, assuming that all politics is artifice, nothing yields higher praise than an image successfully constructed. "Just as TV decries photo-opportunity and sound-bite campaigning yet builds the news around them," wrote communication scholar Daniel Hallin, "so it decries the culture of the campaign consultant, with its emphasis on technique over substance, yet adopts that culture as its own."[4] The candidate who falls off a stage (as Bob Dole did during the 1996 campaign) or holds a press conference with improper lighting will become the object of scorn, while the one who performs in a flawless photo-op will find reporters praising the skill of his operation.

Among the consequences is that reporters will often ignore real evidence about public opinion in favor of their gut feelings about

---

[2] *NBC Nightly News*, June 12, 1999.
[3] Bill Minutaglio, *First Son: George W. Bush and the Bush Family Dynasty*. New York: Three Rivers Press, 2001.
[4] Daniel Hallin, "Sound-Bite News: Television Coverage of Elections, 1968-1988," *Journal of Communication* 42:5-24 (1992).

how image-making is received. Nowhere can this be seen more clearly than in the way reporters view another Republican president, Ronald Reagan. It is commonly accepted and reported that Reagan was a spectacularly popular president who basked in the warm glow of Americans' affections for eight years. But though it gets repeated again and again, this idea is false. When stacked up against other presidents, Reagan's popularity was decidedly mediocre. What are the facts? He averaged an approval rating of 52 percent over the course of his presidency—better than Carter, Ford, Nixon, and Truman but worse than Clinton, George H.W. Bush, Johnson, Kennedy, and Eisenhower. Reagan's best approval of 68 percent was bested at some point by *every* president since polling began under Roosevelt, with the exception of Nixon.[5] Nonetheless, the myth of Reagan's popularity persists to this day.

This myth took hold in no small part because Reagan's handlers were so adept at the staging of public events, and reporters—perhaps believing that ordinary people are easily persuaded—concluded that because the events impressed them, they must have impressed the American people as well.[6] Bush's people are, if anything, even more skillful. With a team combining political operatives with professionals from the television industry, they construct a series of beautifully lit and framed photo opportunities, as they did when Bush gave a speech at Mount Rushmore, the cameras perfectly placed to position his face the correct size and orientation alongside Jefferson, Roosevelt, Lincoln, and Washington.[7] When Bush gives a speech, the banner behind him repeats the message of the day ("Jobs and Growth" or "Protecting America's Homeland") hundreds of times. While a single large typeface would be easier for the assembled audience to see, the smaller repeated type ensures that a camera shot from any angle will carry the message. Michael Deaver, the Reagan adviser revered as the Michelangelo of presidential photo-ops, said in

---

[5] Data on presidential approval ratings are available at www.ropercenter.uconn.edu.
[6] A discussion of this phenomenon can be found in Michael Schudson and Elliot King, "The Illusion of Ronald Reagan's Popularity," in Michael Schudson, *The Power of News.* Cambridge, MA: Harvard University Press, 1995.
[7] Elisabeth Bumiller, "Keepers of Bush Image Lift Stagecraft to New Heights," *New York Times,* May 16, 2003.

admiration, "They understand the visual as well as anybody ever has…they've taken it to an art form."[8]

Just as their predecessors' image of Reagan was shaped by the events Deaver created, the current press corps assumes that the public is invariably swayed by Bush photo-ops, regardless of whether there is any evidence to support that conclusion. In the most celebrated case, the media gave enormous coverage to Bush's landing on the aircraft carrier *Abraham Lincoln* and praised its success in gathering the public behind Bush's declaration of victory in Iraq. But for all the attention given to his glorious landing, the event had no discernible effect on Bush's popularity—zero. The last Gallup poll before the carrier landing showed Bush's approval rating at 70 percent; the first poll after the carrier landing showed his approval at 69 percent.[9] Yet long after Bush's approval fell from its post–September 11 highs, journalists continued to repeat that Bush was enormously popular. And the repetition made it seem true.

THE CHARACTER ISSUE

Senator Tom Harkin said of his late friend and colleague Paul Wellstone, "He never had to proclaim his decency."[10] George W. Bush, on the other hand, proclaims his alleged virtues endlessly, hoping that his words will drown out the silence of his deeds. During his acceptance speech at the 2000 Republican convention, Bush told us, "I do not need to take your pulse before I know my own mind. I do not reinvent myself at every turn. I am not running in borrowed clothes." But the fact is that Bush does exactly that. He adopts the language of others to mask his own agenda and hides his true self behind a persona designed to deceive.

The Bush persona was built by combining cowboy gear with a set of supposed virtues that would separate him from Bill Clinton and from Al Gore. When he ran for president, Bush offered his upstanding character as his primary qualification for office. Taking a cue

[8] Elisabeth Bumiller, "Keepers of Bush Image Lift Stagecraft to New Heights," *New York Times*, May 16, 2003.
[9] Gallup poll results may be viewed at www.gallup.com.
[10] Speech at Wellstone memorial service, October 29, 2002.

from John F. Kennedy, who recited the oath of office on the campaign trail in 1960 to make himself look presidential, Bush ended most of his speeches by raising his right hand and proclaiming, "When I put my hand on the Bible, I will swear to not only uphold the law of the land, but I will also swear to uphold the honor and the dignity of the office to which I have been elected, so help me God!"

The less honorable and dignified parts of the real George W. Bush were kept carefully hidden. Consider what this incident tells us about Bush's "character." In April of 1986, columnist Al Hunt of the *Wall Street Journal* was sitting in a restaurant with his wife and four-year-old son. He saw coming toward him a "clearly lubricated" George W. Bush, who proceeded to unleash a torrent of obscenities on him. "You no-good fucking son of a bitch, I will never fucking forget what you wrote!" Bush said. Hunt was puzzled, but eventually figured out that what had infuriated Bush so much was a recent issue of *Washingtonian* magazine, in which a round-up of pundits predicted the 1988 nominees for president; Hunt had predicted someone other than Bush's father.[11]

Hunt didn't give much thought to the incident for many years until he was asked about it by Bill Minutaglio, a reporter writing a biography of Bush. Then, two weeks later, thirteen years after the incident happened, Hunt received a phone call from none other than George W. Bush, who apologized profusely for spewing expletives at him in front of his family.

This incident might give the picture of an arrogant, angry man ready to lash out at those who get in his way, a picture most at odds with the laid-back portrait his campaign was offering. Bush did not call Hunt to apologize immediately after the incident or after he stopped drinking. Instead, Bush apologized only after Minutaglio told him he had spoken to Hunt about it and the possibility arose that the incident would become a matter of public record; no doubt so that if anyone brought it up he could say he had apologized. When he was indeed asked about it by reporters assembling a profile of the

---

[11] Bill Minutaglio, *First Son: George W. Bush and the Bush Family Dynasty*. New York: Three Rivers Press, 2001, p. 208-9.

candidate for the *Washington Post*, he was also asked why he had
waited thirteen years to apologize. Bush offered this (rather lame and
unbelievable) excuse: "I heard he was angry about it, and it began to
weigh heavy on my mind. I would have done it earlier had I realized
I had offended him."[12] After all, who would think calling someone a
"no-good fucking son of a bitch" in front of his four-year-old son
would offend him?

This incident suggests that the man who claimed a desire to
usher in a "responsibility era" only takes responsibility when not
doing so carries political danger. But the story was little noted.
Where were the media? In the two years of the 2000 campaign, this
incident was mentioned twice on NPR,[13] once in an Associated Press
story,[14] once on *The O'Reilly Factor*,[15] once on Tim Russert's CNBC
show,[16] once in Salon.com,[17] once in *The Economist* magazine,[18] once
by the *Dallas Morning News*,[19] and in two stories about Minutaglio's
book in the *Baltimore Sun*[20] and *New York Post*.[21] In addition to the
Washington Post profile, that adds up to a total of eleven mentions in
all of the news media. Compare that to the false story that Al Gore
claimed to have "invented" the Internet, which was mentioned in
more than 2,500 articles even though it was untrue, a point we'll
discuss in more detail later.[22]

The incident also seems to shed quite a bit of light on Bush's
character. It shows that Bush has a serious mean streak, something

[12] Lois Romano and George Lardner Jr., "1986: A Life-Changing Year," *Washington Post*, July 25, 1999, p. A1.
[13] *All Things Considered*, September 5, 2000; *Weekend Edition Saturday*, September 9, 2000.
[14] Michelle Mittlestadt, "A Rough Morning, a Tough Decision," Associated Press, January 18, 2000.
[15] *The O'Reilly Factor*, Fox News, January 25, 2000.
[16] *Tim Russert*, CNBC, December 4, 1999.
[17] Jake Tapper, "God Is Their Co-Pilot," Salon.com, July 7, 2000.
[18] "A Curse on Both Their Houses," *The Economist*, March 18, 2000.
[19] Carl Leubsdorf, "A Familiar Business," *Dallas Morning News*, June 2, 1999, p. 1A.
[20] Jonathan Weisman, "The Political Rewards of Life with Father," *Baltimore Sun*, January 18, 2000, Telegraph p. 1A.
[21] Cathy Burke, "Book: G.W. Is Dad-icated to Retaking White House," *New York Post*, January 13, 2000.
[22] The press's slander of Gore on this point is discussed in detail in chapter 4.

he has successfully kept hidden from the public. Ann Richards tried unsuccessfully to goad Bush into showing his nasty temper during her debate with him; much to the amazement of his own family, he didn't take her bait.[23] Al Gore may have been trying to do the same thing when he walked up to Bush and stood barely a foot away from him as Bush was giving an answer during their third debate; he didn't succeed either.

But there were plenty of other examples of Bush's mean streak that reporters could have taken note of. In an interview with conservative pundit Tucker Carlson for the magazine *Talk*, Bush mocked the clemency pleas of convicted murderer and born-again Christian Karla Faye Tucker, imitating her begging for her life: "'Please,' Bush whimpers, his lips pursed in mock desperation, 'don't kill me.'"[24] Carlson also reported that Bush had used profanity during their interview; in response, aide Karen Hughes made the absurd allegation that Carlson was lying because Hughes had never once heard Bush use a dirty word. "I've obviously been lied to a lot by campaign operatives," Carlson said later, "but the striking thing about the way she lied was she knew I knew she was lying, and she did it anyway. There is no word in English that captures that. It almost crosses over from bravado into mental illness."[25] During one of his debates with Al Gore, when Bush described how the murderers of James Byrd Jr. would be put to death, a smile covered his face as he discussed the impending executions. When Bush utters a line like "Let's put it this way. [Terrorists who had been killed] are no longer a problem to the United States,"[26] the gleam of pleasure in his eyes leaves no doubt that he means what he says.

So it shouldn't have been a surprise that as the war with Iraq approached, Bush became increasingly excited. Friends and lawmakers who met with Bush just before he launched the invasion found him "upbeat," "chatty," "cocky and relaxed," and "in high

---

[23] Bill Minutaglio, *First Son: George W. Bush and the Bush Family Dynasty*. New York: Three Rivers Press, 2001, p. 8-9.

[24] Tucker Carlson, "Devil May Care," *Talk*, September 1999.

[25] Kerry Lauerman, "'You Burn Out Fast When You Demagogue,'" Salon.com, September 13, 2003.

[26] From the 2003 State of the Union address.

spirits."[27] The most revealing moment came when he thought the cameras were off: before he gave his national address announcing that the war had begun, a camera caught Bush pumping his fist as though instead of initiating a war he had kicked a winning field goal or hit a home run. "Feels good," he said.[28]

In an article analyzing the way the White House's disciplined manipulation of the press had been ratcheted up by the war, the *New York Times* discussed the fact that the Associated Press had distributed a photo of the dramatic fist-pump. The *Times* wrote that the AP "had the gall to publish a picture that showed the president before he began speaking when he made a real, live, spontaneous gesture. The word in the press room the next day was that access to still photographers would be curtailed due to the transgression."[29] Readers were no doubt puzzled by this incomprehensible description, but the *Times* apparently could not bring itself to describe truthfully Bush's evident excitement at sending young Americans and the Iraqis whose well-being he professed to care so deeply about to their deaths—better to just call it a "real, live, spontaneous gesture" and keep Americans from the discomfort that might be occasioned by a glimpse of their president's vulgar callousness. The irony of this act of journalistic cowardice showing up in a story about White House control over the press apparently went unnoticed by the rest of the media, most of who declined to even allude to the fist-pump. Had they described the incident accurately, the *Times* would no doubt also have become the target of the White House's wrath, not to mention that of innumerable conservatives demanding that they support the president in a time of war. A frightened press is a compliant press. After all, we are talking about what ABC News's *The Note* refers to as "inarguably the most beaten down press corps in the modern era,"[30] whose capacity for aggressive journalism has been weakened by relentless criticism

---

[27] Mike Allen, "In Private, Bush Seems Relaxed, Associates Say," *Washington Post*, March 8, 2003, p. A16.

[28] Martin Merzer, Ron Hutcheson and Drew Brown, "War Begins in Iraq with Strikes Aimed at 'Leadership Targets,'" Knight-Ridder Newspapers, March 20, 2003.

[29] David Carr, "Press Secretary Doles Out Answers, But Doesn't Give Away Much," *New York Times*, March 23, 2003, p. B2.

[30] *The Note*, abcnews.com, March 24, 2003.

from the right and an uncompromising, vindictive White House on whom they depend for the production of news.

The fact that Bush was unable to prevent his glee at launching a war from manifesting itself physically should be nothing short of horrifying to any person of conscience, regardless of what one may think about the wisdom of invading Iraq. It cannot be explained by the fact that Bush himself has not seen war firsthand. One need not have crouched in a foxhole with bullets whizzing overhead to appreciate that war's inevitable costs in life and limb should temper one's sense of fun about the enterprise. As Jimmy Carter said when accepting the Nobel Peace Prize, war is sometimes a necessary evil, but it is always evil. But starting his long-sought war seemed to bring George W. Bush nothing but delight.

LIKE FATHER, LIKE SON

Keeping his personality's ugly side under wraps is only one part of what is required to sustain the Bush persona. To appreciate its essence—the regular-guy Texan—you have to understand his father's struggles with his own image: the awkwardness with which the Connecticut preppy attempted to relate to ordinary people, particularly in his adopted state. The elder Bush made two unsuccessful runs for the Senate, in 1964 and 1970, and both times he got out-Bubba-ed, as his opponents convinced voters that Bush was insufficiently Texan, insufficiently Southern, insufficiently down-home, a fancy-pants carpetbagger who was trying to take over on behalf of the eastern establishment. "Elect a Senator from Texas," said his 1964 opponent, Ralph Yarborough, "and not the Connecticut investment bankers." In 1970 Lloyd Bentsen said much the same thing. It worked, and Bush was beaten both times.[31]

By the time he got to the national stage, George Sr. figured out that the key to dealing with his preppy question was not in convincing people that he wasn't one of the elite, but in redefining the elite itself, just as many conservatives had done before him. His attempts to disown his pedigree—like proclaiming his love for pork rinds, an

---

[31] Bill Minutaglio, *First Son: George W. Bush and the Bush Family Dynasty*. New York: Three Rivers Press, 2001.

assertion greeted with universal guffaws—fell flat. So he and his team decided to define their opponent Michael Dukakis, a self-made son of Greek immigrants, as a member of the "Harvard boutique."[32]

This excerpt from a speech given a few days before the 1988 election gives the flavor of Bush's attacks on Dukakis: "Does my opponent respect old-fashioned common sense? I think he's guided more by abstract theories and grids and graphs and computer printouts and the history of Swedish social planning...if you stick too close to the grids and the graphs you can lose your appreciation of what's real—and you can become, for all your intellectual attainment, disconnected from common sense."[33] By the time election day came, Americans were sufficiently convinced that Dukakis wasn't one of them, and gave Bush Sr. the White House.

In the 1992 campaign, Bush renewed his attack, the son of a wealthy senator once more deriding an opponent born of poor parents for being part of the "elite." Clinton "and his advisers talk about industrial policies, economic plans designed by a government elite," Bush said.[34] "He believes that government, kind of a Washington elite, should take the lead in shaping the economy."[35] When he was criticized for implying that Clinton had committed treason by participating in anti–Vietnam War protests while studying at Oxford, Bush said, "You let the liberal elite do their number today, trying to call me Joe McCarthy. I'm standing with American principle."[36] Picking up where insurgent candidate Pat Buchanan left off in his hateful speech at the Republican convention demanding a "cultural war" against liberals,[37] Bush offered, "I don't care what the liberal elite says; family is important."[38] By defining the American "elite" not as an economic one (which would put his family at its very center) but as a cultural or, more specifically, intellectual one,

---

[32] Merrill Hartson, "Bush, Dukakis in Angry Exchange," Associated Press, June 11, 1988.
[33] Speech in South Bend, Indiana, November 1, 1988.
[34] Speech in Schaumburg, Illinois, September 25, 1992.
[35] Speech in Washington, DC, September 30, 1992.
[36] Speech in Cincinnati, Ohio, October 9, 1992.
[37] Molly Ivins gave birth to a thousand Buchanan Nazi jokes when she quipped that his convention speech probably sounded better in the original German.
[38] Speech in Auburn Hills, Michigan, November 1, 1992.

Bush sought to classify his opponents as not only alien from ordinary Americans, but as members of a class with power and influence, repeating it until it seemed true.

George W. Bush understood well the preppy image his father carried and was eager to stake out a contrast to it. But when he made a premature run for Congress in 1978, George W.'s opponent, Kent Hance, did exactly the same thing Yarborough and Bentsen had done to his father, running radio ads mentioning where Bush went to high school (Phillips Andover Academy). Hance would tell this joke, in which a limousine pulls up to a farmer to ask directions to Lubbock:

> The farmer, he chews on the straw for a couple of seconds and points up the dirt road and he says to the chauffeur, "Go on up the road a couple of miles till ya see the cattle guard, then go left and pretty soon you'll be in town."
>
> Well a while goes by and the farmer sees the big fancy limousine coming back down the dirt road. The window rolls down and the chauffeur says, "Forgot to ask, what color uniform is that cattle guard wearing?"
>
> You see, that limousine wasn't from around these parts. I think it had one of them Connecticut licenses. That where you from, George?[39]

Hance won with more than 53 percent of the vote. It was the last time anyone would ever out-Bubba George W. Bush.

So when he was asked as he was preparing to run for governor what the difference between him and his father was, Bush would say, "He went to Greenwich Country Day and I went to San Jacinto Junior High School in Midland."[40] In other words, he was a Connecticut Yankee, but I'm a real Texan. What are the facts? Bush attended San Jacinto Junior High for one year, then went to an elite private school in Houston, followed by spending his high school years at Andover.[41] Bush seldom misses an opportunity to reiterate that he

---

[39] Bill Minutaglio, *First Son: George W. Bush and the Bush Family Dynasty*. New York: Three Rivers Press, 2001, pp. 191-192.

[40] Bush is first quoted saying this in 1989 (David Maraniss, "The Bush Bunch" *Washington Post Magazine*, January 22, 1989, p. W21); he would begin repeating it again in 1992.

[41] Bill Minutaglio, *First Son: George W. Bush and the Bush Family Dynasty*. New York: Three Rivers Press, 2001.

is a real Texan, down to his habit of attributing ordinary American sayings to Texas, as though by speaking them he reveals his provincialism (he once described "show your cards" as "an old Texas expression,"[42] and speaking in Tennessee, offered his mangled version of "fool me once, shame on you; fool me twice, shame on me" as "an old saying in Tennessee—I know it's in Texas, probably in Tennessee").[43]

As in many areas, George W. was far more successful in posing as an anti-elitist than his father. Whether George Sr. actually enjoyed pork rinds as he claimed, nobody believed for a second that his snack-food preference made him an ordinary Joe. But the son, with his love for baseball and plain speakin', managed to make most people forget his Brahmin pedigree.

THE LIBERAL "ELITE"

The effort by Bush and other conservatives to define liberals as the elite continues to this day. Although there may never have been a point in American history in which so much power was held by a party so singularly devoted to the interests of so few, Republicans continue to argue that they speak for the little guy. As author Thomas Frank has written, conservatives have "proceeded to capture and turn every element of the old class-based critique of American life (such as press bias) over the last thirty years. The results are impressive. Not only do billionaire libertarians routinely claim to speak with the vox populi, but class anger in America is channeled almost exclusively at that snooty species known as the 'liberal.'"[44]

Of course, this strategy is not a new one; Aristotle noted that "all people receive favorably speeches spoken in their own character and by persons like themselves."[45] It is all the easier to convince people that you are a person like themselves if you can convince them that your opponent is a person quite unlike themselves. Just as Newt

[42] William Mann, "Cheney Brushes Off France Deadline Offer," Associated Press, March 17, 2003.

[43] Tom Humphrey, "Bush Stumps for Alexander, Civics in Schools," *Knoxville News Sentinel*, September 18, 2002, p. B1.

[44] Thomas Frank, "Let's Talk Class Again," *London Review of Books*, March 21, 2000.

[45] *Rhetoric* II.13.16.

Gingrich once counseled that Democrats should be portrayed as "the enemy of normal Americans,"[46] Republicans, from President Bush on down, endlessly assert that only they and those who support them are real Americans. When he travels to the Midwest or South, Bush calls it a "Home to the Heartland Tour." "Whenever I go home to the heartland," Bush says, "I am reminded of the values that build strong families, strong communities, and strong character, the values that make our people unique."[47] The implication, of course, is that the other parts of America are not so strong in those values—and not so American. When Bush makes this argument, few are so rude as to point out that the man who claimed to be "a uniter, not a divider" has no hesitation in dividing us into the "real" Americans and the not-so-real. And when conservatives say this sort of thing, liberals usually run scared. But they need to stand up and defend what they know to be true, that no one part of America is more American than any other. People who live in Rhode Island or Oregon are no less American than people who live in Oklahoma or Kansas. Nothing about life in Boise is inherently more American than life in New York. No Democrat would dare to suggest that Omaha is not really part of America, but when the Democratic party elected to hold its 2004 convention in Boston, House Majority Leader Dick Armey quipped, "If I were a Democrat, I suspect I'd feel a heck of a lot more comfortable in Boston than, say, America."[48] Armey's formulation may be a tad more vulgar than Bush's, but they are saying the same thing—and they're both wrong.

Bush unifies the various strains of the right's anti-"elite" ideology: the geographic argument, the argument about the alleged bias of the media, and the anti-intellectual argument. In 1953, Arthur Schlesinger Jr. wrote, "Anti-intellectualism has long been the anti-Semitism of the businessman," by which he meant that those at the

---

[46] Ann Devroy and Charles Babcock, "Gingrich Foresees Corruption Probe by a GOP House; Party Could Wield Subpoenas against 'Enemy' Administration," *Washington Post*, October 14, 1994, p. A1.

[47] Scott Lindlaw, "President Fleeing the White House for a Month on the Ranch," Associated Press, August 3, 2001.

[48] Paul Bedard, "Washington Whispers," *U.S. News & World Report*, November 25, 2002.

top of the heap use intellectuals as a scapegoat to distract people from the societal inequities that actually affect their lives: those of wealth and power.[49] Intellectuals are posited as both sinister and powerful, conspiratorially undermining the values of ordinary people.

In order to sustain a fear of intellectuals, the conservative-media apparatus conducts a coordinated effort to elevate any perceived transgression by any liberal associated with education to the status of a major news event. So when one stupid professor in New Mexico says to his class on September 11, "Anyone who can blow up the Pentagon has my vote," the incident receives a torrent of news coverage, spurred on by conservative talk radio, as though the speaker in question were someone of national importance.[50] When the National Education Association puts up a website to help teachers find ways to discuss September 11 with their students, the *Washington Times* writes an appallingly dishonest story distorting the NEA's suggestion to avoid scapegoating all American Muslims into an instruction to avoid blaming al-Qaeda for the attacks; the false charge is then picked up by conservative commentators and columnists who push it onto editorial pages all over the country.[51]

And it needn't only be professors—even lowly college students can be manipulated into providing fodder for the right-wing spin machine. The polemicist David Horowitz, for example, is provided with a steady stream of conservative foundation money essentially to devise ways to outwit nineteen-year-olds. So Horowitz will attempt to place insulting ads in college newspapers—arguing, for example, that African-Americans should be thankful for slavery—and then, when some of the newspapers refuse to run the ads, pose as an aggrieved hero of the First Amendment.[52]

---

[49] Arthur Schlesinger Jr., "The Highbrow in American Politics," *Partisan Review*, March–April 1953, p. 164.
[50] "Professor's Remark on Pentagon Attack Angers State Legislators, UNM," Associated Press, September 21, 2001. A Lexis/Nexis search shows this incident mentioned in more than 200 articles.
[51] The spread of the distortion was documented by Spinsanity: Brendan Nyhan, "The Big NEA September 11 Lie," Spinsanity.org, September 5, 2002.
[52] Erika Hayasaki, "Conservative's Ad Criticizing Antiwar Protests Angers Students," *Los Angeles Times*, September 28, 2001, part 2 page 3.

The conservative-media apparatus is an integrated system in which stories circulate between talk radio, conservative magazines and newspapers, and the Fox News Channel, generating momentum and pushing their way into more mainstream news outlets. The most enthusiastic goal of this media machine is locating and publicizing foolish things said by liberals, no matter how obscure or inconsequential the speaker may be, to inspire mainstream contempt for liberals. The idea that the words of some random professor or student are more important than the actions of the country's leaders may be farcical, but by giving endless attention to these alleged outrages, conservatives sustain the image of liberals as powerful and elitist and conservatives as persecuted and victimized. Were they so inclined, liberals could no doubt find conservative citizens who say stupid things, too. But no one is paying them to undertake the search, while there exists on the conservative side a network of activist foundations willing to pour money into any effort to fight liberals and liberalism.

When ordinary people, told endlessly to be suspicious if not contemptuous of those with too much education, hear people snicker at George W. Bush's inability to put together a grammatical sentence, they sympathize. Far from being damaging, jokes about the president's intelligence and ineloquence serve to distract from his status within the aristocracy, providing evidence that Bush is not one of the elite, indeed is scorned by them. Presidential elections are won and lost over a variety of factors, but which candidate seems the smartest is not one of them. When liberals make jokes about the bizarre tangle of words that sometimes emerges from Bush's mouth, he is only too pleased since it serves the end of separating him from the elite.

Bush will seldom pass up an opportunity to display his contempt for intellectuals. On a European trip in May of 2002, Bush was shocked when an American reporter, David Gregory of NBC News, had the gall to extend to French president Jacques Chirac the same courtesy foreign reporters grant to American presidents: asking a question in the leader's language. Gregory's query in French to Chirac led to this sneering comment by Bush: "Very good, the guy memorizes four words, and he plays like he's intercontinental. I'm impressed. *Que bueno.* Now I'm literate in two languages."[53] Because the idea of an American going out of his way to treat a foreigner with respect was so ridiculous to Bush, he assumed Gregory must have asked the question in French because he was some kind of show-off trying to make Bush look dumb.

THE YALE DILEMMA

Bush's disdain for intellectuals is somewhat unusual, given that they never did him any real harm. The meritocracy did not prevent his aristocratic connections from pushing him along the road of suc-cess—to Andover, then Yale, then Harvard, and ultimately to the White House. There were many he passed along the way who, despite their big brains, were unable to progress as far as George with his ordinary capacities.

But the WASP elite into which Bush was born has a long tradi-tion of resentment of the pointy-headed intellectuals who took over institutions like Bush's alma maters of Yale and Harvard from the men who considered them a birthright. As Richard Hofstadter noted in his 1962 book *Anti-Intellectualism in American Life*, a dis-dain for intellectuals has been present in America since colonial days. This disdain moves in two directions: from the bottom up and from the top down, from both the lower and middle classes for whom the life of the mind seems a decadent luxury and from the aristocrats who see intellectuals as a threat to their birthrights of power and wealth. So it is unsurprising that the meritocratic turn in American society that took hold in the 1960s would have rubbed the Bushes the wrong way. What is notable is the success of the two Georges in convincing ordinary people to share their scorn. Those ordinary people's children might make it to Yale by dint of hard

---

[53] David Sanger, "Skipping Borders, Tripping Diction," *New York Times*, May 28, 2002, p. A10.

work, but they could never share George W.'s good fortune of having a father and a grandfather who could ease his way in as a legacy.

As Mark Crispin Miller has observed, one of the most notable features of Bush's disdain for proper grammar and book learnin' is his lack of concern about it. While Dan Quayle tried mightily to convince people that he was in fact pretty smart and liked to read, Bush doesn't make the same effort. You'd have to be some kind of Ivy League pansy to care about that stuff, he seems to say. "In the matter of his education," Miller wrote, "this president, despite his folksy pretense, is something of an anti-Lincoln—one who, instead of learning eagerly in humble circumstances, learned almost nothing at the finest institutions in the land. When he comments on how many hands he's 'shaked' or frets that quotas 'vulcanize' society, or claims that he has been 'miscalculated,' he is, of course, flaunting not only his costly education but his disdain for it—much as some feckless prince, with a crowd of beggars watching from the street, might take a few bites from the feast laid out before him, then let the servants throw the rest away."[54] Bush is hardly alone in his disdain for higher education; when challenged on his efforts as governor to slash California's education budget, Ronald Reagan asked, "Why should we subsidize intellectual curiosity?"[55]

Bush attended Yale at a time of transition, when the university not only had been opened up to those with less-prestigious pedigrees than the future president (Yale had done away with their quota limiting the number of Jews who could attend), but was also embroiled in the social tumult of the 1960s. By all accounts, Bush and his kind were pleased about neither development. When Prescott Bush and his son George attended Yale, they could feel comfortable that all their classmates were "Their Kind," born of wealth and high position. But by the time George W. got there, William F. Buckley Jr. could sniff disgustedly, "The son of an alumnus, who goes to a private preparatory school, now has less of a chance of getting in than

---

[54] Mark Crispin Miller, *The Bush Dyslexicon*. New York: W.W. Norton, 2001, pp. 14–15.
[55] Brad Knickerbocker, "Reagan and Social Issues," *Christian Science Monitor*, October 2, 1980, p. 12.

some boy from P.S. 109."⁵⁶ Buckley's concerns notwithstanding, it was still little problem for someone like young George—whose grandfather Prescott sat on the Yale board of trustees at the time— to find his way to New Haven.

But Bush was most likely not pleased with what he found there: fellow students who believed that intellectual achievement was more important than fine breeding and who felt that government could help create a world in which everyone had the same opportunities. "These are the ones," Bush later said, "who felt so guilty that they had been given so many blessings in life—like an Andover or a Yale education—that they felt they should overcompensate by trying to give everyone else in life the same thing."⁵⁷ Needless to say, the man who would later move to cut $270 million from the Pell Grant program, cutting off eighty-four thousand students from federal educational aid,⁵⁸ was afflicted with no such impulse for overcompensation. Ann Richards's cutting line about Bush's father—"He was born on third base and thinks he hit a triple"⁵⁹— applies far better to the son.

But when he ran for president, Bush described his college experience not as one where the senator's grandson was forced to compete with those who had actually worked their way into Yale, but rather as an inspiring tale of a plucky regular guy who learned he was as good as those who looked down on him. Appearing on Oprah Winfrey's talk show, Bush discussed his past problems with alcohol, the birth of his children, his feelings about God, and how much he enjoys bringing Laura coffee in the morning. During the campaign Bush tended to avoid situations in which reporters could question him in detail— for instance, late in the campaign NBC offered both candidates a nightly interview for a week; Bush did one, and when Tom Brokaw asked him some difficult questions, he refused to come back. But

⁵⁶ Bill Minutaglio, *First Son: George W. Bush and the Bush Family Dynasty*. New York: Three Rivers Press, 2001, p. 110.
⁵⁷ From a 1994 *Texas Monthly* interview, quoted in Ivins and Dubose, p. 11.
⁵⁸ Greg Winter, "Tens of Thousands Will Lose College Aid," *New York Times*, July 18, 2003, p. A12.
⁵⁹ Richards spoke this line most famously at the 1988 Democratic national convention.

sitting down for an hour with Oprah was virtually risk-free. She didn't spend too much time talking about policy issues, preferring to ask Bush questions like, "When was the last time Laura really chewed you out, and what did you do to tick her off?" When she asked Bush to relate a moment when he had self-doubt, they had this exchange:

Bush: And I got to a place called Phillips Academy, Andover, in Massachusetts, where it was just a whole different world, a completely different environment from where I was raised. And I—I can remember thinking how sm—how, you know, brilliant all of the other kids were and how hard I had to work to catch up. And...

Oprah: Mm-hmm. Were—were—were there many times you thought you weren't smart enough?

Bush: No.

Oprah: No?

Bush: Eventually, I realized that smarts are not only—are not only whether you could write well or whether or not you could do calculus, but smart also is instinct and judgment and common sense.

Oprah: Mm-hmm.

Bush: And there's a lot of folks in my state that—whose judgment and instincts and common sense I respect a lot. They may not even have ever gone to college.

Oprah: Mm-hmm.

Bush: And so smart comes in all different kinds of different ways.

Oprah: I—because I think—you know, my sense is that the American people want a president who's like us, who has felt some of the same things that we've felt and knows what it's like to—to live in the world.[60]

Bush deftly used the question about self-doubt to portray himself as a regular guy who found himself out of place among the sons of the elite at Andover but quickly discovered that his lack of book learning did not signal a lack of intelligence. He was able to simultaneously defend his intelligence and make an anti-intellectual argument. Bush

---

[60] *Oprah*, September 19, 2000.

defines the elite to be scorned not as one of privilege and connections but one of intellectuals. His persona—honest if not too articulate—defines him as an ordinary person with the strengths we associate with the common man. After the taping, Bush aide Karen Hughes told reporters, "We've talked with people who saw it in different cities all over the United States, and the feedback is overwhelmingly positive. 'Home run' is the phrase most frequently being used." Hughes was lying, because at the time she made her claim the show had only been aired in Chicago; it would be aired in other cities later that afternoon, so she could not have "talked with people who saw it in different cities all over the United States."[61] But she didn't have to deceive reporters into pronouncing the *Oprah* appearance a success; reporters praised him as relaxed, affable, and witty. As the *Dallas Morning News* put it, Bush "came across as likable, humorous, and genuine, as when he talked about wanting to be defined by his heart and his love for his country."[62]

JUST A GOOD OLD BOY?

Politicians are fond of telling a story in which a wise person, usually a grandparent, tells the future leader that he can be anything he wants if only he puts his mind to it. Someone probably once spoke these words to a young George W. Perhaps it was his grandfather, the senator, or his father, the president. Like most wealthy patriarchs, they no doubt believed it, just as George believes he earned everything he ever got, including a baseball team, three oil companies, and an easy entry into Yale. During his unsuccessful run for Congress in 1978, Bush remarked to a fellow Republican, "I've got the greatest idea of how to raise money for the campaign. Have your mother send a letter to your family's Christmas card list. I just did and I got $350,000!"[63] The notion that there might be something unusual about George and Barbara's Christmas list hadn't occurred to him.

[61] Frank Bruni, *Ambling into History*. New York: HarperCollins, 2002, p. 171.
[62] "Oprah Politics," *Dallas Morning News*, September 20, 2000, p. 26A.
[63] Evan Thomas and Martha Brandt, "A Son's Restless Journey," *Newsweek*, August 7, 2000, p. 32.

Too much is often made of politicians' personal backgrounds and experiences; after all, the working man hardly ever had a better friend in the White House than the aristocratic Franklin Roosevelt or a greater antagonist than Ronald Reagan, who grew up in a family of modest means. And no president since Abraham Lincoln did more for African-Americans than Lyndon Johnson, who nonetheless retained the vulgar mannerisms of his Southern upbringing. But when we see how George W. Bush reacts to the interests and needs of ordinary people, particularly when it comes to economic matters, his life experience seems highly relevant. Because of the class into which he was born, Bush never found himself needing the kind of job 99 percent of Americans hold at some point, and the vast majority for most of their working lives. Bush was never at the mercy of a boss who could threaten his livelihood, never felt exploited and unappreciated at work, never suffered the petty humiliations so many Americans do at the hands of someone who happens to rank higher than them in their workplace's hierarchy, never went home with aching feet after a long day and no choice but to return the next. Nothing like that for George W. Bush; the jobs he held were ones in which wealthy people connected to his father gave him large sums of money to lose.

So it's little wonder that as president, Bush would undertake a relentless assault on labor unions, seeking to limit their bargaining and political power and attacking their role in the operation of government. After all, the class from which he comes sees unions only as a threat to their prosperity. In one sense they are—unions nibble at the wealth of the capitalist class because they are the means by which working people obtain fair wages and benefits. Bush, of course, never needed a union to stand up for him. He never fretted about whether he could support his family or worried about their health insurance. He never wished the minimum wage was a little higher. He never delayed a purchase until he was on firmer financial footing or wondered whether at the end of the month he could pay all his bills. In short, the struggles and concerns of the ordinary Americans whom he uses as props and rhetorical tools are utterly alien to him. When he asserts that there is no economic problem that cannot be solved with yet another tax break for the wealthy, his narrow experience is painfully obvious.

Yet George W. Bush has succeeded at convincing much of the public that he's just an ordinary Joe. This persona is now firmly lodged in the minds of American journalists and the American public. The vulgar man who would exclaim, "Feels good," upon starting a war is carefully hidden. The son of the elite, his life course determined by his family's wealth and connections, fades from view. And all that remains is the down-home Bush, the simple man with a good heart. No part of the Bush fraud should have been more difficult to pull off. It is not surprising that Bush would try to pass himself off as a homespun, plainspoken, regular guy. What is amazing is that so many Americans—not least the supposedly preternaturally skeptical press corps whose job it is to keep tabs on the truth—believe it.

2.

Dodging Bullets

Triumphs of Spin Control

In order to get elected president, George W. Bush had to convince Americans that a man with little experience, knowledge, perspective, imagination, or vision should be the leader of the free world. But he also had to dodge some bullets. So another aspect of the fraud is how Bush and his political team applied the lessons learned from creating his persona to dealing with the character issue stories that emerged during his campaign. These unsavory stories from his past had the potential to trip up his candidacy because each in its own way threatened to undermine one of the pillars on which his candidacy rested, the ideas that George W. Bush is an ordinary guy, that he tells the truth, and that he takes responsibility for his actions. But through a combination of deft media manipulation and a press corps with a brief attention span, each mini scandal quickly passed into the ether. Thus Bush managed to escape questions about Vietnam, drug use, drunk driving, and his creative business practices with barely a scratch—repeated triumphs of spin control.

It's worth looking back at these stories for two important reasons. First, most people either never learned about them or by now have forgotten what they were all about, and they offer insights to both who George W. Bush is and how he managed to ascend to the most powerful office in the world. Second, they demonstrate how easy it has been for Bush and his advisers to manipulate the press, and one cannot understand the Bush presidency without understanding the submission of the news media.

VIETNAM AND THE NATIONAL GUARD: BUSH GETS A PASS

While he often protests otherwise, the most important thing to know about George W. Bush, the fact that shaped every facet of his life—and even his presidency—is that he is George Bush's son. When he needed money, when he needed connections, when he needed a second chance, the Bush name and the connections that came with it were always enough to get him what he wanted.

In few areas is this clearer than in the way that Bush got out of going to Vietnam. A common complaint from conservatives is that Democratic politicians get treated with kid gloves by reporters while Republicans get raked over the coals. These complaints contribute to the myth of the "liberal" press and the guilt that reporters feel about it. But the claims of bias simply aren't true. There are few cases that offer a clearer test of how the media treats each side than in how reporters approached the questions of Bill Clinton's and George W. Bush's participation in the Vietnam war. Both managed to escape the war that engulfed their generation; both had to face the question when they ran for president. So did the allegedly "liberal" press treat them the same way? Not even close.

Like most young men of his generation, Clinton spent a great deal of time agonizing over the Vietnam War and his own potential participation in it. In college, he wrote a paper about the Selective Service system, advocating a separate classification for conscientious objectors like himself who were not pacifists opposed to war per se but young men opposed to a particular war their government was fighting.[1]

---

[1] My account of Clinton's draft story is drawn largely from David Maraniss, *First in His Class: The Biography of Bill Clinton*. New York: Simon & Schuster, 1995.

While he was doing his Rhodes scholarship at Oxford, Clinton was given his induction notice. After his return from England, with little time before he was to report for service, Clinton began exploring the alternatives to the U.S. Army, including enrolling in an ROTC program in law school, the path he initially favored. However, by that time his chances of actually being drafted had been substantially reduced by policy changes the Nixon administration had undertaken as it sought to extricate the U.S. from Vietnam, something Clinton was probably aware of. When the draft lottery was held at the end of 1969, Clinton's birthday received number 311, making it unlikely that he would have to go to Vietnam.

Bush's statements about Vietnam are even more suspect than those Clinton made, beginning with his whole perspective on the war. Much like Clarence Thomas at his confirmation hearings claiming to have never in his life had a conversation about *Roe v. Wade*, the most contentious legal ruling of the past half-century, Bush claimed that when he and his contemporaries were young men subject to the draft, the Vietnam War just never came up. "I don't remember debates," Bush said. "I don't think we spent a lot of time debating it."[2] In his inspirational campaign biography *A Charge to Keep*, Bush offers the familiar conservative critique of the war: "We could not explain the mission, had no exit strategy, and did not seem to be fighting to win."[3] As the late Lars-Erik Nelson wrote, "If those three missing conditions had been met, we may presume that Bush would have been trudging through the boonies along with Pat Buchanan, Newt Gingrich, Phil Gramm, Dan Quayle, Rush Limbaugh, and the rest of that blowhard army that shunned service in Vietnam because the war was not being fought hard enough."[4]

To the list of those who managed to avoid serving in Vietnam we may add other prominent conservatives like Trent Lott, Dick Armey, Dennis Hastert, Tom DeLay, Bill Frist, Rudy Giuliani, Karl Rove, Richard Perle, Paul Wolfowitz, Bill O'Reilly, Steve Forbes,

---

[2] Mary McGrory, "Flying around the Storms," *Washington Post*, August 1, 1999, p. B1.
[3] George W. Bush, *A Charge to Keep.* New York: William Morrow, 1999.
[4] Lars-Erik Nelson, "Legacy," *New York Review of Books*, February 24, 2000, p. 5.

Ken Starr, Clarence Thomas, Antonin Scalia, Jeb Bush, William Bennett, Bill Kristol, George Will, and Dick Cheney, whose efforts to avoid serving in Vietnam foreshadowed the conscientious precision he would later bring to a string of government jobs. Cheney first got a student deferment, then a marriage deferment. When the rules were changed so that marriage was no longer sufficient to get one a deferment but parenthood was, Lynne Cheney became pregnant. The government lifted the ban on drafting married but childless men on October 26, 1965. The Cheneys' first child was born nine months and two days later.[5]

When asked during his confirmation hearings for his appointment as secretary of defense about his draft avoidance, Cheney replied, "I had other priorities than military service."[6] That is certainly a more reasonable explanation than DeLay's—he once told a Republican group that he and Dan Quayle didn't go to Vietnam because so many black and Latino boys had signed up that there just wasn't any room.[7]

John Ashcroft, who in 2001 argued that criticizing the Bush administration was tantamount to treason, also went to great lengths to avoid fighting in Vietnam. The future attorney general got a series of student deferments then, when he graduated from law school, petitioned to get another deferment granted to those in "critical" civilian jobs. His critical job was teaching business law to undergraduates at Southwest Missouri State University.[8]

It is fascinating that all of these men—with the exception of Quayle, who got plenty of flak for getting into the Guard in circumstances nearly identical to Bush's—were never criticized for hypocritically supporting the war while saving their own skin, while Bill Clinton was vilified and even called a traitor by some because he didn't want to fight in a war he found morally objectionable. In this

[5] Glen Johnson, "Early Knack for Leading Put Cheney on Fast Track," *Boston Globe*, July 26, 2000, p. A12.

[6] Richard Cooper, "A Man of Big But Limited Ambitions—the Perfect Number Two," *Los Angeles Times*, October 19, 2000, p. A1.

[7] Tim Fleck, "Which Bug Gets the Gas," *Houston Press*, January 7, 1999.

[8] Walter Robinson, "In Ashcroft's Past, a Vietnam Deferment," *Boston Globe*, January 16, 2001, p. A1.

interpretation, consistency between belief and action is reprehensible, but hypocrisy is admirable.

In his autobiography, Bush reduces the tumultuous and heart-
rending debates men of his generation had over whether to go to
Vietnam to a few sentences. "I knew I would serve," he says, and
then segues neatly into his father telling him how exhilarating it is
to pilot a plane. Home for Christmas, Bush says he "heard from
contemporaries that there were openings in the Texas Air National
Guard."[9] The last word Bush says about himself and Vietnam is that
during his training he inquired about a program called "Palace
Alert," which rotated National Guard pilots to Vietnam to replace
active-duty pilots, but was told that the program was being phased
out.[10] He would just have to stay safely stateside.

But the facts of the story aren't so simple. Bush followed the
accepted procedure for getting into the Guard—the accepted procedure for the sons of the Texas elite, that is. Ben Barnes, who was
the Speaker of the Texas House of Representatives at the time,
detailed in a sworn deposition in an unrelated lawsuit that he
secured a spot for George at the behest of Sid Adger, a Bush-family
friend. After the request from Adger, Barnes called General James
Rose, who was the head of the Texas Air National Guard, and asked
him to give Bush a spot—after all, the young man's father was a
member of Congress. When asked about the connections used to
obtain his spot, Bush offered his "plausible deniability": "I don't
know if Ben Barnes did or not, but he was not asked by me or my
dad," he said. "I can just tell you, from my perspective, I never
asked for, I don't believe I received special treatment."[11] Did Barnes
act on Bush's behalf? Bush doesn't know. Bush says neither he nor
his father asked Barnes for help—but no one alleged that; they had
a family friend do it. Did Bush receive special treatment? Not, he
believes, from his perspective.

---

[9] George W. Bush, *A Charge to Keep*. New York: William Morrow, 1999, p.
50–51.
[10] George W. Bush, *A Charge to Keep*. New York: William Morrow, 1999, p. 54.
[11] Julian Borger, "Draft Dodge Tale Threatens Bush's Run for Presidency,"
Guardian of London, September 29, 1999, p. 17.

In 1968, there were one hundred thousand young men around the country on waiting lists to get into the National Guard. The Texas Air Guard had a waiting list of five hundred names; it took an applicant about a year and a half to move to the top of the list and get a slot. Although he had scored only a 25 on the pilot aptitude test—the lowest score one could receive and still be accepted—Bush not only didn't get put on any waiting list, he was given a "direct appointment" that made him a second lieutenant right out of basic training. The normal requirements for such an appointment—ROTC experience, rigorous training—were waived for young George.[12]

The Texas Air Guard, which some referred to as the "Champagne Unit," included a number of boys considered too important to be sent to Vietnam, including the sons of Congressman Lloyd Bentsen (later a Senator and U.S. Treasury Secretary), Senator John Tower, and Governor John Connally. Interestingly, there were a few African-Americans in Bush's unit—although their presence might be explained by the fact that they happened to play for the Dallas Cowboys.[13] When Bush was in flight school, President Nixon sent a plane down to fetch him for a blind date with the president's daughter Tricia.[14]

Then there's the question of whether Bush went AWOL, skipping out on part of his service. Although his service was to have continued until October of 1973, the last time Bush participated in a flight drill was April of 1972, a full eighteen months earlier. Soon after, he was suspended from flying duty because he failed to show up for a scheduled physical exam. (The Guard had just added a drug test to the physical. If Bush had taken and failed the drug test, he would have been forbidden from flying. There is no telling whether this played a part in Bush's decision to skip the exam.) Bush requested a transfer to a unit in Alabama because he wanted to work on a Senate race there. But according to official records and

---

[12] Richard Serrano, "Bush Received Quick Air Guard Commission," *Los Angeles Times*, July 4, 1999, p. A1.

[13] Molly Ivins and Lou Dubose, *Shrub: The Short But Happy Political Life of George W. Bush*. New York: Vintage, 2000.

[14] Pete Slover and George Kuempel, "'I Was Young and Irresponsible,'" *Dallas Morning News*, November 15, 1998, p. A1.

National Guard officers in the Montgomery unit in which Bush was to have served, he never showed up.

Asked for an explanation, Bush said through an aide that he had "some recollection" of fulfilling his duty in Alabama; after an exhaustive search, his campaign was unable to produce anyone who could remember serving with him.[15] After the 1972 election, Bush returned to Houston but didn't go back to his old unit as he was supposed to. In May of 1973, his superiors at Ellington Air Force Base reported that they were unable to conduct his yearly evaluation because, "Lt. Bush has not been observed at this unit during the period of this report. A civilian occupation made it necessary for him to move to Montgomery, Alabama. He cleared this base on 15 May 1972 and has been performing equivalent training in a non-flying status with the 187 Tac Recon Gp, Dannelly ANG Base, Alabama."[16] But they were mistaken—Bush was back in Houston and apparently never showed up to the National Guard unit in Alabama when he was there.

Bush later asserted that it was his transfer to Alabama that caused him to stop flying and that he didn't return to flight drills because the plane he was trained on, the F-102, was no longer in use. But as the *Boston Globe* discovered, Bush's statements were false; the F-102 was still in use long after he returned to Houston,[17] and Bush was grounded not because he went to Alabama but because he failed to show up for his physical.

Lastly, there is the question of whether Bush ever completed his obligations before being discharged. Pointing to Guard records including a torn page without Bush's name and no discernable dates, his campaign claimed that he crammed in thirty-six days of duty at his Houston unit in his last three months. Given that Bush's official records show no service whatsoever between May of 1972 and his discharge in October 1973 (by which time he was attending Harvard

---

[15] Walter Robinson, "1-Year Gap in Bush's Guard Duty," *Boston Globe*, May 23, 2000, p. A1.
[16] This document may be viewed at www.talion.com/missing.htm.
[17] Walter Robinson, "Republican Ticket Lets a Military Connection Slip," *Boston Globe*, July 28, 2000, p. A1.

Business School), there is considerable uncertainty as to whether he ultimately satisfied his commitment at all.[18]

Mostly through aides, Bush offered a series of evasions about the missing service—he served in Alabama, but he doesn't remember what he did; he did odds and ends around the base in Houston, but he doesn't remember under whose command; he participated in some drills, but he doesn't remember when. Senator Daniel Inouye, who lost an arm serving his country in World War II, commented that, "During my service, if I missed training for two years, at the least I would have been court-martialed."[19] Bush somehow escaped any disciplinary action. Interestingly, he later told the *National Guard Review* that what the Guard taught him was "the responsibility to show up and do your job."[20]

Another Vietnam veteran, Bush's secretary of state, Colin Powell, had a perspective on cases like Bush's that he probably didn't share with his boss. "I can never forgive a leadership that said, in effect: These young men—poorer, less educated, less privileged—are expendable (someone described them as 'economic cannon fodder'), but the rest are too good to risk," Powell wrote in his autobiography. "I am angry that so many of the sons of the powerful and well-placed and so many professional athletes (who were probably healthier than any of us) managed to wangle slots in Reserve and National Guard units. Of the many tragedies of Vietnam, this raw class discrimination strikes me as the most damaging to the ideal that all Americans are created equal and owe equal allegiance to their country."[21]

During the 1992 primary campaign, a letter Clinton wrote to the head of the University of Arkansas ROTC after the lottery was made public. While Republicans hoped the letter would be the smoking gun proving Clinton had illegally dodged the draft, it actually

---

[18] Walter Robinson, "Questions Remain on Bush's Service as Guard Pilot," *Boston Globe*, October 31, 2000, p. A14.

[19] Susan Milligan, "Bush Pressured on Military Gaps," *Boston Globe*, November 3, 2000, p. A29.

[20] Walter Robinson, "Questions Remain on Bush's Service as Guard Pilot," *Boston Globe*, October 31, 2000, p. A14.

[21] Colin Powell with Joseph Persico, *My American Journey*. New York: Random House, 1995, p. 148.

showed a thoughtful young man, plainly tormented by the conflict between his opposition to the war and fear of dying in it on one hand and his sense of obligation and concerns for his political future on the other. "No government really rooted in limited, parliamentary democracy should have the power to make its citizens fight and kill and die in a war they may oppose, a war which even possibly may be wrong," Clinton wrote. "The decision not to be a resister and the related subsequent decisions were the most difficult of my life."[22]

During the Vietnam War there were 26.8 million American men of draft age. Of those, well over half—nearly sixteen million—avoided going to the war by the various means available: deferments, disqualifications, alternative service such as the National Guard and ROTC, and for a small number, active draft resistance.[23] Neither Bill Clinton nor George W. Bush did anything illegal in avoiding Vietnam, although both carefully manipulated the system in order to avoid going. While Clinton's answers when questioned on his draft status were often vague and seemingly intended to confuse, he never tried to claim that he was indifferent to the war itself. And despite his denials of personal knowledge, no one seriously doubted that Bush got his spot in the National Guard because of his family's connections. One would think, then, that the press would have investigated Clinton's and Bush's answers to Vietnam questions with roughly equal vigor. But this was not the case.

In 1992, there were no fewer than 526 stories about Bill Clinton and the draft in major American newspapers. In all the news outlets covered by Lexis/Nexis, there were 950 stories about the subject. But when the 2000 election rolled around, reporters were decidedly less curious about George W. Bush's Vietnam question. There were seventy-seven stories in 1999 and thirty-eight stories in 2000 in major papers about Bush and the draft. In all news outlets, there were 258 stories in 1999 and only ninety-eight in 2000. This difference is important. The media gave Bush a pass.

---

[22] "Excerpts of Clinton's '69 Letter to ROTC Chief," *Chicago Sun-Times*, February 13, 1992.
[23] Statistics from the *Vietnam Draft Almanac*, cited in Maraniss, p. 176–77.

In other words, during their respective election years, there were nearly ten press stories about Clinton's efforts to avoid serving in Vietnam for every *one* story about Bush's efforts to avoid serving in Vietnam. In major papers, there were almost fourteen Clinton stories for every Bush story.[24] This difference is enormous. The media gave Bush a pass.

The fact that reporters just had a feeling Clinton was dishonest and didn't have the same feeling about Bush led to completely different treatment of the two candidates on a remarkably similar set of questions. While a few print stories appeared on Bush's Vietnam question in mid 1999, television reporters virtually never raised the issue, and when they did they dispatched it quickly. "Did his father pull strings to get him into the National Guard during Vietnam?" Sam Donaldson asked. "'Absolutely not,' said Bush." Well, that settles it, and Donaldson never spoke of it again.[25] On *Meet the Press*, Paul Begala raised the fact that Bush never showed up for his service in Alabama. Karl Rove responded, "Well, that's obviously not true, and the governor has talked about that as have people in Alabama who were with the governor during that period of time." This was not true. In fact, the Bush campaign had been unable to produce a single person among the hundreds of people with whom Bush would have served in Alabama who could recall him being there. Begala responded, "Who served with him? Name one." Rove moved to change the subject: "Nice attempt, Paul, to distract attention from the fact that your candidate is a serial exaggerator."[26] This aggressive scare tactic, accusing your opponent of the exact misdeed you are guilty of, is what I call the "Orwellian Misdirection," and is discussed in more detail in chapter 3.

One would think that the press would have been all over this story. It touched on numerous contentious issues in American social

---

[24] These figures are produced by a search of the Lexis/Nexis "Major Newspapers" file and the "U.S. News Group" file seeking stories mentioning Bill Clinton, Vietnam, and "draft" in the story's lead. Given that the story about Bush was his entry into the National Guard, the search for Bush substituted "National Guard" for "draft." (A search for "draft" produces fewer results. "National Guard" leads to the wealth of stories on the subject.)

[25] *20/20*, ABC, November 17, 1999.

[26] *Meet the Press*, NBC, October 8, 2000.

and political life—the Vietnam War, class privilege, and what should be considered appropriate service in a politician's youth, to name a few. Furthermore, the candidate in question was being evasive at best and more likely plainly dishonest. While Bill Clinton gave maddeningly vague answers to questions about his efforts to avoid Vietnam, at least he stepped up to the cameras and answered reporters' questions. Bush refused to do even that, preferring to send aides out to attest to his faulty memory. So how many stories did the three network news operations do on the question of Bush's Guard service? Twenty? Thirty? If you guessed "zero," you're almost right. The grand total was actually *one*. In July 1999, NBC aired a brief story consisting mostly of Bush's denials that he received preferential treatment in getting his spot in the Guard. The question of the gap in his service was not raised.[27]

The story of Bush's National Guard service does not prove that he doesn't love his country, nor does it show that he's a coward. There is nothing shameful in not wanting to die for a questionable cause—although we should reasonably expect that if you get a spot in the National Guard, you should fulfill your obligation, which apparently Bush didn't do. And sixteen young men from Bush's home of Midland, Texas, gave their lives in Vietnam while George W. Bush was safely stateside.[28] What the story reveals is the kid gloves with which Bush was treated by the national press. After all, the story raised some important questions about Bush, which we would expect reporters charged with vetting candidates on our behalf would pursue. Did his family connections get him out of going to Vietnam? Did he skip out on part of his National Guard service? What does that say about his character? The press apparently found these questions relatively unimportant. The issue was raised briefly in mid 1999, then dropped. Bush was never forced to answer tough questions about it. His remarks about not remembering whether and how he fulfilled his service, despite being contradicted by the memories of Guard officers

---

[27] The story aired at 5:00 A.M. on *NBC News at Sunrise* on July 5, 1999, then again on that morning's *Today* show.
[28] A list of their names can be found at www.buzzflash.com/editorial/03/04/02.html.

and official records, were not described as evasions and lies, although they almost certainly were. Bush got a pass twice: first in 1968, when his father's connections kept him from going to Vietnam, and then again in 2000, when reporters decided not to delve too deeply into his Vietnam question.

USHERING IN THE RESPONSIBILITY ERA

But every potentially damaging story cannot be disposed of with so little effort. Just five days before the 2000 election, a dramatic story broke in the national press: at the age of 30, George W. Bush had been arrested for drunk driving. Although a television station in Maine had learned of the story many weeks before, they decided not to report it. It finally fell to a local Democratic activist who had obtained the relevant court records to inform the press.[29]

Facing a crisis so close to election day, the Bush campaign went into full damage-control mode. Their strategy had two prongs: first, admit to the incident—after all, there was no more concealing it— but portray the admission as admirable forthrightness. Second, do all they could to shift blame to the Gore campaign.

Bush came out to face the press. His explanation for his drunk driving was, "I regret that it happened. But it did. I've learned my lesson."[30] This hopefully was true, since he had driven drunk before. How many times is not clear, although there was at least one other time four years earlier, when at the age of twenty-six Bush drove home from a night of drinking with his sixteen-year-old brother, Marvin, flattening the neighbors' garbage cans on the way. When his father confronted him about his recklessness, Bush challenged him to a fistfight.[31]

No, the lesson Bush seems to have learned from the Maine drunk-driving incident was the same one that was reiterated to him

---

[29] Timothy Burger, "In the Driver's Seat: The Bush DUI," in Larry Sabato (ed.), *Overtime: The Election 2000 Thriller*. New York: Longman.
[30] Timothy Burger, "In the Driver's Seat: The Bush DUI," in Larry Sabato (ed.), *Overtime: The Election 2000 Thriller*. New York: Longman, p. 76.
[31] Bill Minutaglio, *First Son: George W. Bush and the Bush Family Dynasty*. New York: Three Rivers Press, 2001.

again and again—whenever he screwed up, a few calls would be made on his behalf, and at the invocation of his father's name, problems would magically disappear, his slate would be wiped clean, and he would be free to screw up again. It isn't too surprising, therefore, that not long after he moved into the White House his daughter would think that despite the fact that her father was the president of the United States, in the relatively small city of Austin she could order drinks in a bar with a fake ID and no one would recognize her. I raise this not to condemn Jenna Bush—hers was rather typical American adolescent behavior—but because it shows that she absorbed well the lessons of her father's life.

When asked if he had been given a sobriety test during his arrest, Bush replied, "No. I admitted I was wrong." What are the facts? As his campaign was forced to acknowledge the next day; Bush had in fact been given a sobriety test.[32] Bush himself and his aides attempted to deflect the story by alleging falsely that the Gore campaign was responsible for the story, and consequently it was they and not Bush who had some explaining to do. The first question Bush was asked was why he had waited until he had no choice to admit to his arrest. The man who had dubbed his 1994 campaign plane *Accountability One* saw the opening to deflect blame off himself. "I think that's an interesting question," Bush said. "Why now, four days before an election?" Using repetition to make it seem true, he came back four more times to the point: "I do find it interesting that it's come out four or five days before an election....It's a regrettable incident that I find interesting that four or five days before the election is coming to the surface....And that's the interesting thing about this. Here we are with four days to go in the campaign and we're discussing something that happened twenty-four years ago....I think the interesting thing is that why five days before an election all of a sudden it pops...." At that point a reporter jumped in with, "Why, do you think?" Bush responded, "That's your job. I got my suspicions."

---

[32] Timothy Burger, "In the Driver's Seat: The Bush DUI," in Larry Sabato (ed.), *Overtime: The Election 2000 Thriller*. New York: Longman, p. 77.

In case any reporters missed the point, aide Karen Hughes added, "I think the American people are tired of this kind of 'gotcha' politics, are tired of this kind of last-minute dirty tricks, and I think the Democrats owe the American people an explanation."[33]

Meanwhile, *Dallas Morning News* reporter Wayne Slater told other journalists that he asked Governor Bush in 1998 whether he had ever been arrested after 1968 (meaning after Bush's arrests for college pranks), and Bush responded that he hadn't. This was clearly a lie. When Slater began to ask for details, Karen Hughes jumped in and declared the interview over.[34]

Bush also appears to have lied in order to get his license to drive in Maine reinstated two years later. In a hearing conducted over the telephone, he told a hearing officer that he drank only once a month and had an "occasional beer," a characterization that is at odds with the amount of drinking he had admitted to on many occasions.[35] The Republicans who argued so strenuously that if Bill Clinton perjured himself in a deposition he was unfit for the presidency seemed to be somewhat less outraged by Bush's deception in this proceeding.

I raise these issues not to criticize Bush for having had a drinking problem; alcoholism has been rightly recognized as a disease, not a failure of character, that affects millions of Americans. Whether he would be characterized as an alcoholic, it is to Bush's credit that he was able to stop drinking. What is troubling is not even the less savory aspects of Bush's personality that his drinking seems to have brought out—the nastiness of his berating of Al Hunt or the reckless disregard for the lives of others evident in his drunk driving. Rather it is the hypocrisy evident in the way he dealt with questions about these events when they were revealed that is so problematic.

In the close of a campaign, it is not surprising that a candidate should seek to limit the effects of a damaging revelation by attempting to deflect criticism onto his opponent. But if a candidate makes

---

[33] Press conference, November 3, 2000.

[34] Anne Kornblut, "Bush Camp Fires Back on Drunk Driving Story," *Boston Globe*, November 5, 2000, p. A35.

[35] Steve Kurkjian and David Armstrong, "Bush Downplayed Drinking: '78 Comments Got License Back," *Boston Globe*, November 4, 2000, p. A11.

"responsibility" and "integrity" a central part of his message, then he must be held to a higher standard when it comes to taking responsibility and showing integrity. If you argue that you should be elected because of your political experience, then your record deserves extra scrutiny. If you argue that you should be elected because you were successful in business, then your business dealings should be examined in detail. And if you argue that you should be elected because you have extra doses of integrity and you are someone who takes responsibility, then when the time comes to step up to the plate and admit you did wrong—whether last week or when you were thirty—then you shouldn't try to pin the blame on somebody else.

Just days before, Bush had proclaimed that he wanted to usher in a "responsibility era." "For too long," Bush said, "our culture has sent the message, if it feels good, do it and if you've got a problem, just go ahead and blame somebody else. Each of us must understand that's not right. Each of us must understand that we are responsible for the decisions and choices we make in life."[36] But when he got into hot water over concealing his drunk-driving arrest, Bush blamed the Democrats.

Bush tried to assert that he was being forthright by admitting to the drunk-driving incident. But at that point there was no denying it—the police records were there in black and white. Just as Bill Clinton admitted to his affair with Monica Lewinsky only when the infamous blue dress underwent DNA testing and there was incontrovertible proof, Bush admitted to the DUI only when it was impossible to conceal the truth any longer.

There is another interesting parallel between the Lewinsky scandal and Bush's handling of the DUI revelation. After his grand-jury testimony, Clinton gave a brief televised address finally admitting his affair with Lewinsky. Although many on his staff wanted the president to be wholly contrite and humble, Clinton included in his statement criticism of Independent Counsel Kenneth Starr and

---

[36] James Dao, "Bush, Wooing Pennsylvania, Attacks Gore's Character," *New York Times*, October 27, 2000, p. A26.

mentioned his own family as a reason for his prior evasions. "I can only tell you I was motivated by many factors," Clinton said. "First, by a desire to protect myself from the embarrassment of my own conduct. I was also very concerned about protecting my family."[37] The reaction from the press was ferocious. To take just one example, *USA Today*, perhaps the most obsessively neutral newspaper in the country, said, "Clinton said Monday that he acted as he did to protect his family. But that, too, is a familiar excuse, and one that rings ever more hollow. In truth, he has put his family's interests second to his passions, and then when caught, used them as a shield to create sympathy for himself."[38]

In 2000, Bush gave precisely the same explanation as to why he had hid his drunk-driving arrest, citing his children three times during his press conference. "I made the decision that, as a dad, I didn't want my girls doing the kinds of things I did, and I told them not to drink and drive....I didn't want to talk about this in front of my daughters....As I mentioned to you, I'm a dad. I'm trying to—trying to teach my children right from wrong. I chose the course that—that to my daughters I was going to tell them they shouldn't drive and drink and that's the course of action I took."[39]

Yet for some reason, when Bush used his children as justification for hiding his criminal record, we did not see, for example, Orrin Hatch saying about Bush as he had about Clinton, "Wasn't that pathetic? I tell you, what a jerk."[40] Quite the contrary—Republicans fanned out to explain why Bush's use of his family as an excuse for hiding his misdeeds from the American public was the height of nobility. Appearing on the *Today* show, William Bennett complimented Bush for the "manly way" he dealt with the issue,[41] then went on Fox and CNN to declare that it was no big deal because Bush was honest about it and took responsibility. On the Sunday shows, the

[37] Televised address, August 17, 1998.
[38] "Clinton's Hollow Apology Puts Nothing to Rest," *USA Today*, August 18, 1998, p. 12A.
[39] Press conference, November 3, 2000.
[40] "Clinton's Attack on Starr Leaves Republicans Furious," *Atlanta Journal and Constitution*, August 18, 1998, p. 1A.
[41] *Today*, November 3, 2000.

hosts dispatched the issue with a few brief items. When Jeb Bush told Sam Donaldson, "Let's move on," Donaldson obediently replied, "All right, let's move on."[42] What discussion there was concerned, of course, the impact the revelation might have on the race's outcome, not on what it said about Bush's character.

The day after the drunk-driving arrest was revealed, Bush stood before a banner asserting "Honesty Works," and proclaimed, "It's become clear to America over the course of this campaign that I've made mistakes in my life. But I'm proud to tell you that I've learned from those mistakes."[43] And what did he learn? Number one, don't get caught. Number two, if you get caught, blame your opponent.

Bush was much more successful early on in wriggling away from rumors that he had taken cocaine as a young man. Whenever the issue of his possible drug use came up, Bush bobbed and weaved, saying things like, "When I was young and irresponsible, I was young and irresponsible," which he repeated a number of times, or the even more blurry, "There were things I did that were mistakes, but I think inventorying mistakes is a mistake."[44] (Bush often uses the power of tautology to confuse his listeners, making them believe he is actually saying something. For instance, on his plans to invade Iraq, he offered, "When I say I'm a patient man, I mean I'm a patient man."[45]) He said that what he did as a youth was irrelevant, and asserted that the fact that reporters couldn't find anyone to admit to have snorted blow with him must mean it never happened: "If I had done anything in the past that would have disqualified me for being in public office, you'd have found it."[46] Bush thus tried to get reporters to write that the rumors were groundless, without actually denying it himself. One can't help but believe that his reluctance to issue a denial might have something to do with what could happen if such a denial were proved false. While Bush

[42] *This Week*, November 5, 2000.
[43] Dana Milbank, "Parallel Phrases on the Peccadillo Circuit," *Washington Post*, November 4, 2000, p. C1.
[44] Sam Howe Verhovek, "Is There Room on a Republican Ticket for Another Bush?" *New York Times Magazine*, September 13, 1998.
[45] Speech in Crawford, TX, August 26, 2002.
[46] Jake Tapper, "Prodigal Son," Salon.com, April 9, 1999.

was quite forthcoming in discussing his excessive use of alcohol, when the subject of illegal drugs came up he resolutely insisted that admitting anything would set a bad example for young people.

Then one day, Bush made the mistake of, for all intents and purposes, admitting he had done illegal drugs. "Not only could I pass the background check and the standards applied to today's White House," he said in August 1999, "but I could have passed the background check and the standards applied on the most stringent conditions when my dad was the president of the United States—a fifteen-year period."[47] In other words, he would be able to prove that he had not taken drugs in the last fifteen years. This would appear to be, quite plainly, an admission on Bush's part that he had taken illegal drugs. If I asked you if you had ever gone over Niagara Falls in a barrel, would you answer, "Not in the last 25 years"? Of course not—if you didn't want to answer the question you wouldn't, but if the answer was no you'd say no.

Bush's admission was a big story…for two days, accompanied by a lot of self-flagellation on the part of the press for even asking in the first place. The strongest criticism came from primary opponent Gary Bauer, who called Bush's statements "Clintonian."[48]

There is an interesting footnote to the question of Bush's drug use. In 1973, Bush spent a number of months working at Project PULL, a Houston program offering tutoring and other services to poor children. As Mark Crispin Miller has observed, this was pretty much the only altruistic thing Bush ever did in his life and just the sort of thing politicians love to trumpet to show their strong character. Yet Bush never mentioned it when running for president.[49] The suspicion some have (for which there is no concrete evidence) is that his time there was some sort of court-ordered community service, and his failure to discuss it is in order to avoid having reporters look too deeply.

---

[47] "Bush Expands His Drug Denial to the Past 25 Years," Associated Press, August 20, 1999.

[48] Andrew Cain, "Clinton Takes a Stand on Cocaine, Says He Never Used It," *Washington Times*, August 24, 1999, p. A1.

[49] Bush never spoke of it on the stump, but there was a reference made during a biographical video shown at the Republican convention.

This is not to say that having taken illegal drugs at some point in his life should have disqualified Bush from the presidency—indeed, it places him with the majority of American adults born after World War II and an increasing number of politicians.[50] But since reporters were not able to get anyone on record as saying they had done drugs with Bush, the issue was permanently dropped in mid 1999. As they have so many times since, reporters gave Bush a pass.

A SERVANT TO HIS CLASS

If there is one group of people that truly knows George W. Bush, whose members have been behind him every step of his political career, it is the corporate benefactors who have financed his campaigns and had the benefit of his friendly ear when decisions were being made. Although he has sometimes tried to rewrite his history as that of a small businessman ("I understand small business growth—I was one."[51]), Bush's business career is mostly the story of a string of very wealthy people who lost money financing his plans. Some would assert that experience in the world of business is excellent preparation for the presidency, and thus Bush was more experienced than his thin political résumé indicated. Indeed, candidates at all levels proudly assert their status as "a businessman, not a politician." But when it comes to Bush, this assertion would be misleading. If being a successful businessman indicated the presence of some set of abilities that made one qualified to hold executive office in government, no one can argue that Bush's experience in the business world could be termed "successful." He ran three oil companies into the ground, only to be bailed out by his father's friends. Bush's company, Arbusto, did so poorly that eventually people began calling it "El Busto."[52] Although Laura Bush once said, "I know something about business leaders who

---

[50] Polls show that around half of adults born after WWII admit to having tried marijuana. Given people's understandable reluctance to admit illegal behavior to a stranger over the phone, the actual number is certainly higher; how much higher is impossible to say.

[51] Dana Milbank, "What's on W's Mind? Hard to Say," *Washington Post*, May 5, 2000, p. C1.

[52] Richard Cooper, "To the Manner Born, Bush Finds His Own Way," *Los Angeles Times*, July 30, 2000, p. A1.

bring business smarts and common sense to government. I married one,"[53] Bush was hardly a "business leader" who had anything resembling "business smarts."

Nonetheless, when he took office, America's corporations knew they had a friend in the White House: someone who would slash consumer and environmental regulations; oppose efforts to protect worker's rights; and above all, work tirelessly to cut taxes on corporations and the wealthy. Although Bush may not have been successful as a businessman, he was one of them.

As President Bush endlessly told us during his 2000 campaign, he is a man of honesty and integrity. He takes responsibility. He does what's right. He sets an example for our children. He tells the truth. So when the Enron scandal began to break, and Bush was asked by reporters about his relationship with Enron chairman Kenneth Lay, one would have been forgiven for expecting Bush to admit that his ties to Enron are substantial. For the record, Lay is an old Bush-family supporter. Lay raised and contributed money for the senior Bush, who made him chairman of the organizing committee for the 1992 Republican convention in Houston. No company gave George W. more money over the course of his political career than Enron:

- Lay's first contributions to Bush were during his unsuccessful run for Congress in 1978. The Lays gave Bush $47,500 for his 1994 race and $75,000 toward his reelection bid in 1998.
- Enron and its employees gave Bush a total of $312,500 for his two governor's races.
- During the 2000 presidential campaign, Bush flew around the country on a corporate jet provided by Enron.
- Enron contributed $100,000 to Bush's inaugural committee; Lay and Enron CEO, Jeffrey Skilling, each chipped in $100,000 of their own.

---

[53] Herbert Sample, "Simon Receives Help of First Lady," *Sacramento Bee*, June 13, 2002, p. A4.

- During the Florida recount, the Bush campaign set up a recount fund, limiting contributions to $5,000. Both Lay and his wife gave the full amount.
- Enron gave the Republican party $1,138,990 in 2000; Lay himself gave the GOP $333,910 in soft-money donations between 1998 and 2002.[54]

So let's just say the financial ties are pretty strong and go back a ways. But when Bush answered the reporters' questions about Ken Lay and Enron, you would have thought he was talking about somebody he barely knew. "He was a supporter of Ann Richards in my run in 1994," Bush said. "And she named him the head of the Governor's Business Council. And I decided to leave him in place, just for the sake of continuity. And that's when I first got to know Ken, and worked with Ken, and he supported my candidacy."[55]

In other words, he did not have political relations with that company. This is certainly true of part of Bush's statement, that Lay "was a supporter of Ann Richards in my run in 1994." Like Clinton's denial of his relationship with Monica Lewinsky, Bush's statement is "true" under a tortured interpretation of the term "supporter." What are the facts? Yes, Lay contributed money to Richards's 1994 campaign, but he and his wife contributed three times as much to Bush during that race. And there was little question, particularly given the support Lay and Enron had given Bush's father and the Republican party, whom Lay really "supported." Bush wanted his listeners to believe that Lay favored Richards over Bush in that race, which was plainly not the case. Consequently, the statement is a lie under the most useful definition of the term, which is whether the speaker intends that the listener will come to a false conclusion.

As Bush continued, he said one thing that was simply ridiculous then another that appeared to be an outright lie. He accurately said that Richards appointed Lay to the Governor's Business Council, then asserted that "I decided to leave him in place, just for the sake

---

[54] Figures from Texans for Public Justice and the Center for Responsive Politics.
[55] Bennett Roth and R.G. Ratcliffe, "Ken Who? Bush Team Plays Defense," *Houston Chronicle*, January 11, 2002, Business p. 1.

of continuity." At this sentence, the reporters in the room must have had to stifle their giggles. Bush kept Lay on the commission for any number of reasons—to reward a contributor, loyal Bush family friend, and supporter and powerful Texas businessman, perhaps, but for the most part probably because he and Lay shared a common perspective on the role of government regulation of business. When they have the power to change the makeup of commissions, governors rarely keep people around "for the sake of continuity."

Bush then spoke what was almost certainly a lie, that after he took office in 1995, "that was when I first got to know him." In fact, Lay first wrote George W. Bush a check during his 1978 congressional campaign. George W. and Lay were both actively involved in Bush's father's 1992 reelection campaign. Before he became governor, George W. worked with Lay on Houston's bid to host the elder Bush's presidential library. "That's when I probably spent a little more quality time with George W.," said Lay.[56] So did Bush "first get to know" Lay only after he took office in 1995? No. To avoid the conclusion that Bush was lying, one has to employ a Clintonesque semantic deconstruction, arguing that the phrase "got to know" could be interpreted as meaning, say, "shared a hot tub with," and since they didn't do that prior to 1995, Bush hadn't really gotten to know Lay. But that is neither the interpretation most people would make nor the one Bush wanted people to make. His intention was to deceive his listeners into thinking his relationship with Lay was less substantial and of shorter duration than it in fact was. As Bush wrote to Lay in a 1997 birthday letter, in a voice plainly his own and not that of some junior staffer, "One of the sad things about old friends is that they seem to be getting older—just like you!…Laura and I value our friendship with you."[57]

Bush's denials of a relationship with Lay are hardly the most egregious lies a politician has ever uttered. But we should recall how Bill Clinton's one big lie was so similar to the way Bush explained his relationship with Enron. When Clinton said, "I did not have sexual relations with that woman," he meant the term to refer only

[56] Bruce Nichols, "Enron Chief Masters Power of Persuasion," *Dallas Morning News*, July 22, 2001, p. 1H.
[57] This letter can be seen on thesmokinggun.com.

to sexual intercourse; however, he knew and hoped that most people would hear him to mean that he had never had any intimate contact with Lewinsky whatsoever. Clinton was then branded, not only by Republicans but by reporters as well, as practically the worst liar in the history of American politics. Bush's denials during the intense journalistic scrutiny of Enron, by contrast, led few reporters to reevaluate or question their judgment of Bush's fundamental integrity.

As the Enron scandal began to balloon, Bush aide Mary Matalin complained that the Democrats were just making too much of things. "They act like there's some billing records or some cattle scam or some fired travel aides or some blue dress," Matalin said.[58] Had sex been involved, that would have been something awful. But thousands of people losing their jobs and their life savings? Stockholders defrauded? Documents destroyed in an apparent attempt to avoid detection by government authorities? A company that now appears to be little short of a criminal enterprise sitting in the White House making energy policy and determining who will regulate its activities? These questions were of little concern to an administration that claims to be committed to responsibility and accountability.

ECONOMIC CORRUPTION

A pop quiz: Which well-known Texas businessman:

- had a company that set up a phony Cayman Island subsidiary in order to dodge American taxes;
- took a huge loan from his company;
- sold a huge amount of his company's stock just before it was revealed that the company had engaged in accounting fraud, sending the stock price tumbling; and
- was investigated by the SEC for violations of federal securities law?

If you answered Ken Lay of Enron, you'd be half-right. This list also describes the conduct of George W. Bush at Harken Energy

---

[58] Richard Berke, "Parties Weigh Political Price of Enron's Fall" *New York Times*, January 11, 2002, p. A1.

Corporation. Among the shady, sleazy, unethical, and possibly illegal actions taken by the executives at Enron, one stands out for its moral bankruptcy. As the house of cards that was the company's finances began to teeter, the top management at Enron began a massive sell-off of their stock. They apparently knew that once the actual value of the company was revealed, the share price would plummet and their nest eggs would be worthless. What makes this action so reprehensible is that the majority of Enron's employees—who had been encouraged to load up their 401(k)s with Enron stock—and all of its shareholders were not privy to this knowledge and consequently lost everything.[59]

Bush no doubt understood the Enron scandal quite well because in 1990, when he was an officer of the Harken Energy Corporation, Bush did exactly the same thing. As the nonpartisan Center for Public Integrity reported, before he became the governor of Texas, Bush not only violated federal securities law, he sold off a huge amount of stock just before his company's shares went down the toilet, leaving unknowing investors holding the bag.

The parallels between Enron and Harken are striking. Bush's failing oil company, Spectrum 7, had been bought by Harken Energy for $2 million in Harken stock in 1986. Although Spectrum 7 had virtually no value, what did have value, and what Harken purchased, was the Bush family name. By 1990, Harken—on whose board Bush now sat—was losing money rapidly. But the company hid the fact from investors through some creative accounting, for which they were later reprimanded by the SEC. On June 22, 1990, Bush sold Harken stock worth $848,560 at $4 per share. Just weeks later, the company issued a quarterly report revealing millions of dollars in losses. The stock then began to fall, reaching $1 per share by the end of the year. By getting out before things hit the fan, Bush saved himself more than $600,000.[60]

---

[59] A number of books have already been written about the implosion of Enron; see for example Mimi Swartz and Sherron Watkins, *Power Failure: The Inside Story of the Collapse of Enron*. New York: Doubleday, 2003.

[60] John Dunbar, "A Brief History of Bush, Harken, and the SEC," Center for Public Integrity.

Bush has offered different explanations of his stock sale, saying at various times that he "needed to liquefy" the stock in order to pay off a loan, or alternatively that he "just [doesn't] like to carry debt."[61] Whatever the truth, Bush may have felt a little sheepish about bailing out, because instead of filing a report detailing his stock sale within ten days, as is mandated for corporate officers by federal securities law, he didn't get around to informing the SEC until nearly nine months later. This was not the first time Bush found the law inconvenient; he failed to meet the filing deadline on three prior occasions. Was what Bush did illegal? If he sold his stock on the basis of inside information, the answer is yes. Did Bush have inside information?

Before he dumped his stock, Bush served on Harken's audit committee, whose responsibility was to keep track of the company's finances. In the weeks before his stock sale, Bush received memos revealing that the company was about to report a huge loss and would have trouble refinancing its debt.[62] If he read the memos sent to him, he would have had inside information. Nonetheless, Bush later claimed, "I absolutely had no idea [that Harken was about to report a $23 million loss] and would not have sold it had I known."[63] There are only two possible conclusions: either Bush never read these memos and remained blissfully unaware of the company's condition—in which case he was negligent—or he lied about how much he knew and committed an act of insider trading by selling his stock. When the Enron scandal began to creep its way toward him, Bush proclaimed himself "outraged" that the company's executives would do something so terrible. "I thought the captain was supposed to be the last one off the sinking ship, not the first one," an aide quoted Bush as saying. "This stinks."[64] Indeed.

[61] Anthony York, "Memos: Bush Knew of Harken's Problems," Salon.com, July 12, 2002.

[62] Anthony York, "Memos: Bush Knew of Harken's Problems," Salon.com, July 12, 2002.

[63] Mark Curriden, "Records Show What Bush Knew before Stock Sale," *Dallas Morning News*, September 7, 2000, p. 6A.

[64] Lois Romano, "For Kenneth Lay, A Bright Career in Dim Twilight," *Washington Post*, February 3, 2002, p. A1.

The SEC could find no definitive proof Bush knew about the accounting shenanigans that led to the plunge in Harken's stock, and declined to pursue criminal charges against him. Of course, at the time, Bush's father was president, the chair of the SEC was a close Bush family friend, and Bush's former lawyer was now the commission's general counsel.[65] It was neither the first nor the last time he was bailed out in a moment of crisis by some conveniently placed connections.

Although Bush claimed, "I was exonerated" by the SEC over the Harken deal, a letter from the commission said the fact that they were not pursuing the case "must in no way be construed as indicating that [Bush] has been exonerated or that no action may ultimately result from the staff's investigation."[66]

For a time, it seemed as though every new revelation of corporate malfeasance was followed a few days later by a revelation that Bush himself had engaged in precisely the unethical conduct companies like Enron and WorldCom were being criticized for. "The president is concerned about corporations in America who take advantage, set up operations outside of America, in an effort to lower their taxes," said White House press secretary Ari Fleischer solemnly in July of 2002. The next day it was revealed that Harken set up a subsidiary in the Cayman Islands in an effort to lower their taxes while Bush was there (Dick Cheney's Halliburton used the same move). Fleischer, who was admittedly in an unenviable spot, suggested that the fact that the Harken subsidiary didn't make any money meant that there was nothing wrong with the behavior he had just condemned on the president's behalf.[67] In other words, since Bush and his company tried and failed to dodge American taxes, he hadn't done anything wrong—had he tried and succeeded, that might have been a different story. Granted, most people would consider attempting unsuccessfully to commit a crime to be slightly

[65] Mike Allen and George Lardner Jr., "Harken Papers Offer Details on Bush Knowledge," *Washington Post*, July 14, 2002, p. A1.

[66] George Lardner Jr. and Lois Romano, "The Life of George W. Bush," *Washington Post*, July 30, 1999, p. A1.

[67] This little bit of hypocrisy was pointed out by Jonathan Chait of the *New Republic*, "Stupid Is, Stupid Does," tnr.com, August 1, 2002.

less serious than successfully committing the crime, but the attempt is criminal nonetheless. But anyway, it didn't matter, said Bush's communications director, since Bush "has no recollection" of the Cayman tax dodge.[68]

The accounting firm that helped Harken construct its financial house of cards was Arthur Andersen, which performed similar services for Enron. An Arthur Andersen promotional video produced in 1997 shows then–Halliburton CEO Dick Cheney extolling the virtues of the accounting firm. Cheney was particularly taken with the fact that Andersen provided services "over and above just sort of the normal by-the-books auditing arrangement."[69] Andersen's willingness to go over and above all that by-the-books stuff got Halliburton into some hot water, as the SEC began an investigation into Cheney's former company in 2002. Employing some of the same creativity they did at Enron, Andersen helped Halliburton hide losses and report more than $100 million in revenues it hadn't actually received. Such practices, which may not be quite illegal, are referred to by those in the know as "aggressive"—although if you were a Halliburton shareholder, you'd probably consider them to be fraud. The company, of course, denied that its CEO had any clue about the way the company he was in charge of counted its profits—Cheney, they said, was a "hands-off" chief executive.[70]

When the Harken story began to gather steam and the administration decided Bush had to come out against corporate fraud, he gave a speech outlining a hastily drawn ten-point plan for corporate responsibility. "I challenge compensation committees," Bush firmly said, "to put an end to all company loans to corporate officers,"[71] such as the $180,000 in sub-prime rate loans he got from Harken Energy when he served on their board during the 1980s. His plan also said, "Corporate leaders should be required to tell the public promptly

---

[68] Timothy Burger, "Bush Unaware of Firm's Tax Move, Aide Says," *New York Daily News*, August 1, 2002.

[69] Anita Raghavan and Jean Cummings, "Cheney Praised Andersen Work in Video," *Wall Street Journal*, May 10, 2002, p. C1.

[70] Alex Berenson, "Halliburton and Inquiry by the S.E.C.," *New York Times*, May 30, 2002, p. C1.

[71] Speech on Wall Street, July 9, 2002.

whenever they buy or sell company stock for personal gain," just as he had failed to do when he sold nearly a million dollars in Harken stock.

When asked what he knew about Harken's scheme to falsely boost revenue through the "sale" of a subsidiary called Aloha Petroleum to its own officers (Harken loaned the officers the money to buy Aloha, then declared the sale as income), Bush said he just didn't remember, and reporters would have to check the minutes of the board meetings. When they asked for those minutes, the White House said Bush didn't have them, and he wasn't going to ask Harken for them. The company, of course, refused to release them as well. Bush also refused to ask the SEC to release all its documents relating to Bush and Harken. The matter, said Bush, had been "fully vetted," so stop asking.[72] The media complied.

Bush's professions of ignorance were plainly disingenuous—according to Harken documents retrieved from the SEC by the Center for Public Integrity via a Freedom of Information Act request, Bush was present at multiple board meetings where the Aloha scheme was discussed, and, as a member of the Harken board's audit committee, would have been more than familiar with the details. When the company settled on the plan—under which the Harken execs would pay $1 million for Aloha, but the company's accountants (again Arthur Andersen) would magically record a $7.9 million profit—Bush and his fellow board members gave the go-ahead.[73]

This scheme was plainly fraudulent, an early precursor the kind of "creative accounting" pulled by Bush's supporter Enron. Bush described the SEC forcing the company to restate its profits as "an honest disagreement about accounting procedures,"[74] but that's like John Dillinger saying he and the FBI had an honest disagreement about bank withdrawal procedures. It is meant to convey a false impression.

During his speech to Wall Street, Bush did take the opportunity to reiterate his firmly held belief that the rich are different. "In the

---

[72] Mike Allen, "Memo Cited Bush's Late SEC Filings," *Washington Post*, July 3, 2002, p. A4.
[73] Internal Harken documents detailing these facts can be found at the Center for Public Integrity, www.publicintegrity.org.
[74] Press conference, July 8, 2002.

long run," he said, "there is no capitalism without conscience. There is no wealth without character."[75] In other words, those who accumulate wealth through chicanery ultimately lose their wealth. If you see somebody who's been rich for a long time—or somebody who has had their wealth passed down through a couple of generations—it's only because he's a person of character, someone who is wealthy because he *deserves* to be.

We should recall that it was Newt Gingrich's Republican-led Congress that got the ball rolling by passing, as part of their "Contract with America," the Private Securities Litigation Reform Act of 1995, a bill that by shielding corporate officers and accountants from lawsuits opened the door to a corporate crime wave. President Clinton vetoed it, but his veto was overridden. President Bush's first budget proposed eliminating fifty-seven staff positions at the SEC, including thirteen positions in the office of full disclosure, thirteen positions in the office of investment-management regulation, and twelve positions in the office of the prevention and suppression of fraud.[76]

SILENT WATCHDOGS

The reaction to Bush's speech about the Enron scandal from at least some of the press was positive. *Newsweek*'s Howard Fineman wrote, "The president didn't go far enough for the Democrats, of course. But they are easy to dismiss as donation-grubbing insiders eager for a way to cover their rears and find an issue for the fall."[77] Even for reporters less sycophantic than Fineman, the shockingly brief and belated press coverage of Bush's involvement in the fraud committed during his tenure at Harken was friendly to the president in a critical way: almost none of it went into any substantial detail about the substance of the charges, what had actually occurred at Harken, what Bush knew about it, or what he did in response. Instead, the coverage was speculative and strategic, focused on the question of whether

[75] Speech on Wall Street, July 9, 2002.
[76] Anthony York, "The Hypocrite in Chief," Salon.com, July 2, 2002.
[77] Howard Fineman, "Living Politics: McCain Remains Bush's Top Nemesis," *Newsweek* Web exclusive, July 10, 2002.

the Harken story would hurt Bush politically. Reporters politely refrained from doing much real investigation about what he had actually done wrong.

pass again

As a point of reference, let's compare the Harken story to another tale of questionable prepresidential finances. The Whitewater "scandal," in which Bill and Hillary Clinton were involved in a failed land deal in Arkansas, was the target of an Independent Counsel investigation that spent more than $70 million in taxpayer funds. And how much money was involved? Approximately $220,000. A lot of money to you and me, perhaps, but a rather insubstantial amount in the context of national affairs. The numbers involved in Harken are substantially larger: the $848,560 Bush made on his timely sale of Harken stock, the $20 million in losses Harken hid from shareholders, and the $8 million in sham "profit" it created out of thin air with the Aloha deal.

The *New York Times*—a single newspaper—ran more than *one thousand* articles discussing Whitewater.[78] The *Times*'s coverage of the failed land deal was, to put it mildly, overblown. After reporter Jeff Gerth broke the story (with an account riddled with errors, as Gene Lyons detailed in his book *Fools for Scandal*), the Grey Lady continued to flog the story for years, even after the Independent Counsel could unearth no wrongdoing on the Clintons' part. Like the prosecutor who proclaims his certainty that the man he convicted is guilty even after he is exonerated by DNA evidence and someone else confesses to the crime, the *Times* held to the end that, well, after we spent all that energy investigating it, they must have done *something* wrong, even if we can't quite say what it was.

Since they're the bastion of the liberal media, the *Times* must have investigated the Harken scandal with a vigor similar to that they put into the Whitewater scandal, right? Well, not exactly.

---

[78] This figure—1,091 articles in the *New York Times* between the beginning of 1992 and the day Clinton left office—was obtained by searching the Lexis/Nexis archives seeking articles mentioning Whitewater in the story's lead and Clinton anywhere in the story, but excluding all stories mentioning "Lewinsky" in the lead.

While they published more than one thousand articles mentioning Whitewater, the grand total for Harken was...nine.[79]

As Bush said in a radio address while the Enron scandal was brewing, "Employees who have worked hard and saved all their lives should not have to risk losing everything if their company fails."[80] Hard to argue with that. The Enron and Harken cases prove what most ordinary people understand: careful government regulation is necessary to rein in the distortions that unfettered markets engender. Contrary to what Treasury Secretary Paul O'Neill argued, the Enron failure does not prove "the genius of capitalism."[81] It highlights its dark underbelly, where the Ken Lays and George Bushes of the world get rich and people without the benefit of inside information and powerful friends lose everything.

The Harken non-scandal was truly remarkable for its brevity and the lack of seriousness with which it was treated by the press. As he has so many other times, George W. Bush was able to walk away from responsibility with barely a scratch.

Should the press have gone after these stories more aggressively? The answer is slightly different in each case. On Vietnam, the answer is unquestionably yes. Bush used family connections to get a plum spot in the National Guard, leapfrogging over other less fortunate young men to stay out of harm's way. He also failed to fulfill the commitment he had made to the Guard, then offered ridiculous and implausible explanations for his conduct. With the exception of the *Boston Globe* and to a lesser extent the *Los Angeles Times*, the only news outlets to investigate the story with any real energy, the press failed in its responsibility to the American public to fully vet the candidates' biographies. On the drunk-driving incident, the press failed by focusing on the tactical aspect—what would the effect be on the race's outcome?—and failing to explore what light Bush's hiding the story and then attempting to blame the Democrats for it

---

[79] This figure was obtained using the same search methodology as the Whitewater figure—articles in the *Times* mentioning Harken in the lead and Bush anywhere in the story. All of these appeared between March and August 2002.

[80] Weekly radio address, February 2, 2002.

[81] H. Josef Hebert, "Cabinet Members Say They Didn't Inform Bush about Enron Calls for Help," Associated Press, January 13, 2002.

shed on his character. The question of Bush's drug use may have been the least relevant to whether he should have been elected president, although he got away with some pretty squirmy evasions on the subject. On the Harken issue, the press failed miserably, once again failing to call Bush on his evasions and lies and asking only whether the story would hurt him politically. In each case, Bush and his people managed to make the best of a potentially bad situation, cajoling, intimidating, and at times deceiving the press into writing the story almost exactly as they wanted.

The 2000 campaign and what has occurred since show the Bush machine's mastery of spin control. Each of these stories revealed something about George W. Bush that for other politicians might have been fatal. More importantly, other politicians facing almost identical issues were far more aggressively investigated by the press.

While Bill Clinton spent nearly his entire presidency under a state of siege from an aggressive, adversarial press corps, reporters have treated Bush with deference and respect. Every potential scandal is dispatched with a few days' worth of mildly critical coverage before the press's attention moves on to some other story, never to raise the fundamental questions that might bring Bush's claims of a flawless integrity into question. With every bullet Bush dodges, the idea that the media have a liberal bias becomes more and more absurd. It is a record of successful press manipulation that has continued nearly unabated to this day.

3.

"That's Trustworthiness"

A Strategy of Lies

> "I think if you say you're going to do something
> and don't do it, that's trustworthiness."
> —*George W. Bush, in an August 2000 interview with CNN*

As the old joke goes, you can tell a politician is lying when his lips are moving. But while there have been many dishonest presidents in American history, there has never been a presidency so organized around deception as a fundamental operating principle as that of George W. Bush. When he ran for president, Bush promised he would "repair the broken bonds of trust between Americans and their government."[1] What he has delivered instead is perhaps the most dishonest administration in American history.

Bush is certainly not one for pandering. He seldom adopts positions simply because they are popular. His agenda is clear and unambiguous, if you look past the cloud of contradictory rhetoric inside which it is hidden. He is well aware, furthermore, of which parts of the agenda are popular and which aren't. When one of his goals is greeted with opposition or indifference, he accomplishes its enactment with a web of deception built on absurd syllogisms and

---

[1] Speech in Austin, TX, March 7, 2000.

sprinkled with a few outright falsehoods to sow misunderstanding and confusion among the American public.

Journalists are loath to call a president (with the exception of Bill Clinton) a liar, or even write the words "The president lied." Ben Bradlee, the legendary *Washington Post* editor, told journalist Mark Hertsgaard, "We have not developed a way to say to the reader, 'The president spoke last night, but he told a lie, so we're not going to tell you what it is.'"[2] Instead, they point out deceptions with euphemisms, attempting in a round-about way to lead the reader to draw connections between the statement and the truth. But somehow, saying the president lied is beyond the bounds of propriety.[3] During the 2000 campaign, Howell Raines, editor in chief of the "liberal" *New York Times*, even barred columnist Paul Krugman from saying Bush was lying.[4]

Later, Krugman's fellow *Times* columnist Nicholas Kristof penned a rather extraordinary testimonial to Bush's sincerity that reveals just how eager even ostensibly liberal journalists have been to proclaim what an honest guy Bush is. During the 2000 campaign, Kristof had heard that as a boy Bush was rejected from the St. Johns private school in Houston, and when he asked him about it, Bush "indignantly" denied it. The next day, a Bush staffer called Kristof to say that Bush had checked with his parents, and it turned out that he had in fact been rejected from St. Johns. What Kristof wrote in relating the tale in early 2003 is truly remarkable: "I found his willingness to confirm this unflattering detail an impressive example of his political integrity, and it was this kind of honesty that won Mr. Bush the respect of many journalists who were covering him."[5] The fact that Bush said something untrue then admitted his mistake is evidence to Kristof, and apparently to other journalists, of impressive integrity. Just as journalists found the most trivial inaccuracies

---

[2] Mark Hertsgaard, *On Bended Knee: The Press and the Reagan Presidency*. New York: Shocken Books, 1988, p. 331.
[3] Eric Alterman pointed this out in "Bush Lies, Media Swallows," thenation.com, November 7, 2002.
[4] Howard Kurtz, "Wealth of Opinions," *Washington Post*, January 22, 2003, p. C1.
[5] Nicholas Kristof, "A Boy and His Benefits," *New York Times*, January 24, 2003.

to be proof of pathological mendacity when spoken by Al Gore, admitting to faulty memory about an inconsequential event decades before yields Bush a glowing tribute.

So let's not mince words: George W. Bush is a liar. Whether he lies to his wife or his friends is something I could not care less about, and I suspect most Americans would agree. What Bush does is far worse: he lies to the American people about things that matter. He lies about who he is and what he believes; he lies about what he has done; and he lies about what he plans to do.

In this Bush is the inverse of Bill Clinton—Bush's lies are legion but have nothing to do with whom he sleeps with. While many on both the right and left took issue with Clinton's policies, Clinton did not try to deceive Americans about what those policies were. Bush, on the other hand, lies not to protect himself from embarrassment but to conceal the nature of his ideology and plans. Bush tells more lies about policy in a week than Bill Clinton did in eight years. Even the lies he tells about who he is as a person, which were detailed in the previous chapters, are told in the service of a narrow partisan agenda. While Bill Clinton lied about his personal life to save his own skin, George W. Bush does something far worse: he deceives Americans about the things he does that will actually affect their lives.

Columnist Michael Kinsley offered one explanation for this peculiar perspective on honesty, which Bush seems to share with his father, that one may lie about political matters but still consider one-self an honest person. "This derived," Kinsley wrote, "from the cherished preppy-snob distinction between life and games. In life one must be decent and honest and must not seem to be trying too hard. But in games—including politics—one must be ruthless, and one must win. One is not really misbehaving because it's only a game."[6] Bush is certainly ruthless when it comes to politics. One of the many things the 2000 campaign revealed about his vaunted "character" is that when power is on the line, he has no qualms about lying, whether about himself or his opponents.

---

[6] Michael Kinsley, "Lying in Style," *Slate*, April 18, 2002.

The Federal Trade Commission, which polices the accuracy of advertising, considers certain claims to be outside the definition of "false advertising" if they are so patently absurd that no one could believe them to be true. Claims like, "Our new shampoo will change your life!" are considered "puffery," and no action is taken against them. When a candidate says, "I'm running for Congress because I want to change the way they do business in Washington," he is being no less absurd. Maybe he wants to change the way they do business in Washington and maybe he doesn't, but he's running for Congress because he wants to be a Congressman. In both cases, we let the lie slide.

Perhaps some of what Bush says should be considered puffery, such as his claims to be a regular guy who understands the needs of ordinary people (or, as he put it, "I know how hard it is for you to put food on your family"[7]) or his assertions that his tax cuts do not disproportionately benefit the wealthy. But the problem with many of Bush's lies, ridiculous though they may be, is that so many people end up believing them.

Bush does occasionally lie about trivial things, but for the most part his lies are large and comprehensive. This is the reason I assert that Bush is among the most dishonest presidents America has seen. Long ago, Bush made his peace with the idea that in order to accomplish his goals, he would have to deceive the American public. Once you do that, the lies flow like water.

THE ORWELLIAN MISDIRECTION

Like many on the right, Bush utilizes a particularly diabolical kind of lie, which I call the Orwellian Misdirection, as a staple of argumentation. In this move, the speaker accuses his opponents of the very thing of which he is guilty. The Orwellian Misdirection often has the intended effect of befuddling one's opponent, making him change the subject in a retreat to firmer ground.

For instance, when questioned about his extraordinary fund raising during the 2000 campaign, Bush accused his opponents of being

---

[7] Bob Herbert, "Lessons in Reality," *New York Times*, February 21, 2000, p. A19.

the real profligate fundraisers. During the primaries, he tagged John McCain as the creature of special interests, saying McCain had raised "more money than anybody" from Washington lobbyists. This was simply untrue; in fact, at that point Bush had raised *five times* as much from lobbyists and their immediate families as McCain had.[8] Then, in his first debate with Al Gore, Bush responded to a question about campaign-finance reform by saying, "This man has outspent me; the special interests are outspending me." Like many he told, this ridiculous lie (Bush spent more than $185 million in 2000, more than any other candidate in history[9]) went unremarked by the watchdogs in the press.

There may be no more consistently offered Orwellian Misdirection than the charge of "class warfare," which Republicans regularly thrust at Democrats. Ask yourself: when was the last time you heard a journalist refer to Republican efforts to attack unions, to undermine enforcement of fair labor regulations, to cut programs like food stamps, or to fight against increases in the minimum wage as "class warfare"? The charge is only applied to Democrats. Consider this: the ABC News political unit put out a call for anyone who came across "suspect" political communication in the 2002 campaign to send it in to their "Watchdog," including "messages that are false, logically flawed, racist or race-baiting, religion-baiting, sexist, class-warfaring, or deeply personal." Notice how engaging in "class warfare"—in other words, suggesting that politicians should serve the interests of working people—is put in the same classification as lies and race-baiting.

In this perverse formulation, it is not the *act* of pimping for the rich at the expense of everyone else that constitutes class warfare but only the *observation* that someone is doing so. As far as Republicans are concerned, class warfare can only move in one direction—

[8] Jim Yardley and Frank Bruni, "Bush Takes Tougher Line and Emphasizes Reform," *New York Times*, February 8, 2000, p. A22.
[9] The most commonly cited figure on Bush's 2000 fundraising is $100 million; the $185 million covers all the money his campaign spent during that campaign, including both private and public funds. For more information on federal campaign fundraising and spending, see the Center for Responsive Politics, www.opensecrets.org.

upward. Any salvos in the other direction are nothing more than attempts to stimulate the economy. This exchange between Gore adviser Bob Shrum and Bush adviser Karen Hughes during the 2000 campaign summarizes in two lines how "debates" about the fairness of tax policy proceed and how the right uses the charge of class warfare to squash discussion of equity:

> **Shrum:** Half of the benefits in Governor Bush's tax proposal go to people who make $250,000 a year or more.
> **Hughes:** There you go again, class warfare.[10]

In order to defend Bush's tax plan, Hughes avoids addressing the substance of Shrum's (accurate) argument—instead, she tries to define any discussion of the fairness of Bush's plan as out of bounds, shifting the focus from whether Bush's plan is fair to whether Shrum's argument is fair. Of course, nothing terrifies Republicans more than the idea of people voting according to their class. It's all well and good for the rich to do so, but if everyone of modest means took a clear-eyed look at the two parties and voted according to who was on their side, Republicans would be routed. Preventing this from happening requires not only devising what Lee Atwater called "wedge issues" that define Democrats as alien from the values of ordinary people, but arguing that any discussion of class—especially how Republican policies benefit the rich—is off-limits.

Journalists are all too willing to wag a finger at any Democrat who might attempt to raise the issue of economic inequity. As a class, reporters are well-educated, fairly well paid (some more than others), and, when it comes to their economic opinions, more conservative than liberal. For instance, a 1998 poll of journalists found them to be to the right of the public on a range of issues from NAFTA to taxes to entitlement cuts to the extent of corporate power in America. When asked which sources they used when writing stories about economic issues, 82 percent said they consulted government officials

---

[10] *This Week*, ABC, August 20, 2000.

or business representatives "nearly always," while only 10 percent said the same about labor representatives or consumer advocates.[11] These are hardly the reporting practices of a press gripped by liberal bias.

The Orwellian Misdirection can be trotted out in a wide range of circumstances. Consider the case of Miguel Estrada, the arch-conservative judge Bush appointed early in his term to sit on the D.C. Circuit Court (the last stop before the Supreme Court). Democrats were concerned both about Estrada's ideology and his temperament; Estrada's supervisor in the Solicitor General's office said about him, "I think Estrada lacks the judgment and he is too much of an ideologue to be an appeals court judge."[12] When Democrats on the Judiciary Committee delayed Estrada's confirmation hearings in order to examine his record more closely, Trent Lott (who was forced to step down as Senate majority leader after making comments seeming to support Strom Thurmond's segregationist presidential campaign) had the gall to charge his Democratic colleagues with racism, saying they were holding up Estrada's nomination "because he's Hispanic."[13] A conservative group later ran ads about the Estrada nomination showing a young Hispanic boy looking for a job while a white store owner takes down his "help wanted" sign. "Call the Senate Democrats," the ad said. "Tell them it's time for intolerance to end." The charge Republicans made over and over—that Democrats opposed Estrada because they are racists—was as despicable as it was ridiculous.

Utah Senator Orrin Hatch played the same tune when Democrats questioned Priscilla Owen's nomination to the 5th Circuit Court of Appeals. Owen was the true definition of a "judicial activist," someone who goes beyond the law to produce the outcomes she favors. Even her colleagues on the all-Republican Texas Supreme Court often found her opinions indefensible, particularly on abortion (President Bush's counsel, Alberto Gonzales, who served with Owen on the Texas

[11] David Croteau, "Examining the 'Liberal Media' Claim: Journalists' Views on Politics, Economic Policy and Media Coverage," Fairness & Accuracy in Reporting.
[12] Bill Miller, "Appeals Court Nominees Share Conservative Roots," *Washington Post*, May 23, 2001.
[13] John Lancaster, "Some Detect GOP Hypocrisy on Hispanics," *Washington Post*, April 15, 2001, p. A19.

court called one of her decisions "an unconscionable act of judicial activism.") Owen was also widely criticized for failing to recuse herself from cases involving the corporations that funded her campaigns—then ruling in their favor.[14] But Senator Hatch argued that Democrats—including, presumably, the women senators balking at her nomination—were opposing Owen "because she is a woman in public life who is believed to have personal views that some maintain should be unacceptable for a woman in public life to have." This sexist approach, he said, "represents a new glass ceiling for woman jurists, and they have come too far to suffer now having their feet bound up just as they approach the tables of our high courts."[15] The conservative Utah Republican's defense of women's rights—after all, it's not easy to get the glass ceiling and foot binding into a single sentence—was eloquent. But no serious person could believe that the Democrats were opposing Owen's nomination because she was a woman.

Sadly, this repugnant tactic has become standard Republican operating procedure, as was in evidence when Democrats objected to another Bush judicial nominee, Alabama Attorney General William Pryor. A right-wing extremist on any number of issues, Pryor has devoted himself to destroying what he calls the "so-called separation of church and state," because, as he said in 1997, "God has chosen, through his son Jesus Christ, this time and this place for all Christians...to save our country and save our courts."[16] The hesitation of Democratic senators on the Judiciary Committee to see Pryor given a lifetime appointment to the federal bench led to charges that they were evincing an anti-Catholic bias (Pryor is an observant Catholic, though he does not feel himself bound by the Church's opposition to the death penalty). When Alabama Republican Jeff Sessions—a Methodist—accused the Democrats of being anti-Catholic, the Catholic Democrats Patrick Leahy and Richard Durbin were not amused.

---

[14] Kris Axtman, "The Case of Judges v. Ideology," *Christian Science Monitor*, January 23, 2003, p. 2.

[15] Anthony York, "Owen's Fate in Feinstein's Hands," *Salon*, July 24, 2002.

[16] Michelle Goldberg, "Defining Judicial Deviancy Down," Salon.com, June 13, 2003.

In all fairness, although the Republicans have of late made the scurrilous charge of religious and ethnic bias their favorite piece of mud to sling, Democrats are on occasion guilty of variations on the Orwellian Misdirection as well. In 2002, South Carolina Senate candidate Alex Sanders—who opposed the death penalty, a principled stand that didn't win him many votes—ran an ad accusing his opponent, Lindsay Graham, of voting against the death penalty for terrorists. "It's a question of judgment—Lindsay Graham's judgment," the ad said.

Nonetheless, the Orwellian Misdirection remains a rhetorical tool largely of the right. During the 2002 congressional elections, some Republican candidates started accusing Democrats who had supported government investment of Social Security funds in the stock market (which would pool the risk, as opposed to the Republicans' favored plan of individual accounts) of supporting the dreaded "privatization" of Social Security—which almost every Republican supports. John Thune of South Dakota, who favored individual accounts, ran an ad against his Senate opponent Tim Johnson claiming that "Johnson supports a Social Security privatization plan."[17]

Thune, like many other Republican candidates, was following the instructions of the National Republican Congressional Committee, which sent out a memo to its candidates telling them to run as fast and as far from Social Security "privatization" as possible—not the concept, but the word itself. Despite the fact that diverting Social Security funds to private accounts has for some time been Republican gospel, and up until 2002 everyone, Democrats and Republicans, called it "privatization" or at the very least "partial privatization," the NRCC was now proclaiming that "'privatization' is a false and misleading word insofar as it is being used by Democrats to describe Republican positions on Social Security."

NRCC spokesman Steve Schmidt all but acknowledged that Republicans were hoping to deceive voters on the issue, so they could

---

[17] *Inside Politics*, CNN, August 21, 2002.

chasten Democrats and work to partially privatize Social Security later. "In order for there to be an honest debate on Social Security, Democrats have to lose this election," he said. "Only after they've lost another election where they've put all their chips on the Social Security issue will honest-minded Democrats step forward to work on the issue."[18]

A variant of this tactic can work as well—not claiming to be for what you are against but claiming to be against something no one is for. If Bush opposes something popular, instead of stating his opposition forthrightly he will proclaim that what he actually opposes is something unpopular. This is how Bush finesses his opposition to affirmative action. Bush understands that while majorities of Americans support efforts to ensure diversity in education, everybody is against "quotas." So when Bush decided in early 2003 to side with white students suing the University of Michigan over its admissions procedure, in which extra points were awarded for being a member of a minority (as well as being an athlete or coming from the largely white Upper Peninsula), he proclaimed that what he was really opposing was quotas—in fact, he repeated the word no fewer than four times in his brief statement explaining his opposition.[19]

The problem, of course, is that quotas don't exist at the University of Michigan or anywhere else. They were made illegal by the landmark 1978 *Regents of the University of California v. Bakke* case. But saying he opposed affirmative action because he opposed quotas had worked for him before. In his final debate with Al Gore, Bush tactically answered a question about affirmative action by repeating the word "quota" five times. Gore tried to call him on it, saying, "with all due respect, Governor, that's a red herring. Affirmative action isn't quotas. I'm against quotas. They're illegal." Bush responded, "If affirmative action means quotas, I'm against it. If affirmative action means what I just described, what I'm for, then I'm for it."

When the Supreme Court decided the Michigan case, ruling that the undergraduate system—in which points were awarded for

---

[18] Jonathan Weisman, "GOP Disavows Social Security 'Privatization,'" *Washington Post*, September 13, 2002, p. A10.
[19] Statement in Washington, DC, January 15, 2003.

membership in a minority group—was unconstitutional but the Michigan law school's more "holistic" method of seeking racial diversity in each incoming class was permissible, the decision accorded with most Americans' beliefs about how affirmative action should be carried out. So Bush quickly reversed his position, saying about the decision he had argued against, "I applaud the Supreme Court for recognizing the value of diversity on our nation's campuses."[20] Bush nonetheless remained strangely silent on the topic of affirmative action for children of alumni, which no one doubts played a role in getting a certain C student into Yale.

In cases like Social Security privatization and the touchy issue of efforts to enhance class privilege, Republicans rely on the Orwellian Misdirection because it can be so effective. It substitutes counter-attack for engagement, using a kind of "I know you are but what am I" that sends any reasonable argument spiraling into absurdity. The original criticism is inevitably lost, the less likely to be brought up again. The truth and the facts disappear.

Too Dumb to Lie?

The success of lies that politicians tell is determined by the willing-ness of the press to uncover them and punish their purveyors. When journalists are aggressive and skeptical, politicians learn quickly that lying has costs and are persuaded to stick to the truth. But when reporters decide that a politician is honest and show him that they don't particularly care if he lies, he will be emboldened to deceive on a grander and grander scale, unconcerned about the prospect of being exposed. This is just what happened to George W. Bush.

During the 2000 campaign, reporters determined to get inside the candidates' heads framed their coverage around what they believed to be each man's Achilles heel. For Gore, it was the idea that he was an overambitious, self-aggrandizing liar who would say any-thing to get elected. For Bush, it was the idea that he was too inex-perienced and blockheaded to handle the world's most important

---

[20] Dana Milbank, "As 2004 Nears, Bush Pins Slump on Clinton," *Washington Post*, July 1, 2003, p. A11.

job. Although both of these pictures were uncomplimentary, they worked to Bush's advantage in a number of important ways. First, one may disprove the notion that one is unintelligent by displaying a command of important facts and ideas, as Bush was thought to have done in his debates with Gore (a questionable conclusion, but one that was nonetheless made). But no number of honest statements can undo the conclusion that one is untrustworthy. Second, reporters find honesty to be a more important quality in a candidate than intelligence, making Gore's caricature likely to result in more critical coverage. A 2001 study by a group of scholars found that reporters rated honesty as more important in a candidate than experience or having solutions to the country's problems.[21]

But most importantly, if reporters think one candidate is smart but dishonest while the other is dumb but honest, the second candidate is free to lie pretty much whenever he wants. When Gore said something that turned out to be inaccurate in any way, reporters assumed he was being willfully deceptive. When Bush said something untrue, on the other hand, reporters assumed he had just made a mistake because, after all, he's not too bright.

The way this worked to Bush's advantage can be seen in one of the most brazen lies he told during the 2000 campaign, concerning a patients' bill of rights, an immensely popular proposal to prevent HMOs from denying needed care to consumers. When public desire to curb HMO abuses reached a pitch in 1995, Governor Bush dug in his heels. The Texas legislature passed a patients' bill of rights; Bush vetoed it. The legislature tried again in its next session; despite Bush's lobbying against it, they passed another version, this time with a veto-proof majority. With no choice left, Bush allowed the bill to become law without his signature.

But when he began running for president, Bush reconstructed this episode as evidence of his record of bipartisan accomplishment. In the last of their three debates, Al Gore accused Bush of not supporting a patients' bill of rights. "Actually, Mr. Vice President, it's not

[21] Judith Trent et al, "Image, Media Bias, and Voter Characteristics," *American Behavioral Scientist* 44: 2101-2124 (2001).

true; I do support a national patients' bill of rights," Bush said. "As a matter of fact, I brought Republicans and Democrats together to do just that in the state of Texas to get a patients' bill of rights through." This was no off-the-cuff exaggeration. Bush was not taking credit for something in which he was only peripherally involved; he was taking credit for something that happened despite his determined opposition. And the press let the lie stand.

The episode demonstrates that the only thing that will stop a politician like Bush from lying is if reporters call him on the lie. In this case, journalists were so busy poring over every statement Gore made that they couldn't be bothered to check if Bush was telling the truth. When he got away with the lie, he figured he could just keep on making it; and he did. Bush knew he could lie about the patients' bill of rights—during the primary campaign he aired ads that said, "while Washington deadlocked, he delivered a patients' bill of rights that's a model for America." Reporters failed to point out that the claim was false.

While Gore's exaggerations may have put him more at the center of events than he actually was, they didn't deceive anyone about what his positions or goals were. For instance, he cosponsored early versions of campaign-finance reform but not the McCain-Feingold campaign-finance-reform bill as he once said.[22] In contrast, Bush deceived people both about what he had done and what he intended to do. His lie about the Texas patients' bill of rights is a perfect example. The critical deception is not simply that he took credit for a bill he actually opposed but that he was trying to fool voters into thinking he actually believed in genuine patient protections and would work to see them enacted into law, which he did not and would not. Needless to say, despite what he claimed as a candidate, Bush never lifted a finger to enact a patients' bill of rights once he was in the Oval Office.

Stories about a reply Bush gave to a foreign journalist's question about Slovakia illustrate the way his caricature was far less damaging

[22] Robert Parry, "He's No Pinocchio," *Washington Monthly*, April 1, 2000, p. 23.

than Gore's. "The only thing I know about Slovakia is what I learned first hand from your foreign minister, who came to Texas," Bush said. "I had a great meeting with him. It's an exciting country. It's a country that's flourishing. It's a country that's doing very well."[23] Numerous stories revealed that the person Bush had met was not the Foreign Minister of Slovakia but the Prime Minister of Slovenia. The incident was used as one of a litany of examples in stories with titles like, "The Question Dogs George Bush: Is He Smart Enough?"[24]

While those stories were certainly uncomplimentary, had it been Al Gore, the article would have read something like this: "It was later revealed that the man Gore had met was not the foreign minister of Slovakia, but the prime minister of Slovenia. Bush aides charged that this was the latest in a long line of Gore deceptions. A psychologist has a slightly different explanation: 'Gore may not be consciously trying to lie, but he wants to ingratiate himself with the person he's meeting,' says Georgetown University professor Biff Headshrinker. 'He's trying, somewhat awkwardly, to make a connection, even if it means fudging the facts.' But the incident raises an issue—the question of honesty—political insiders see as Gore's Achilles heel." If you were reading the newspaper during the 2000 campaign, this invented article probably has a familiar ring.

But because Bush's caricature was about intelligence, not honesty, the possibility that he might have been lying was not raised. Consequently, no moral judgment was made about the statement—it was simply an honest mistake and one that would seem to most Americans to be completely understandable. Slovenia and Slovakia? Why ten years before they weren't even countries! While we do not know whether this particular statement was a mistake or not, almost any lie Bush uttered could be and was dismissed in this way: well, he's not too bright, so he must have just been mistaken. (Bush's confusion

---

[23] "Hot Spots Put Texan Bush on the Spot," *St. Petersburg Times*, June 23, 1999, p. 3A.
[24] Kevin Merida, "Shades of Gray Matter: The Question Dogs George Bush: Is He Smart Enough?" *Washington Post*, January 19, 2000, p. C1.

over the two eastern European nations actually turned out to have some consequence four years later, when Slovakia agreed to have its name added to the Bush administration's "coalition" of supporters for its war on Iraq. The Bush administration mistakenly announced that Slovenia had joined the coalition, sparking outraged protests in the Slovenian capital of Ljubljana.[25])

Because Gore was characterized as the dishonest one, Bush was free to lie without consequence. Bush understood he could therefore lie about Gore on just about any subject. "He's the biggest spender we've ever had in the history of politics,"[26] Bush said of Gore—an absurd suggestion, but one that reporters felt was unnecessary to correct. (Of course, the biggest government spender was Franklin Roosevelt; during the height of World War II, government spending accounted for more than 40 percent of GDP, peaking at 43.7 percent in 1944. The post-war champ was Ronald Reagan, who campaigned as an advocate of limited government; at the height of his military buildup, government spending accounted for 23.5 percent of GDP.[27]) Bush's ads accused Gore of having a prescription-drug plan that "forces seniors into one HMO, selected by the federal government," which lied on two counts: Gore's plan didn't force anyone to do anything, and the "federal HMO" to which it referred was Medicare, which is not an HMO at all.

In a particularly egregious case, in May 2000 Bush falsely asserted that Gore had been a member of the National Rifle Association. When Gore said that he had never been an NRA member and reporters asked Bush about it, Bush pointed out that he had ended his false accusation with the phrase "if I'm not mistaken"—as though that forgave the lie—then told reporters that it was their responsibility to discover the truth and Gore's responsibility to prove that he wasn't a member. When he was then asked where he got the idea that Gore was an NRA member, Bush responded, "A little

[25] Al Kamen, "They Got the 'Slov' Part Right," *Washington Post*, March 28, 2003, p. A21.
[26] Kevin Sack, "For Limited Government? That's Me, Says Gore," *New York Times*, October 25, 2000, p. A23.
[27] The annual Budget of the United States Government contains historical tables in which these data may be found.

birdie."[28] By this logic, Bush could have accused Gore of being a child molester, and it would have been Gore's responsibility to prove that he wasn't. Ask yourself: would the press, which was so vigilant about policing Gore's every word for veracity, have allowed Gore to get away with something like that?

Of course, whether Bush added "if I'm not mistaken" to his deception is utterly meaningless. Although we can define "lying" in a number of ways, the definition that many scholars who have contemplated the issue have settled on and the one that is most satisfactory when it comes to leaders speaking to citizens is that the lie lies in the intention of the speaker. If the speaker intends to deceive those who listen, then he has lied, no matter the syntax he has employed or the qualifiers he has offered.

A POLICY OF DECEPTION

Once Bush was elected, deception became not just a technique of argumentation but a key component of policy-making, nowhere more so than on the issue of Iraq. In arguing for his war, Bush said that Iraq had "a growing fleet of manned and unmanned aerial vehicles" that could be used "for missions targeting the United States"[29]—but the unmanned aircraft Iraq was attempting to construct didn't have the range to get anywhere near the United States. He said that Iraq had tried to buy uranium from Africa, a charge based on fabricated evidence. He said Iraq had tried to buy aluminum cylinders "used to enrich uranium for a nuclear weapon"— but the type of cylinders Iraq was seeking were of virtually no use in enriching uranium, instead being intended for conventional rockets.[30] Even though this was the consensus of virtually every expert who examined the issue, Bush continued to repeat that the aluminum tubes were meant for enriching uranium, even in his 2003 State of the Union address. Others in the administration took up

[28] Frank Bruni, "Gore and Bush Clash Further on Firearms," *New York Times*, May 8, 2000, p. A8.
[29] Speech in Cincinnati, October 7, 2002.
[30] Jody Warrick, "U.S. Claim on Iraqi Nuclear Program is Called into Question," *Washington Post*, January 24, 2003, p. A1.

the charge as well—Condoleezza Rice said on CNN that the aluminum tubes were "only really suited for nuclear weapons programs, centrifuge programs."[31]

Bush also said that an International Atomic Energy Agency report found Iraq six months away from having nuclear weapons, and argued that the report settled the issue of whether to invade. "I would remind you that when the inspectors first went into Iraq and were denied, finally denied access, a report came out of the Atomic—the IAEA—that they were six months away from developing a weapon. I don't know what more evidence we need," he said.[32] But the IAEA had concluded nothing of the sort—what they had said in a 1998 report was that in 1991, before the Gulf War, Iraq had been somewhere between six and twenty-four months from developing a nuclear weapon. The IAEA's findings in 1998 were that they had "neutralized Iraq's nuclear weapons programme and that there were no indications that Iraq retained any physical capability to produce weapon usable nuclear material."[33]

Bush also said that unions were holding up homeland-security legislation over a dispute on radiation detectors for the Customs Agency and the dispute could take "a long time" to resolve, delaying terrorism readiness. But in fact, the dispute had been resolved months before.[34] Over at the CIA, analysts complained that, according to the *New York Times*, "they had felt pressured to make their intelligence reports on Iraq conform to Bush administration policies."[35] It soon became obvious that just as the administration uses polls not to assess what Americans think but to figure out how to sell policies on which they've already decided, Bush pressured the intelligence agencies not to provide him with objective

---

[31] *Late Edition with Wolf Blitzer*, September 8, 2002.

[32] Dana Milbank, "For Bush, Facts Are Malleable," *Washington Post*, October 22, 2002, p. A1.

[33] Mohamed ElBaradei, "The Status of Nuclear Inspections in Iraq," statement to the United Nations Security Council, January 27, 2003.

[34] Dana Milbank, "For Bush, Facts Are Malleable," *Washington Post*, October 22, 2002, p. A1.

[35] James Risen, "C.I.A. Aides Feel Pressure in Preparing Iraqi Reports," *New York Times*, March 23, 2003.

information but to give him justification, phony or not, for the war he knew he wanted to launch. In an unprecedented application of not-so-subtle pressure, Dick Cheney made multiple visits to CIA headquarters in the days before the war to make sure that the analysts were producing reports that told the administration what it wanted to hear. According to veteran intelligence official Ray McGovern, "During my 27-year career at the Central Intelligence Agency, no vice president ever came to us for a working visit."[36]

In his presentation before the United Nations, Secretary of State Colin Powell repeated some of Bush's deceptions and added a few of his own. He offered the discredited story of the aluminum tubes (saying "most United States experts" believed them to be for enriching uranium, which was false), then quoted from an intercepted telephone call between Iraqi officials purporting to show them scrambling to clean up a chemical-weapons lab before inspectors arrived. But it turned out that Powell's description of the translation was a distortion, including the invention of a quote ("make sure there is nothing there") to make it sound as though there were chemical weapons at the site being discussed.[37]

Powell also said that Iraq had produced four tons of VX nerve agent: "A single drop of VX on the skin will kill in minutes." (Pause for effect.) "Four tons." But what is the truth? He conveniently neglected to mention that most of that four tons had been destroyed by UN weapons inspectors, and what remained was likely degraded since it had been produced so long before. Powell also showed photos of what he claimed was a facility "clearly intended [to produce] long-range missiles that can fly 1,200 kilometers" and noted that a new roof had recently been put on the facility, making it impossible for spy satellites to see inside. What he didn't say was that UN inspectors had repeatedly visited that very site and found no banned weapons. He showed a video of an Iraqi jet spraying "simulated

[36] Ray McGovern, "Cheney and the CIA: Not Business As Usual," *Hartford Courant*, June 27, 2003, p. A13.
[37] Gilbert Cranberg, "Powell's UN Report Apparently Contains False Information," *Sarasota Herald-Tribune*, February 24, 2003.

anthrax"—but neglected to mention that the video was more than a decade old, predating the first Gulf War.[38]

Powell is generally regarded as the voice of moderation and integrity in the Bush administration, and that reputation is precisely what made his presentation to the UN so persuasive to so many. But this evidence suggests that no less than the rest of the administration, Powell was happy to willfully deceive the American people and the rest of the world if it served the purpose of justifying the invasion of Iraq. No one noticed that in 2001, Powell had said of sanctions against Iraq, "Frankly they have worked. He has not developed any significant capability with respect to weapons of mass destruction. He is unable to project conventional power against his neighbors."[39]

But since they regard him so highly, the press declined to investigate the charges Powell made before the UN too closely. Instead, they hailed his appearance as having settled once and for all the question of whether we should invade Iraq. The editorials the following day were nearly unanimous. Speaking for many liberal commentators, the *Washington Post*'s Mary McGrory wrote, "I don't know how the United Nations felt about Colin Powell's 'J'accuse' speech against Saddam Hussein. I can only say that he persuaded me, and I was as tough as France to convince."[40] "Secretary of State Colin Powell's strong, plain-spoken indictment of the Saddam Hussein regime before the UN Security Council Wednesday embodies something truly great about the United States," said the *Chicago Sun-Times.* "Those around the world who demanded proof must now be satisfied, or else admit that no satisfaction is possible for them."[41] "In a brilliant presentation as riveting and as convincing as Adlai Stevenson's 1962 unmasking of Soviet missiles in Cuba, Powell proved beyond any doubt that Iraq still possesses and continues to develop illegal weapons of mass destruction," said the

[38] Charles Hanley, "Point by Point, a Look Back at a 'Thick' File, a Fateful Six Months Later," Associated Press, August 10, 2003.
[39] A transcript of these remarks, made in Cairo, may be found here: http://www.state.gov/secretary/rm/2001/933.htm.
[40] Mary McGrory, "I'm Persuaded," *Washington Post*, February 6, 2003, p. A37.
[41] *Chicago Sun-Times*, February 6, 2003, p. 37.

New York Daily News. "The case for war has been made. And it's irrefutable."[42] The *Hartford Courant* said Powell's presentation was "masterful,"[43] while the Portland *Oregonian* found Powell's presentation "devastating" and "overwhelming...We think he made his case."[44] The headline in the *Dallas Morning News* read, "Only the Blind Could Ignore Powell's Evidence."[45] The editors of the *San Antonio Express-News*, who also found his presentation "irrefutable," thought you didn't have to be blind to disagree, but you did have to be an Iraqi sympathizer. "Only those ready to believe Iraq and assume that the United States would manufacture false evidence against Saddam would not be persuaded by Powell's case," they said.[46]

But you didn't have to believe Iraq to know that the Bush administration would in fact present false evidence in its march to war. When confronted by reporters about some of the lies Bush was telling to convince Americans that we had to invade Iraq immediately if not sooner, press secretary Ari Fleischer asserted that nothing the president had said was inaccurate. "The president's statements are well documented and supported by the facts," Fleischer said. "We reject any allegation to the contrary," he added helpfully.[47]

Bush successfully built support for the Iraq war on the proposition that if America didn't attack Iraq, Iraq would surely attack America with its weapons of mass destruction, the phrase repeated again and again like a mantra. (Once the war began, Bush quickly shifted the war's rationale—instead of, "Operation Secure America from Iraqi Invasion," the war was christened, "Operation Iraqi Freedom," as though it had been about liberating the Iraqi people all along. Military and civilian personnel were instructed to refer to the invasion as a "war of liberation" and Iraqi fighters as "death

---

[42] "Powell! Right in the Kisser!" *New York Daily News*, February 6, 2003, p. 36.
[43] "Iraq's Flimflam Exposed," *Hartford Courant*, February 6, 2003, p. A10.
[44] "The Facts Accumulate against Iraq," *Oregonian*, February 6, 2003, p. B8.
[45] "Iraqi Proof: Only the Blind Could Ignore Powell's Evidence," *Dallas Morning News*, February 6, 2003, p. 18A.
[46] "Our Turn," *San Antonio Express-News*, February 6, 2003, p. 8B.
[47] Dana Milbank, "For Bush, Facts Are Malleable," *Washington Post*, October 22, 2002, p. A1.

squads.")[48] But if, as the administration's supporters asserted, the case for invading Iraq was so airtight, why then did the administration find it necessary to tell so many lies in making that case?

Without question, there was a legitimate case to be made for the war on Iraq. But the administration couldn't muster the courage to make its case on the facts, choosing instead to build support through deception. As one official at the Defense Intelligence Agency said, "The American people were manipulated."[49]

There was yet another motivation for the Iraq war that was kept out of view. The war was intended to "send a message" that the United States was global lord and master, and any country that failed to do our bidding risked an invasion. "We were not lying," said one administration official when asked why the war was sold to Americans on the basis of supposedly threatening weapons and Iraqi liberation instead of its true purpose as a giant flexing of muscle. "But it was just a matter of emphasis."[50] In a rare moment of candor, Deputy Secretary of Defense Paul Wolfowitz admitted that Iraq's alleged weapons of mass destruction were put forward as the reason for going to war for bureaucratic reasons: "The truth is that for reasons that have a lot to do with the U.S. government bureaucracy," Wolfowitz told *Vanity Fair*, "we settled on one issue that everyone could agree on, which was weapons of mass destruction."[51]

Did Bush's string of lies on Iraq lead the press to the conclusion that he is, in fact, a liar? Hardly. This is how "liberal" *Washington Post* columnist Richard Cohen described his thinking on the issue: "In his kiss-and-not-tell book, David Frum, the former White House speechwriter, tells us about George W. Bush's insistence on honesty—on refraining from even politically acceptable exaggeration. I accept what he has to say. Yet it's apparent that when it comes to making the case for war with Iraq, both Bush and his

---

[48] Bob Kemper, "Agency Wages Media Battle," *Chicago Tribune*, April 7, 2003.
[49] Nicholas Kristof, "Save Our Spooks," *New York Times*, May 30, 2003, p. A27.
[50] John Cochran, "Reason for War?" abcnews.com, April 25, 2003.
[51] Cited on *Meet the Press*, NBC, July 27, 2003.

aides have tickled the facts so that everything proves their case."[52] Cohen considers the administration's lies merely "tickling the facts" and nonetheless "accepts" that Bush is a steadfastly honest character.

But it wasn't only columnists like Cohen. Even as a few journalists actually went to the trouble of comparing what Bush had said in the run-up to the war to the facts, they shied away from the conclusion to which such a comparison inevitably led. When the heat over his dishonesty on Iraq was turned up, Bush claimed that he launched the invasion only after giving Saddam Hussein "a chance to allow the inspectors in, and he wouldn't let them in."[53] This is what ordinary people call a lie and a poor one at that, since as everyone knew, UN weapons inspectors had been allowed in Iraq, and Bush himself rejected the idea of giving them more time to complete their work. But the *Washington Post* could only say that Bush's statement "appeared to contradict the events leading up to war."[54] A piece in the *New York Times*'s Week in Review entitled "Bush May Have Exaggerated, But Did He Lie?" discussed a number of the lies he had told, yet managed to find him innocent of the charges, declaring that "a review of the president's public statements found little that could lead to a conclusion that the president actually lied."[55] Why knowingly making factually inaccurate statements did not constitute "actually" lying they did not say.

Reporters' obsession during the 2000 campaign with Al Gore's alleged exaggerations—and their stubborn refusal to even ask whether Bush was as honest as he said—seem in retrospect to be a stunning act of professional negligence. While Gore may have on occasion burnished the importance he played in past events, it was Bush who was willing to look the American people in the eye and lie about matters of life and death. While reporters were contemplating

---

[52] Richard Cohen, "Powellian Propaganda?" *Washington Post*, February 13, 2003, p. A31.
[53] Press avail, July 14, 2003.
[54] Dana Priest and Dana Milbank, "President Defends Allegation on Iraq," *Washington Post*, July 15, 2003.
[55] David Rosenbaum, "Bush May Have Exaggerated, But Did He Lie?" *New York Times*, June 22, 2003, Week in Review p. 1.

whether Bush's SAT scores were high enough, they had ample evidence on which to base the conclusion that he is dishonest. This was the character flaw that mattered, and reporters failed the public by neglecting to warn them.

THE PROPAGANDA WAR

Bush cultivated the image of the dolt so successfully that reporters came to assume that he should not even bear responsibility for the words that come out of his own mouth. The administration tries to claim that if he lies when giving a speech, well, he didn't write the words—or as one White House official put it, the president "is not a fact-checker."[56] But if he lies when speaking extemporaneously, well that's just Bush being Bush. So he can tell Polish television that "We found the weapons of mass destruction,"[57] referring to two trailers found in Iraq that the Pentagon later admitted showed no evidence of having ever produced biological or chemical weapons, instead more likely having been used to produce hydrogen for weather balloons,[58] or say that he went to war because Saddam Hussein wouldn't allow UN inspectors into Iraq, or claim that the International Atomic Energy Agency says Saddam is six months from obtaining nuclear weapons—all statements known to be false the moment he said them—and pay no price. He can even lie about his own lies—for instance, when he told reporters that doubts about the validity of the uranium story only emerged "subsequent to the [State of the Union] speech"[59]—with barely anyone noticing.

---

[56] Richard Stevenson, "White House Tells of How Bush Came to Talk of Iraq Uranium," *New York Times*, July 18, 2003, p. A6.

[57] This was Bush's statement in an interview on Polish television on May 29, 2003: "We found the weapons of mass destruction. We found biological laboratories. You remember when Colin Powell stood up in front of the world, and he said, Iraq has got laboratories, mobile labs to build biological weapons. They're illegal. They're against the United Nations resolutions, and we've so far discovered two. And we'll find more weapons as time goes on. But for those who say we haven't found the banned manufacturing devices or banned weapons, they're wrong, we found them."

[58] Douglas Jehl, "Iraqi Trailers Said to Make Hydrogen, Not Biological Arms," *New York Times*, August 9, 2003, p. A1.

[59] Ronald Brownstein, "A 'Straight Shooter' Takes Hits," *Los Angeles Times*, July 27, 2003, p. 23.

These lies were greeted without comment by reporters. The fact that, in contrast, the false claim that Iraq sought uranium from Niger actually became controversial might lead one to believe that the only lie for which Bush is held responsible is the lie somebody else writes for him. If this is true, reporters have decided that stupidity and dishonesty are mutually exclusive. Once Bush was declared stupid, he became, in their eyes, *prima facie* honest. As Richard Cohen put it in yet another defense of Bush's integrity, "His judgment and his competence are being questioned—his honesty as well. But the president is no liar. More likely, he is merely an uncritical man who believed what he was told."[60] Why is it unfathomable that Bush actually believed Iraq was a threat but also decided that, since Americans weren't feeling sufficiently threatened, he would win their consent with a campaign of deception? As I have argued, Bush is no dummy. But even if you believe he is, why can't he be both dumb *and* dishonest?

The uranium-from-Africa issue also offers a lesson in the dynamics of media manipulation. Ordinarily, the Bush White House is characterized by a numbing message discipline and an absence of leaks, with every administration official parroting precisely the chosen party line no matter what the facts. Though reporters may grumble, they feel they have little choice but to print the White House line. As George Condon, the Washington bureau chief of the Copley News Service, said, "They are the best I've seen at getting their message out and making it difficult for you to get beyond that message."[61] In the case of the uranium charge in Bush's 2003 State of the Union, however, the administration's story kept changing and the White House made the mistake of blaming the CIA for its troubles, causing CIA officials in their resentment to open up to journalists. The press therefore had something new to offer on the subject on an almost daily basis for a while, ensuring that the story would have "legs." However, the

---

[60] Richard Cohen, "Bush the Believer," *Washington Post*, July 22, 2003, p. A17.
[61] Rachel Smolkin, "Are the News Media Soft on Bush?" *American Journalism Review*, August/September 2003.

other lies that Bush told in the speech, like so many of his lies, were not fully investigated by the press.

To make matters worse, White House officials were blatantly, obviously dishonest in their attempts to make the story go away. Condoleezza Rice, for instance, said, "It was a case that said he is trying to reconstitute. He's trying to acquire nuclear weapons. Nobody ever said that it was going to be the next year."[62] But the fact is, somebody did say just that: the president of the United States. "Should Iraq acquire fissile material, it would be able to build a nuclear weapon within a year," he said in his address to the United Nations on September 12, 2002. Two days later, he repeated the claim in his weekly radio address: "Should his regime acquire fissile material, it would be able to build a nuclear weapon within a year." In his radio address two weeks after that, he said it yet again: "This regime is seeking a nuclear bomb and, with fissile material, could build one within a year."[63] Earlier, Rice had pulled an Orwellian Misdirection on the administration's Iraq claims, asserting that those who accused them of overhyping the threat of Iraq were engaging in "revisionist history."[64] A few days later, Bush picked up the charge, saying that his critics, by actually examining the veracity of what he had said before the war, were trying to "rewrite history—revisionist historians is what I like to call them."[65]

In one of the bright lights of reporting on the hyped nuclear threat, the *Washington Post* aggressively went after the story of the administration's deception, carefully analyzing what the White House had said and what the truth was. But on the day that their definitive piece on the subject was printed,[66] the *Post*'s editorial page,

[62] *The NewsHour With Jim Lehrer*, July 30, 2003. Thanks to the *New Republic* for pointing out this whopper.
[63] Bush quotes from address to the United Nations, September 12, 2002 and weekly radio addresses, September 14 and 28, 2002.
[64] Walter Pincus, "Officials Defend Intelligence," *Washington Post*, June 9, 2003, p. A1.
[65] David Sanger, "In Speech, Bush Reiterates Threat Hussein Posed, but Makes No Mention of Weapons Search," *New York Times*, June 17, 2003, p. A13.
[66] Barton Gellman and Walter Pincus, "Depiction of Threat Outgrew Supporting Evidence," *Washington Post*, August 10, 2003, p. A1.

which had aggressively supported the war, ridiculed Al Gore for suggesting "that we were all somehow bamboozled into war" in a speech that they said "validated just about every conspiratorial theory of the antiwar left." Should Democratic presidential candidates follow Gore in attacking the administration for deceiving the public, said the *Post*, "they will all go off the cliff."[67] Later, Walter Pincus, the *Post* reporter who had detailed the disconnect between the Bush administration's arguments and the truth, explained why the stories he wrote during the run-up to the war were buried deep inside the paper: "The *Post* was scared."[68] Again, a frightened press is a compliant press.

One of the most appalling footnotes to the Niger story came after former ambassador Joseph Wilson wrote an op-ed detailing the fact that the CIA had sent him to Niger to check out the story; after he returned he reported back that it was almost certainly false. In retaliation, two administration officials told columnist Bob Novak that Wilson must have been sent because his wife is a CIA agent. Novak didn't *discover* Wilson's wife's identity—they came to him. "I didn't dig it out, it was given to me," he said.[69] One might ask, by whom? It was later revealed that the two leakers had told at least five other reporters about Wilson's wife, but only Novak would print her name. "Clearly, it was meant purely and simply for revenge," a senior administration official told the *Washington Post*.[70] Revealing the name of a covert agent is a federal crime punishable by up to ten years in jail.

By publicly identifying a covert CIA operative, the White House not only may have destroyed her career by making her useless as an asset to the agency, but compromised every operation she had ever been involved in. As an example of the damage it caused, the revelation exposed the CIA front company Wilson's wife had listed as an employer as part of her cover, meaning that others who used the

---

[67] "Mr. Gore's Blurred View," *Washington Post*, August 10, 2003, p. B6.

[68] Ari Berman, "The Postwar *Post*," *The Nation*, September 29, 2003.

[69] Timothy Phelps and Knut Royce, "Columnist Blows CIA Agent's Cover," *Newsday*, July 22, 2003, p. A4.

[70] Mike Allen and Dana Priest, "Bush Administration Is Focus of Inquiry," *Washington Post*, September 28, 2003, p. A1.

front company would be exposed as CIA operatives as well.[71] And what was her assignment at the CIA? Combating the proliferation of weapons of mass destruction.

Almost from the moment September 11 occurred, the Bush administration began planning to use the attacks as a pretext for an invasion of Iraq. The administration went through a ridiculous charade on the subject, insisting for months that Bush had not in fact made up his mind as to whether he would invade. In fact, Bush ordered the Pentagon to begin planning for an invasion of Iraq only six days after September 11.[72] Bush was beaten to the punch only by Defense Secretary Donald Rumsfeld, who waited *five whole hours* after the attacks to begin exploring whether September 11 could be used as a pretext for a war on Iraq. "Go massive," an aide's notes of their meeting quote Rumsfeld as saying. "Sweep it all up. Things related and not."[73]

There was never any doubt that George W. Bush would have his war. September 11 merely provided the justification, as the administration peddled invented tales of links between Saddam Hussein and al-Qaeda and nightmare scenarios of doom. They understood that if they hinted at connections between Iraq and al-Qaeda, despite an utter lack of evidence for such a relationship, enough Americans would conclude that revenge for September 11 could reasonably be exacted on Saddam Hussein. Months after it had been definitively identified as fiction by both the CIA and FBI, Dick Cheney continued to peddle a story about lead hijacker Mohammed Atta meeting an Iraqi intelligence officer in Prague. When his interviewer asked whether that report was credible, Cheney responded, "I think a way to put it would be it's unconfirmed at this point"[74] (the story had been downgraded in Cheney's mind from a year before, when he claimed it was "pretty well confirmed"[75]). In fact, Atta was in the

---

[71] Walter Pincus and Mike Allen, "Leak of Agent's Name Causes Exposure of CIA Front Firm," *Washington Post*, October 4, 2003, p. A3.
[72] Glenn Kessler, "U.S. Decision on Iraq Has Puzzling Past," *Washington Post*, January 13, 2003, p. A1.
[73] "Plans for Iraq Attack Began on 9/11," CBSNews.com, September 4, 2002.
[74] *Meet the Press*, September 8, 2002.
[75] *Meet the Press*, December 9, 2001.

United States at the time the alleged meeting took place.[76] Cheney repeated the tale of the fictional meeting as late as September 2003.[77] Cheney even described Iraq as "the geographic base of the terrorists who had us under assault now for many years, but most especially on 9/11."[78] Of course, the geographic base of the terrorists who carried out the September 11 attacks was Afghanistan. That's why we invaded that country one month after those attacks. When Cheney was asked directly whether Saddam was involved in planning September 11, he replied, "We don't know."[79] Vincent Cannistraro, a former CIA counter-terrorism expert, commented that Cheney's "willingness to use speculation and conjecture as facts in public presentations is appalling. It's astounding."[80]

But Cheney was even more inventive in spinning out apocalyptic predictions. "Many of us are convinced that Saddam Hussein will acquire nuclear weapons fairly soon," he said, unconcerned by the lack of evidence to support his supposed conviction. "Armed with an arsenal of these weapons of terror and a seat atop 10 percent of the world's oil reserves, Saddam Hussein could then be expected to seek domination of the entire Middle East, take control of a great portion of the world's energy supplies, directly threaten America's friends throughout the region, and subject the United States or any other nation to nuclear blackmail." Cheney went on to aver that "There is no doubt" that Hussein was amassing weapons "to use against our friends, against our allies, and against us." To support this contention, Cheney said, "We now know that Saddam has resumed his efforts to acquire nuclear weapons. Among other sources, we've gotten this from the firsthand testimony of defectors—including Saddam's own son-in-law."[81] Cheney managed two lies here. First, the

---

[76] Peter Canellos and Bryan Bender, "Questions Grow Over Iraq Links to Qaeda," *Boston Globe*, August 3, 2003, p. A1.

[77] *Meet the Press*, September 14, 2003.

[78] *Meet the Press*, September 14, 2003.

[79] *Meet the Press*, September 14, 2003.

[80] Anne Kornblut and Bryan Bender, "Cheney Link of Iraq, 9/11 Challenged," *Boston Globe*, September 16, 2003.

[81] Speech to the Veterans of Foreign Wars, Nashville, TN, August 26, 2002.

United States "now knew" nothing about Iraq's nuclear program from Saddam's son-in-law because Saddam had him killed in 1996. Second, what the son-in-law, Hussein Kamel, had told American intelligence officials in 1995 was that Saddam had a nuclear program before the 1991 Gulf War but that it had not been restarted after the war.[82]

When Iraqi soldiers would be storming the beaches at Coney Island, Cheney would not specify, but we could be sure it was any day. When the administration sent to Congress its resolution authorizing the Iraq war, it cited "the high risk that the current Iraqi regime will…launch a surprise attack against the United States."[83] Just before the war began, Cheney went on *Meet the Press* and said that Saddam Hussein "has, in fact, reconstituted nuclear weapons,"[84] an assertion so absurd that it could only have been made by a liar or a fool, and Dick Cheney is no fool. Tim Russert didn't bother to ask him for clarification.

Of course, the timing of the unveiling of the imminent Iraqi invasion was critical. Explaining why the administration waited patiently and then began issuing grave warnings of the Iraqi threat in September 2002, just two months before the midterm elections, chief of staff Andrew Card said, "From a marketing point of view, you don't introduce new products in August." Karl Rove added that it wouldn't look right to sound the drumbeats of war while the president was on one of his many lengthy vacations.[85] But that weekend, Dick Cheney declared it "reprehensible" that anyone would dare to suggest what Card and Rove had confirmed to be true, "that somehow, you know, we saved this and now we've sprung it on them for political reasons."[86] Press secretary Ari Fleischer echoed the attack: "Even the suggestion that the timing of something so serious could be done for political reasons is reprehensible."[87]

[82] Barton Gellman and Walter Pincus, "Depiction of Threat Outgrew Supporting Evidence," *Washington Post*, August 10, 2003, p. A1.

[83] Resolution sent to Congress on September 19, 2002.

[84] *Meet the Press*, March 16, 2003.

[85] Elisabeth Bumiller, "Bush Aides Set Strategy to Sell Policy on Iraq," *New York Times*, September 7, 2002, p. A1.

[86] *Meet the Press*, September 8, 2002.

[87] Dana Milbank, "Democrats Question Iraq Timing," *Washington Post*, September 16, 2002, p. A1.

So the public-relations campaign for the Iraq war went forward, and just as Bush, Cheney, and the rest of the administration hoped, many Americans arrived at a series of false conclusions about Iraq. A survey conducted in January 2003 by the Knight-Ridder News Service found that 65 percent of Americans thought that Saddam Hussein and al-Qaeda were working together, a false belief Bush labored mightily to implant in the public mind, despite being refuted by his own intelligence agencies. Donald Rumsfeld said the evidence of a link between Saddam and al-Qaeda was "bullet-proof"—but wouldn't say what that evidence was.[88] (Rumsfeld also said of the weapons of mass destruction, "We know where they are." When the alleged weapons remained stubbornly missing, Rumsfeld said, "Sometimes I overstate for emphasis.")[89] The best the administration could come up with was that, according to President Bush, a "very senior al-Qaeda leader" had gone to a hospital in Iraq. By that logic, the Bush administration has ties to al-Qaeda too, since people associated with the terrorist group have been found in the United States. It was only later revealed that even on this absurdly tenuous evidence for an Iraq–al-Qaeda link, Bush was lying: as American intelligence officials knew quite well, the man in question, Abu Mussab Zarqawi, was not a member of al-Qaeda but of an entirely different terrorist group.[90]

In fact, as Greg Thielmann, who served under Bush as an intelligence officer in the State Department, told the Associated Press, "There was no significant pattern of cooperation between Iraq and the al-Qaeda terrorist operation."[91] The Congressional intelligence committees found the same thing in their investigation of September 11: there was, according to one government official, "no link between Iraq and al-Qaeda." The report was completed in December of 2002, but its release was delayed until

[88] Eric Schmitt, "Rumsfeld Says U.S. Has 'Bulletproof' Evidence of Iraq's Links to Al Qaeda," *New York Times*, September 28, 2002, p. A9.
[89] Luncheon at the National Press Club, September 10, 2003.
[90] Walter Pincus, "Report Cast Doubt on Iraq-Al-Qaeda Connection," *Washington Post*, June 22, 2003, p. A1.
[91] John Lumpkin and Dafna Linzer, "Intelligence Experts Say Iraq Nuclear Evidence Was Thin," Associated Press, July 19, 2003.

after the war was over.[92] But even months after what the White House called "major combat operations" in Iraq had ended, the misperception persisted: in August of 2003, a Harris poll found that 50 percent of Americans believed that "clear evidence that Iraq was supporting al-Qaeda has been found in Iraq."[93]

The public misperception was hardly limited to general questions about who might be connected to whom. Exactly half of those surveyed by Knight-Ridder also thought that there were Iraqis among the September 11 hijackers. Only 17 percent correctly answered that none of the hijackers were Iraqis, a group outnumbered by the 21 percent who thought "most" of the hijackers were Iraqis. The poll's most compelling finding was that the less someone actually knew about the Iraq situation, the more likely he or she was to support military action to oust Saddam.[94] Support for Bush's policy was thus dependent on ignorance created by the misperception he worked so hard to create.

When a *Time*/CNN survey taken in early February 2003 asked people how likely it was that Saddam Hussein was personally involved in the September 11 attacks, 38 percent said "somewhat likely" and a further 34 percent said "very likely." And the failure to find any such connection did nothing to diminish this belief: in September 2003, a nearly identical 69 percent of Americans told the *Washington Post* that it was at least somewhat likely that Saddam was personally involved in September 11.[95]

Despite their use of the specter of terrorism as justification for invading Iraq, even the Bush administration was not so brazen as to claim directly that Saddam was involved in September 11. But their hints, insinuations, and speculations had their intended effect. They knew that if "Saddam" and "al-Qaeda" were repeated in the same paragraph often enough, that if they mentioned

---

[92] Shaun Waterman, "9-11 Report: No Iraq Link to Al-Qaeda," United Press International, July 23, 2003.

[93] Harris poll taken August 12–17, 2003.

[94] Martin Merzer, "Unilateral Iraq Attack Losing Support," *Milwaukee Journal Sentinel*, January 12, 2003, p. 3A.

[95] Dana Milbank and Claudia Deane, "Hussein Link to 9/11 Lingers in Many Minds," *Washington Post*, September 6, 2003, p. A1.

September 11 every time they spoke about Iraq, then the twin visions of fear and hatred would become entwined in enough minds to create the passive consensus necessary for the war to proceed.

BUSH AND HIS PREDECESSORS

In order to understand George W. Bush's particular brand of mendacity, it is useful to compare him to his predecessors, particularly two whose dishonesty is often discussed: Bill Clinton and Ronald Reagan. Each lied in a unique way, and each was largely judged by a single set of lies: Clinton for those he told about Monica Lewinsky and Reagan for those he told about the Iran-Contra affair.

When the Iran-Contra story broke, Reagan first said, "The charge has been made that the United States has shipped weapons to Iran as ransom payment for the release of American hostages in Lebanon, that the United States undercut its allies and secretly violated American policy against trafficking with terrorists. Those charges are utterly false. The United States has not made concessions to those who hold our people captive in Lebanon. And we will not. The United States has not swapped boatloads or planeloads of American weapons for the return of American hostages. And we will not."[96] As the world would soon learn, this was a lie: Reagan had approved the sale of arms to Iran in exchange for the release of American hostages held in Lebanon. According to then–Defense Secretary Caspar Weinberger's notes, Weinberger told Reagan the sale of arms to Iran was illegal, but Reagan told him to go ahead with the arms-for-hostages deal anyway.[97]

At each subsequent press conference and public statement about the affair, Reagan kept repeating that he was trying to get to the bottom of things because he wanted the truth to come out. He thus attempted to evade responsibility for his own actions by posing as an investigator trying to discover what he himself did. Finally, on

[96] Statement by Ronald Reagan, November 13, 1986.
[97] Thomas Blanton, "Now It Can Be Told: The Coverup Worked," *Boston Globe*, January 22, 1994, p. 11.

March 3, 1987, in an address to the nation, Reagan admitted that he had been lying, while not really admitting anything. "Let's start with the part that is the most controversial," he said. "A few months ago I told the American people I did not trade arms for hostages. My heart and my best intentions still tell me that is true, but the facts and the evidence tell me it is not."

How do we interpret this rather incredible statement? Psychologists Michael Milburn and Sheree Conrad argue that Reagan's extraordinary capacity for denial can be traced to the fact that he grew up with an alcoholic father.[98] At the time, the prevailing interpretation was that his heart was in the right place, but he just got carried away. But it would be more accurate to interpret it as evidence of some sort of delusional disorder. Reagan was unable to reject the fantasy he had constructed even in the face of irrefutable evidence that the fantasy was untrue. It didn't "feel" like a lie. His signature was on the order authorizing the sale of arms to Iran, but his *heart* continued to tell him it was not. The key word here is "still." He knows what really happened, but his heart and best intentions *still* won't let him believe it. Intentions and emotions are given a weight equal to that of facts and evidence in determining the truth. Imagine if Bill Clinton had said that despite the presence of the infamous blue dress, his heart and best intentions still told him that he had never been involved with Monica. Such a statement would not only be laughable, it would be evidence of a denial so deep as to be pathological.

For Reagan, fiction was merely another form of truth; the actor has been truthful not if his words were factual but if the presentation was sincere. Compare their reaction to getting caught: Clinton performed a careful semantic deconstruction in order to convince you (and himself) that even if he deceived you, he did not actually lie. Though Reagan attempted to convince America that he had not lied to them, his evidence was not the content of his prior statement but the content of his heart.

---

[98] Michael Milburn and Sheree Conrad, *The Politics of Denial*. Cambridge: MIT Press, 1996, p. 127–128.

The most marked difference between the two is that while Reagan seemed oblivious to, or at least unconcerned with, the distinction between truth-telling and lying, Bill Clinton, in his own unusual way, hates to utter what he considers a "lie." Given the events of 1998, this may seem like a strange assertion, but an examination of the Lewinsky affair reveals the extraordinary lengths Clinton will go to avoid certain kinds of statements and to convince himself and others that while he may have deceived, misled, or hoodwinked in a given situation, he did not in fact "lie."

During the Lewinsky affair, it was revealed and much discussed that Clinton does not consider oral sex to be adultery. He told Monica Lewinsky as much and apparently had told others the same thing before. This appears to be the reason that he and Lewinsky never consummated their affair. The natural question would be, why does this distinction matter? If his wife happened upon him with another woman, one assumes she would be equally distressed whether they were having intercourse or oral sex. I submit that Clinton maintains this belief so that he can tell his wife he has not committed adultery and assure himself that he has not lied to her. Whether this conversation ever takes place, he has prepared for it. To an ordinary person this seems irrelevant; the act of betrayal is far more significant than the label one attaches to the necessary deception involved. But to Clinton, the semantic distinction enables him to resolve his internal conflict in such a way as to convince himself that he has not acted immorally, while also enabling him to satisfy his desires.

Of course, few believe his affair with the intern was the first time Clinton strayed from his marriage. When the Gennifer Flowers story broke during the 1992 primaries, a friend then working on Clinton's campaign staff told me with a shake of his head, "Gennifer Flowers may be the only woman in Arkansas Bill Clinton *hasn't* slept with." Clinton's testimony in the Paula Jones deposition proved my friend wrong: whatever his contacts with the female population of

Arkansas, Clinton admitted to having sex with Flowers (although the truth of her allegation of a twelve-year affair remains an open question).

But consider the events of January 1998. The Lewinsky story broke, and Clinton kept a previously scheduled interview with Jim Lehrer. Of course, Lehrer asked him about the charges. If Clinton were the inveterate liar many believe him to be, what would he have said? He could have said that he never laid eyes on her, that he never touched her, etc. But instead, he replied that "There is no improper relationship" and "There is no sexual relationship."[99] Now Bill Clinton is many things, but stupid is not one of them. He must have known that this first statement would have been read over, and any observer would hear it and assume that if there *is* no relationship, surely there *was* one.

A few days later, Clinton answered the charges in a formal press conference. Once again, he could have told a lie, but instead he said that he "did not have sexual relations with that woman." At the time, this seemed like a blanket denial (and it became Exhibit A in the argument that Clinton is a liar), but the revelation of wrangling over definitions in the Paula Jones deposition quickly made clear that this phrase was meant to convey something specific. As Clinton later testified to the grand jury, his interpretation was that receiving oral sex did not fall under the definition of the term "sexual relations." Whether that interpretation is reasonable is beside the point. In January, he was not in a legal arena but talking to reporters, and through them to the country. If his intention was simply to deny the affair, he surely could have chosen a more persuasive verbal formulation here as in the Lehrer interview. Instead, he chose a formulation that would allow him later to claim that he did not "lie." Nonetheless, Clinton's statement is understood by most people as a lie, and properly so, since his intent was to deceive his listeners.

Of course, this was precisely the defense Clinton's legal team argued persuasively to the Senate to answer charges that Clinton

[99] *The Newshour with Jim Lehrer*, January 21, 1998.

had committed perjury in his videotaped grand-jury testimony. In that context the distinction was a relevant one, since a deception which is less than a lie may subject one to less legal jeopardy. In a statement to the country, however, such a distinction is essentially meaningless. The only reason to choose those particular words was to be able to claim later that the statement was not a lie. Although we may never know what was in Clinton's head, it is possible (if not likely) that he understood at that point that the full story would inevitably be revealed. With a press corps whose reaction to the story was nothing short of gleeful and an independent counsel who had demonstrated a limitless enthusiasm for investigating every nook and cranny of Clinton's sexual life, the chances that the truth would not eventually be known were next to nil.

Was it his hope, then, that the ultimate verdict would be that he is an adulterer but not a liar? If so, his worst fear came to pass: he is considered not merely slick, willing to sell out his allies, or lacking in courage, but a liar.

Clinton conducted himself as a lawyer, operating on the legal definition of perjury, which is concerned with the words themselves, not the intention of the speaker. If done carefully enough, one may deceive one's listeners in court without committing perjury; in a case often noted during the Lewinsky affair, the Supreme Court found that a defendant who had answered a question on whether *he* held any Swiss bank accounts by saying, "the company had an account there," did not commit perjury when in fact he had held such accounts.[100] His words were true though the intent was to deceive. In daily life, on the other hand, most people would agree with the definition of a lie stating that the determining factor is whether the intent of the speaker is to deceive the listener. For Clinton, however, the test of truth lies in the words themselves, exclusive of whatever lies in the mind of the speaker or the listener. For Reagan, the test of truth was his heart—if his intentions were

---

[100] *Bronston v. United States* 409 US 352 (1973).

good, regardless of whether he deceived you, he told a version of the truth. When reporters complained that the anecdotes he used to justify his policy positions seemed to be made up, his aides responded that Reagan *believed* in the welfare queen and the man buying vodka with food stamps, so it was acceptable for him to use them in argumentation whether they were inventions or not. According to one press aide, Reagan wouldn't tell tall tales "unless he thought they were accurate."[101] Confronted about one such lie, Reagan spokesman Larry Speakes said, "Well, it's a good story, though. It made the point, didn't it?"[102]

In her paean to the former president, *When Character Was King*, Reagan speechwriter Peggy Noonan testified to the Gipper's honesty. Now, Reagan had some good qualities, but his relationship to the truth was, shall we say, complex. But Noonan managed to write the following:

Ronald Reagan loved the truth. We all do or say we do but for Reagan it was like fresh water, something he needed and wanted.

He loved the truth for a number of reasons, a primary one of which is that he thought it, in our current political circumstances, uniquely constructive. He thought that by voicing it you were beginning to make things better.

He thought the truth is the only foundation on which can be built something strong and good and lasting—because only truth endures. Lies die. He thought that in politics and world affairs in his time there had been too many lies for too long, and that they had been uniquely destructive. And so his public career was devoted to countering that destructiveness by speaking the truth, spreading it and repeating it.

He wanted to put words into the air that were honest and have them take the place of other words that were not.

He wanted to crowd out the false with the true.[103]

[101] Robert Pear, "Reagan Unverified on Fraud Stories," *New York Times*, March 25, 1982, p. A20.
[102] Lou Cannon, "Reagan Seeks to Calm Hill Fears of Inflexibility on Budget Issues," *Washington Post*, April 17, 1982, p. A6.
[103] Peggy Noonan, *When Character Was King*. New York: Viking, 2001, p. 200.

The one who believed such things would truly be a noble man. Of course, other than George W. Bush it would be hard to think of a president to whom those words applied *less* than Ronald Reagan. After all, we're talking about the man who argued that trees cause more pollution than automobiles,[104] who lied to the American people about Iran-Contra, who upon meeting Israeli Prime Minister Yitzhak Shamir claimed to have liberated Jews from concentration camps when he actually spent World War II in Hollywood then repeated the tall tale a few months later to famed Nazi hunter Simon Wiesenthal,[105] who again and again told stories featuring himself and others that turned out to have occurred only in movies he had seen. It would have been no less absurd to write, "We all say that infidelity is morally wrong, but Bill Clinton believed it with every fiber of his being," or, "We all support openness in government, but for Richard Nixon it was the very essence of the democracy he so loved." Noonan's description of Reagan is only slightly more ridiculous than Bush speechwriter David Frum's assertion in his book *The Right Man* that Bush "scorned the petty untruths of the politician."[106]

Where Reagan and Clinton differ from Bush, apart from the size and scope of their lies (most far smaller than Bush's) is their desire to convince us, each in his own way, that they had in fact told the truth. Bush lies brazenly and repeatedly, apparently unconcerned about getting caught. Even when his lies are pointed out, he often continues to repeat them in an effort to make them sound true.

Nonetheless, Bush does occasionally tell lies in the fashion of Reagan or Clinton. While the Pentagon was busily planning the invasion of Iraq, Bush and his aides were denying that any plans existed. They managed this deception with a Clintonesque linguistic trick, saying that there was no invasion plan "on the president's desk." "There's no

---

[104] Martin Schram, "Nation's Longest Campaign Comes to an End," *Washington Post*, November 4, 1980, p. A1.

[105] Lou Cannon, "Dramatic Account about Film of Nazi Death Camps Questioned," *Washington Post*, March 5, 1984, p. A2.

[106] David Frum, *The Right Man: The Surprise Presidency of George W. Bush.* New York: Random House, 2003.

plan on the president's desk," a senior official told the *Boston Globe* on the condition of anonymity.[107] "There are no plans to attack Iraq on the president's desk," said a State Department spokesman.[108] "There's no plans on the president's desk to take any type of military action," said Ari Fleischer.[109] Colin Powell added, "There is no war plan on the president's desk this morning."[110] A BBC reporter asked Powell, "On Iraq, we keep hearing there are no plans on the president's desk to invade Iraq. What does that mean?" Powell responded, "It seems to me a rather clear declaratory sentence: There are no plans on the president's desk."[111]

All these officials were trying to fool Americans into believing that the fact that the plan was not physically lying on the desk in the Oval Office meant that it was not in the works, which of course it was. Bush approved the war plan on August 29, 2002, a full six months before the war actually began.[112]

When the press got around to discussing the fact that Bush used a fictitious story about Iraq seeking uranium from Africa in his 2003 State of the Union address, administration officials adopted a Clintonesque semantic deconstruction strategy. According to CIA officials, the White House wanted to assert that Saddam Hussein had sought the uranium, but the CIA objected, knowing that the story was false. So a decision was made to just attribute the uranium story to the British, thereby insuring a measure of deniability if they were to get caught.

And get caught they did. So how did the administration of the man who promised to restore honor and dignity to the White House react? Let's compare these two statements:

---

[107] Anthony Shadid, "US Seeks Solid Ally in Effort to Oust Hussein," *Boston Globe*, March 2, 2002, p. A10.

[108] Tom Raum, "Bush Must Placate Nervous Republicans as He Ponders Iraq Strategy," Associated Press, August 20, 2002.

[109] White House briefing, June 5, 2002.

[110] John Lumpkin, "U.S. Considers Actions against Iraq," Associated Press, February 14, 2002.

[111] State Department press release, May 31, 2002.

[112] Rowan Scarborough, "U.S. Rushed Post-Saddam Planning," *Washington Times*, September 3, 2003.

- As you know, in a deposition in January, I was asked questions about my relationship with Monica Lewinsky. While my answers were legally accurate, I did not volunteer information.

- It didn't rise to the standard of a presidential speech. But it's not clear that, it's not known, for example, that it was inaccurate. In fact, people think it was technically accurate.[113]

The first statement, made by Bill Clinton, sent conservatives into paroxysms of rage. "Legally accurate"? Who cares, they said—you were trying to deceive us. The second statement was made by Donald Rumsfeld, defending Bush's uranium charge. Oddly, no Republicans were seen expressing their outrage over Rumsfeld's rather derivative defense of the president's honesty.

Bush has been equally willing to follow Reagan's lead, inventing stories in order to enhance a quip or argument. Once, discussing parenting with a state representative from Virginia, Bush said, "I've been to war. I've raised twins. If I had a choice, I'd rather go to war."[114] Of course, Bush never went to war, much like Ronald Reagan never liberated a concentration camp.

After his tax cut destroyed the surplus, Bush adopted a Reaganesque strategy of rewriting his own history. Before September 11, he began to say that during the campaign he had said he would run a deficit if there was a war or a recession. After September 11, Bush added "national emergency" to the list of the conditions he purportedly had given for running a deficit. In a statement from his ranch on April 26, 2002, he said, "I want to remind you what I told the American people, that if I'm the president—when I was campaigning, if I were to become the president, we would have deficits only in the case of war, a recession, or a national emergency."

But if he ever said such a thing during the campaign, it appeared in none of his speeches and was not recorded by any reporter. In truth,

---

[113] *This Week With George Stephanopoulos*, ABC, July 13, 2003. Thanks to Media Whores Online for pointing out this neat little parallel.
[114] "Bush Says Raising Twins Not Easy," Associated Press, January 27, 2002.

during the campaign Bush always said there was plenty of money to go around—enough for his tax cut, leaving the Social Security surplus untouched, spending on all the other government programs, and paying down the national debt. When that turned out to be untrue, he did not simply blame the recession and the terrorist attacks but said that he had prepared people for the eventuality. But in fact, the only statement remotely resembling what he now claimed he had said long before was in an August 2000 interview when Bush said he would be willing to run a deficit in order to cut taxes during a recession—although he never mentioned war or national emergency.[115]

But in 2002, at various times he claimed to have made the statement to reporters or more helpfully, "some guy" or "the guy," as in, "I remember campaigning in Chicago one time, and the guy said, 'Would you ever deficit spend?'"[116] No record of that conversation exists, but perhaps "the guy" visited Bush in his hotel room, where they pored over the federal budget. Even after reporters began questioning Bush aides on it, Bush continued to repeat the fabrication. Only after months of relentless criticism over his repeated lie did someone convince Bush to drop the line from his speeches.

In another example of a Reaganesque tall tale, at a town-hall meeting in Orlando, a third grader asked Bush how he felt when he first heard about the terrorist attacks in New York. "Well, Jordan," he said, "you're not going to believe what state I was in when I heard about the terrorist attack. I was in Florida. And my chief of staff, Andy Card—actually I was in a classroom talking about a reading program that works. And I was sitting outside the classroom waiting to go in, and I saw an airplane hit the tower—the TV was obviously on, and I used to fly myself, and I said, 'There's one terrible pilot.' And I said, 'It must have been a horrible accident.'"[117]

Why Bush would fabricate this story to tell a child is unclear, but what is clear is that it was a fabrication (one that he told at least twice).

[115] James O'Toole, "Bush Happy Race Is Close," *Pittsburgh Post-Gazette*, August 29, 2000, p. A-1.
[116] Remarks at fundraiser for Pennsylvania governor candidate Mike Fisher, April 8, 2002.
[117] Stephanie Schorow, "What Did Bush See and When Did He See It?" *Boston Herald*, October 22, 2002, p. 48.

Bush's assertion that he "saw the airplane hit the tower" and responded, "There's one terrible pilot" is plainly false. He could not have seen the first plane hit the tower on television, because the first plane hitting the tower was not broadcast on television (while some amateur video of the first impact later surfaced, no television cameras were trained on the towers until afterward). Bush was informed about the first plane by aides just before entering the classroom. And he could not have had that reaction when he saw video of the second plane hitting the second tower because he was informed of the second plane by chief-of-staff Andrew Card while he was still sitting in the classroom. So by the time he saw any video, he already understood that the World Trade Center attacks were the work of terrorists, not some "terrible pilot."

This is a rather trivial fib, you might say. True enough. But if Reagan was so used to acting that the very notion of truth had lost meaning for him, George W. Bush knows quite well the difference between the truth and a lie. Does he no longer care? He knows that even if reporters point out his inaccuracies, because of their belief in his honesty, they will never call him a liar and that his reputation as a man of integrity will remain intact. As often as not, Reagan's lies were ad-libbed, a response to a question or a spontaneous remark. Bush's lies, on the other hand, are usually the product of careful strategizing, spoken with his eyes glued to the index card on which a staffer has carefully written the message of the day. What was so distinctive about the flap over Bush's claim that Iraq had sought uranium from Africa was that the administration actually admitted they were wrong.[118] Ordinarily, the Bush strategy is to forge ahead, never admit you made a mistake, never give an inch, and if all else fails stage another photo-op where the president can talk tough. Eventually the press will just lose interest. This strategy has been enormously successful, allowing Bush to escape responsibility for any number of falsehoods.

Bush no doubt learned valuable lessons about truth in politics from his father. When it was revealed that the elder Bush had lied

---

[118] As Timothy Noah of *Slate* put it, "The yellowcake lie landed on Page One solely because it occasioned a brief and fatal departure from the Bush White House's press strategy of stonewalling." Timothy Noah, "Why This Bush Lie? Part II," slate.com, July 16, 2003.

about his opponents during his 1984 debate with Geraldine Ferraro, his press secretary, Peter Teeley, scoffed at the notion that Bush would pay a price. "You can say anything you want during a debate, and 80 million people hear it," Teeley said. When the reporter interviewing him asked what then happens if journalists exposed the candidate's statement as untrue, Teeley responded, "So what? Maybe 200 people read it, or 2,000 or 20,000."[119] Let's be clear about what this means: the lie is seen by millions, and the correction by journalists is seen by a fraction. And exploiting this is an accepted practice.

But an even more apt aphorism was offered by Ronald Reagan's spokesman Larry Speakes. Asked to explain his boss's penchant for inventing tales out of whole cloth, Speakes memorably said, "If you tell the same story five times, it's true."[120] The Bush administration learned, no doubt to their delight, that Speakes was right. Iraq is about to invade the United States; Osama Bin Laden has been "marginalized"; the only way to create jobs is to give tax breaks to millionaires; I'm a uniter, not a divider—if repeated often enough, no assertion is too ridiculous to be taken seriously.

George W. Bush knows all too well that when it comes to lying, he can get away with pretty much whatever he wants. He can fib about his opponents, distort his own record, bring the United States to war with an endless progression of lies, but the reporters citizens trust to describe the world to them will never dare to call him a liar, so long as he doesn't lie about sex. With the megaphone of the presidency and a usually timid opposition, he can dissemble, distort, and deceive with little cost.

But as William Bennett once wrote, "persistent lies by a person in high public office are not merely 'personal'; they have to do with the public interest. Public office is a public trust, and people who violate it ought to be held accountable."[121] Agreed.

---

[119] Fay Joyce, "Bush's Plane Forced to Make Quick Dive to Avoid Collision," *New York Times*, October 19, 1984, p. A1.

[120] This quote appeared in an article written by Lars-Erik Nelson, December 16, 1983.

[121] William Bennett, "A Lifetime of Lies," *Wall Street Journal*, October 11, 2000, p. A26.

4.

The Emperor's Fashion Critics

How to Make the Press Love You

If there is a modern president who has received kinder coverage from the press than George W. Bush, it's hard to think who he might be, particularly when you consider the vigor with which reporters went after his predecessor. As Marvin Kalb, the former longtime journalist and now a senior fellow at Harvard's Shorenstein Center put it, "This White House very wisely and very effectively created a message system that made it seem as [if] the Bush administration walked on water, and the media went along for the walk."[1] Any discussion of the Bush fraud must therefore address the news media and their seemingly limitless willingness to give Bush the benefit of the doubt, forgive his serial dishonesty, praise his character, and pass along his spin points. Bush's most notable contribution to American journalism may be the dramatic increase in the use of the notation "[sic]" occasioned by his emergence on the national scene. But while reporters may snicker at his malapropisms, they have toward Bush a strange combination of awed deference and low standards, never tiring of proclaiming that he has "exceeded expectations" no matter how many political victories he achieves.

In few areas has the press been more compliant with the Bush administration's media manipulation than in the adjectives they use

---

[1] Rachel Smolkin, "Are the News Media Soft on Bush?" *American Journalism Review*, August/September 2003.

to describe the president. When Bush labors to associate his policies with manliness and describe anything else as weak (he once derided an alternate version of a tax cut as "little bitty"[2]), reporters respond by describing his "swagger"[3] and calling his policies "muscular."[4] The most obvious case is the administration's favorite word to portray Bush, the talismanic "bold." Whatever Bush does, on matters foreign or domestic, administration officials hail its "boldness," and reporters repeat the word as they have been instructed. Here are some sample headlines from the first months of 2003: "A Blueprint with Bold Letters" (*Los Angeles Times*);[5] "Bush Offers Bold Tax Cuts" (*Baltimore Sun*);[6] "Bush Pushes Surprisingly Bold Plan to Jump-Start the Economy" (Associated Press);[7] "Bush Goes with the Bold Stroke" (*Washington Post*);[8] "Bush's Bold New Plans Could Give Democrats Big Targets" (*Dallas Morning News*);[9] "Bush Takes Bold Step to Help Poor Battle AIDS" (*San Francisco Chronicle*);[10] "Bush's Bold Agenda, Soaring Stakes" (*Christian Science Monitor*);[11] "Bold Step for Bush" (*New York Times*).[12]

---

[2] Dana Milbank, "Bush: Iraq May Have Destroyed Weapons," *Washington Post*, April 25, 2003, p. A10.

[3] Some samples: Foreign officials "could not help but see a swagger in Bush's recent actions" (Elisabeth Bumiller, "Bush, at NATO Meeting, Firms Up His 'Posse,'" *New York Times*, November 22, 2002, p. A12); "Bush seemed to have his swagger back" after the fall of Saddam Hussein's government (David Greene, "Bush Lets Pictures Speak for Themselves," *Baltimore Sun*, April 10, 2003, p. 26A); "From his Stars-and-Stripes lapel pin to his six-shooter swagger, Bush has come to symbolize a largely cohesive American response to the calamity of Sept. 11." (Bob Deans, "Bewilderment, Fear Transform into Anger, Determination," *Atlanta Journal and Constitution*, September 1, 2002, p. 2D.

[4] For instance, the *Los Angeles Times* described his "forward-leaning, muscular foreign policy" (Sonni Efron, "Diplomats on the Defensive," May 8, 2003, p. 1), the *San Francisco Chronicle* called the Bush Doctrine "unapologetically muscular" (Carolyn Lochead, "The Bush Doctrine: Aftermath of War, May 4, 2003, p. A3), while the *New York Times* described Bush's approach as "muscular and sometimes aggressive" (David Sanger, "Bush to Outline Doctrine of Striking Foes First, September 20, 2002, p. A1.).

[5] Ronald Brownstein, January 8, 2003, p. 1.

[6] David Greene, January 8, 2003, p. 1A.

[7] January 8, 2003.

[8] Dana Milbank, January 9, 2003, p. A1.

[9] David Jackson, January 11, 2003.

[10] Sabin Russell, February 1, 2003, p. A3.

[11] Linda Feldman, March 5, 2003, p. 1.

[12] James Bennett, March 15, 2003, p. A6.

As Josh Marshall has observed, the press's image of the Bush administration as a team of super-competent managers managed to survive an utter lack of policy successes. This is particularly true in the case of Dick Cheney, who during the first two years of the Bush administration committed an unusually long series of blunders requiring feverish backtracking by the administration nearly every time he opened his mouth in public, yet continued to be regarded as some kind of bureaucratic Kasparov.[13] Because the Bush administration is punctual, dresses formally, and doesn't run to the press to launch not-for-attribution recriminations against one another, reporters assume they know what they're doing. But whether it's foreign-policy disasters like the Middle East and North Korea or domestic screw-ups like alienating Jim Jeffords and temporarily losing the Senate majority, the lack of promised changes to Social Security or the return of the deficit, the Bush administration has demonstrated a nearly infinite capacity for incompetence, and the press has demonstrated a nearly equally limitless willingness to look the other way.

Early on in the 2000 primary campaign, Bush held daily press conferences to answer reporters' questions. One day, the reporters decided to devote the time to a single topic—potential court nominations—and attempted to pin Bush down on what sort of people he would appoint and what he meant by "strict constructionists" (a Republican code phrase meant to signal anti-abortion activists that the candidate would appoint only pro-life judges while fooling the rest of the people into thinking that all the candidate really cares about is adherence to the Constitution). Bush dodged the questions, then sent staffers out to announce that there would be no more daily press conferences. Answering reporters' questions, said a press aide, was no longer "in our best interests."[14]

But Bush soon realized that the secret to avoid seeing his slip-ups in the press wasn't steering clear of situations in which he might slip up but getting the reporters to like him so they'd be less likely to

---

[13] Joshua Micah Marshall, "Vice Grip," *Washington Monthly*, January/February 2003; "Confidence Men," *Washington Monthly*, September 2002.

[14] Frank Bruni, *Ambling into History: The Unlikely Odyssey of George W. Bush*. New York: HarperCollins, 2001, pp. 49-50.

point them out. The man who, when he worked for his father, saw journalists only as the enemy and saw no need to be polite to them—sometimes responding to a question with, "No comment, asshole"[15]—had come to understand the value of good press relations. Indeed, in his time as governor of Texas he had carefully cultivated the Austin press corps in a manner described by *Dallas Morning News* reporter Wayne Slater as "open, sometimes goofy and self-effacing, forever pursuing [reporters'] favor with an unpretentiousness that became his signature style in Austin."[16] Bush turned on the same charm with the national press on the campaign trail. His success in gaining their affections enabled him to glide through the campaign while seldom facing difficult questions.

But at times, Bush's cultivation of the press could manifest itself in rather appalling ways. For instance, *New York Times* reporter Frank Bruni relates that at a memorial service for seven people killed when a deranged man opened fire in a Texas church, Bush couldn't keep from making funny faces at the reporters behind him: "As preachers preached and singers sang and a city prayed, Bush turned around from time to time to shoot us little smiles. He scrunched up his forehead, as if to ask us silently what we were up to back there. He wiggled his eyebrows, a wacky and wordless hello."[17]

Bush understood that there may be nothing reporters value more in a candidate than that elusive quality known as "authenticity." And how does one establish that one is "authentic"? For Bush, doing so meant joking around and bestowing on each reporter a nickname, a technique he learned early in life to create the illusion of friendship, intimacy, and affection by making others believe they mean something to him. Bruni described how Bush "touched those of us around him a lot...He pinched our cheeks or gently slapped them, in an almost grandmotherly, aren't-you-adorable way."[18]

---

[15] Bill Minutaglio, *First Son: George W. Bush and the Bush Family Dynasty*. New York: Three Rivers Press, 2001, p. 223.

[16] Wayne Slater, "On Message," *American Journalism Review*, April 2001, p. 50.

[17] Frank Bruni, *Ambling into History: The Unlikely Odyssey of George W. Bush*. New York: HarperCollins, 2002, p. 17.

[18] Frank Bruni, *Ambling into History: The Unlikely Odyssey of George W. Bush*. New York: HarperCollins, 2002, p. 25.

When reporter Seth Mnookin joined the Bush press entourage to write a story for *Brill's Content* about how the campaign was being covered, he found himself an immediate target of the Bush act:

> Within five minutes of meeting me for the first time, Bush developed some shorthand to signify our intimate connection. Since the press was writing about Bush, and I was writing about the press, he and I were joined together in a kind of enemies-of-my-enemies equation. Now—I've spent a total of about five days traveling with the Bush press corps—whenever Bush sees me, he sticks out his right hand, wrapping his middle finger around his index finger. And then, as he's waving his hand back and forth, he shouts out, "Me and you, right?"[19]

This performance was greeted with raves. The entire press corps agreed that while Al Gore was wooden and stiff, George W. Bush displayed what the reporters described as an admirable degree of comfort within his skin. Cokie and Steve Roberts wrote that Bush was "a man completely comfortable in his own skin."[20] "He's just so obviously comfortable in his own skin," said *Time* magazine's Karen Tumulty.[21] On the primary campaign trail, CNN reporter Bill Delaney described him as "every bit as comfortable in his own skin, as he's often described, as ever."[22] On *Good Morning America*, *Advertising Age's* Bob Garfield looked at Bush's television ads and pronounced, "he looks comfortable in his own skin."[23] Richard Reeves wrote that Bush "seems comfortable in his own skin, which makes him a very appealing fellow."[24] Even back when he was in college, the *New York Times* told us, Bush was "entirely comfortable in his own skin."[25] Reporters were convinced that while they

---

[19] Seth Mnookin, "The Charm Offensive," *Brill's Content*, April 2000, p. 129.
[20] Cokie and Steve Roberts, "Tale of Two Campaigns: Sun Shines on Bush, While Storms Lash Gore," *Dallas Morning News*, July 24, 2000, p. 17A.
[21] *Hardball*, CNBC, September 6, 1999.
[22] *Inside Politics*, CNN, September 7, 1999.
[23] *Good Morning America*, ABC, October 25, 1999.
[24] Richard Reeves, "May I Trouble You, W?" *Tulsa World*, December 23, 1999.
[25] Nicholas Kristof, "The Texas Governor: Ally of an Older Generation Amid the Tumult of the 60's," *New York Times*, June 19, 2000, p. A1.

were seeing a false presentation when Gore spoke to them, because Bush seemed more relaxed, he must have been revealing the real man beneath the candidate. Of course, Bush's interactions with reporters were no less a performance than Gore's—just a more convincing one.

One of the consequences of this personal adoration was that Bush found it all too easy to deflect difficult questions. No reporter bothered to press Bush about what he might do if there were a terrorist attack during his presidency; the only person who asked Bush detailed questions about terrorism during the 2000 campaign was David Letterman. Appearing on Letterman's show, Bush was surprised to find himself forced to discuss policy. Letterman asked him what he would do about a terrorist attack. "If I find out who it was, they'd pay a serious price," Bush said. "I mean a serious price."

"Now, what does that mean?" Letterman asked.

"That means they're not going to like what happened to them," Bush said to the cheers of the crowd.

But Letterman actually wanted an answer. "Now are you talking about retaliation or due process of law?" he asked.

"Heh-heh," Bush said. "I'm talking about gettin' the facts and lettin' them know we don't appreciate it and there's a serious consequence...and I'll decide what that consequence is."[26]

Looking back, this interview is quite revealing. It demonstrates Bush's preference for tough talk over considered action, his lack of concern with legal procedures, and his inability to answer questions that don't lead directly to crowd-pleasing sound bites. But fortunately for Bush, the press corps was not as concerned with matters of substance as David Letterman was.

THE REGULAR GUY VS. THE PHONY

"One of the advantages Bush had in the 2000 campaign" noted Susan Page of USA Today much later, "was that the press always

---

[26] Jake Tapper, "Meet the Press, with David Letterman," Salon.com, October 21, 2000.

liked him."[27] But Bush got the better of press coverage in the 2000 campaign not simply because he was treated so kindly but also because Al Gore was treated so poorly. While there are many influences on the coverage a candidate receives, one factor is inescapable: you can't get good press if the reporters dislike you. And in 2000, the reporters disliked Al Gore. They bristled at his inaccessibility, they derided his campaign's strategy, and most of all, they thought he was a phony.[28]

The disparate treatment started early on. A study by the non-partisan Project for Excellence in Journalism found that during a five-month period from February to June 2000, the most common theme in stories about Gore was that he was "scandal-tainted," while the most common theme in stories about Bush was that he was "a different kind of Republican."[29] There were few whose writing more reflected this view than the two reporters Gore most needed on his side, those representing the two most important news outlets in America: Katherine (Kit) Seelye of the *New York Times* and Ceci Connolly of the *Washington Post*. Candidates know that if they want the press on their side, the first thing they have to do is get the *Times* reporter and, to a lesser extent, the *Post* reporter to like them. But if Gore tried to make Seelye and Connolly like him, it sure didn't work. Their writing dripped with a contempt unusual for reporting in establishment newspapers devoted to the ideal of objectivity. This may seem surprising to some, the idea that the "liberal" *Times* and *Post* would be hostile to a Democratic presidential candidate. But allow me to offer a few examples.

As the campaign wound down, Gore paid a visit to his home state of Tennessee. This is how Seelye described the event: "Mr. Gore held a rally here, near Knoxville, on the airport tarmac, with Air Force Two in the background and airplanes coming and going. He said he was glad to be 'home.'...He also made an appeal based on

---

[27] Samantha Nelson, "*USA Today* Editor: Bush Can't Rely on War in 2004," *Daily Northwestern*, April 29, 2003.

[28] Portions of this section were previously published in the *American Prospect*: Paul Waldman, "Gored by the Media Bull," *American Prospect*, Volume 13 number 24, January 13, 2003.

[29] "A Question of Character," Project for Excellence in Journalism, 2000.

what he described as his hard work for the state—as if a debt were owed in return for his years of service."[30] Seelye put "home" in quotation marks to remind her readers that Gore is really a creature of Washington and his connection to Tennessee is phony, then practically pleaded with Tennesseans not to vote for him. While these kinds of characterizations are not inherently illegitimate, they belong in a journal of opinion—the *Weekly Standard,* perhaps, or the *National Review*—not a newspaper that touts its objectivity.

Seelye's use of quotation marks to show her disdain for Gore was in evidence in the lead of a March 23 story: "Perhaps it was best not to call attention to the incongruity. Vice President Al Gore has been trumpeting his 'passion' for overhauling the campaign finance system, even while scooping up money and emerging from the primary season as the richest candidate in the race. But today, while holding perhaps his most successful fund-raising session, he refrained entirely from mentioning his newfound 'priority' of eliminating the large, unregulated contributions known as soft money."[31] Gore was "the richest candidate in the race" for about twelve seconds because at the time he momentarily had more money in the bank than Bush, though Bush spent dramatically more than him in both the primaries and the general election, and Gore had supported a ban on soft money for years.

After putting the most uncomplimentary spin on everything Gore said or did, Seelye chastised the vice president for seizing on a remark Bush made when he accused Gore of wanting "the federal government controlling the Social Security, like it's some kind of federal program." "The vice president never allowed," Seelye wrote, "that Mr. Bush's comment might have been a slip of the tongue or a poorly worded thought, instead milking the idea that it was just plain dumb."[32] Of course, Seelye herself seldom allowed

[30] Katherine Seelye, "Attacks Grow Sharp as Time Dwindles," *New York Times,* November 4, 2000, p. A1.
[31] Katherine Seelye, "Gore, Mum on Reform, Raises $700,000," *New York Times,* March 23, 2000, p. A24.
[32] Katherine Seelye, "Attacks Grow Sharp as Time Dwindles," *New York Times,* November 4, 2000, p. A1.

that anything Gore said could have been a slip of the tongue. In one of the most egregious cases in the campaign, Seelye and Connolly misquoted Gore at an event in New Hampshire to write stories saying he had claimed to have discovered toxic waste at Love Canal, when all Gore actually said was that he had held the first Congressional hearings on the topic.[33]

Time magazine writer Margaret Carlson, who serves as a "liberal" on various Beltway gabfests, admitted to radio host Don Imus during the campaign that though Bush was lying with regularity, reporters just enjoyed exposing Gore's fabrications more. "You can actually disprove some of what Bush is saying if you really get in the weeds and get out your calculator, or you look at his record in Texas," Carlson said, discussing the tedious work that would have to be done to evaluate Bush's truthfulness. "But it's really easy, and it's fun, to disprove Gore. As sport and as our enterprise, Gore coming up with another whopper is greatly entertaining to us."[34]

Other journalists admitted in a *Rolling Stone* article by Eric Boehlert the ill will reporters held toward the vice president. "There was a fair amount of animus as time wore on with Gore," said James Warren of the *Chicago Tribune*. A network correspondent said, "There just developed among a certain group of people covering Gore, particularly the print people, a real disdain for him. Everything was negative. They had a grudge against [Gore]. I don't know how else to put it." Another reporter traveling with the Gore campaign said, "I felt there was an ethic on the plane that Gore was a bad guy. I had the sense that [reporters] were harsher on him and more critical of him, and never gave him the benefit of the doubt."[35]

At one primary debate with Bill Bradley, reporters watching the debate in an adjacent room actually booed and hissed Gore's

---

[33] Katherine Seelye, "Gore Borrows Clinton's Shadow Back to Share a Bow," *New York Times*, December 1, 1999, p. A20; Ceci Connolly, "Gore Paints Himself as No Beltway Baby," *Washington Post*, December 1, 1999, p. A10.
[34] Quoted in Eric Boehlert, "The Press vs. Al Gore," *Rolling Stone*, December 6–13, 2001.
[35] Eric Boehlert, "The Press vs. Al Gore," *Rolling Stone*, December 6–13, 2001.

answers. Slate.com columnist Mickey Kaus, hardly a fan of Gore's, was surprised when he went to New Hampshire during the primaries and began talking with other reporters. "What I underestimated," Kaus wrote, "what, indeed, has startled me—is the extent to which reporters aren't simply boosting Bradley for their own sake (or Bradley's). It's also something else: *They hate Gore.* They really do think he's a liar. And a phony."[36] After the same debate in which the press hooted Al Gore, CNN's William Schneider actually managed to attribute even the vice president's bodily functions to manipulative calculation. Gore, Schneider said, "even perspired, perhaps that was planned, to make himself look like a fighter."[37] Al Gore must be the only human being on the planet who can sweat at will. Try to think of a more absurd criticism of a candidate you've heard from someone purporting to be a journalist.

Bush, on the other hand, was considered to be a regular guy, "comfortable in his own skin," so when he wore different clothes at different times or sweated when it was hot, it was unworthy of note. After getting beaten by John McCain in New Hampshire, Bush unveiled a new slogan: he was now a "Reformer with Results." But reporters did not say that Bush was "reinventing himself," as they said so often about Gore. Instead, he was merely retooling his *campaign.*[38] McCain's response summed it up: "If he's a reformer, I'm an astronaut."[39]

Let's be clear about this: did Al Gore sometimes exaggerate his importance in events, attempting to show that his role was more central than it actually was? Yes. Did he do this more often than other politicians? Arguable, but perhaps. But nevertheless, on this question Gore got a bum rap.

---

[36] Mickey Kaus, "Gore's Press Problem," slate.com, January 31, 2000.
[37] CNN, October 28, 1999.
[38] For instance, the *St. Louis Post-Dispatch* said that Bush "changed both the style and substance of his campaign to counter McCain's momentum" ("Bush Pitches Himself as 'Reformer with Results' in Dig at McCain," *St. Louis Post-Dispatch,* February 8, 2000, p. A9), while the *Hartford Courant* referred to Bush's "new style of campaigning as a 'reformer with results'" (David Lightman, "A No-Show's Good Showing," *Hartford Courant,* February 9, 2000, p. A7).
[39] Ron Fournier, "Bush Defeats McCain in S.C. Primary," Associated Press, February 20, 2000.

But wait, you say. The man claimed he invented the Internet, for gosh sakes. But what is the truth? What you probably don't know—and who can blame you, given how often the claim was repeated—is that he did *not* in fact claim he invented the Internet. In an interview with CNN's Wolf Blitzer in March 1999, Gore said this:

> During my service in the United States Congress, I took the initiative in creating the Internet.[40]

Note that the word "invented" is absent from this statement. Gore was talking about the role Congress played in the development of the Internet, providing the funding that turned a tiny network linking a few universities into what would eventually become the World Wide Web. Among politicians Gore was something of a visionary in this area; it is no exaggeration to say he "took the initiative" in securing federal money to expand the Internet.

But as soon as Gore made the statement, Republicans and reporters decided that Gore had claimed to be the computer engineer who had invented packet switching and file transfer protocol. Four days after the interview, CNN's Miles O'Brien and Bob Franken had some on-air fun at Gore's expense:

> **O'Brien:** Senate Majority Leader Trent Lott now jokingly claims credit for taking the initiative in inventing the paper clip. And House Majority Leader Dick Armey says, if Gore invented the Internet, well then, by God, Armey created the interstate highway system. Our Bob Franken, not many people know, invented the reporter's notebook, didn't you, Bob?

> **Franken:** That's right. And if Dick Armey invented the interstate highway system, he should be ashamed of himself. I invented the Capitol over here, by the way.

---

[40] *Late Edition with Wolf Blitzer*, CNN, March 9, 1999.

O'Brien: You invented the speed trap on the interstates; that's it.[41]

But reporters know the facts, right? They wouldn't repeat a mis-quote time after time, would they? Well, actually they would: a Lexis-Nexis search seeking stories mentioning Al Gore and using the phrase "invented the Internet" or "invent the Internet" between Gore's interview with Blitzer in March 1999 and election day of 2000 produces 2,684 articles.[42] The notion, "Al Gore said he invented the Internet," became shorthand for his dishonesty. The fact that it wasn't true was too inconvenient for reporters—who are supposed to have a handle on this sort of thing—to go back and check. "Somewhere along the line," ABC News political director Mark Halperin later said, "the dominant political reporters for most dominant news organizations decided they didn't like him, and they thought the story line on any given day was about his being a phony or a liar or a waffler. Within the subculture of political reporting, there was almost peer pressure not to say something neutral, let alone nice, about his ideas, his political skills, his motivations."[43]

As citizens we have a right to expect that reporters will put aside their personal feelings—whether about an issue or a candidate—and report the story as fairly as they can. This is the heart of jour-nalistic integrity. But in 2000, Gore couldn't overcome the suspicion and resentment that reporters had of him, which had been building for years. And Bush's back-slappin', nickname-givin', regular-guy routine had its desired effect: journalists were soft on him, not bothering to expose his lies or question him too harshly.

Although George W. Bush's 2000 victory can be attributed to any number of things, a look at the progression of the race shows that what saved him were the debates—or rather, not the debates them-selves but the press's reaction to them. Al Gore had turned around a significant deficit with his highly successful convention and was

---

[41] CNN Saturday Morning News, March 13, 1999.
[42] This is a search of the Lexis/Nexis News Group File, using the following search string: "Gore and (invent the Internet or invented the Internet)."
[43] Howard Kurtz, "By Stepping Aside, Gore Stands Out," *Washington Post*, December 23, 2002, p. C1.

leading Bush by as much as ten points in the two weeks leading up to the first debate. But the trap was set before the debate took place.

The press accepted two premises in setting expectations for the first debate, neither of which was true: 1) Bush was both inexperienced and unskilled at debating; and 2) Gore was an extraordinarily skilled debater. Bush aide Karen Hughes called Gore "the best debater in politics today,"[44] a laughable assertion but one bested only by aide Karl Rove, who called Gore "the world's most preeminent debater, a man who is more proficient at hand-to-hand debate combat than anybody the world has ever seen."[45] Similarly, *Time* magazine described Gore as "one of the most effective debaters on the political scene,"[46] while the *New York Times* said, "Mr. Gore is a far more accomplished debater than Mr. Bush."[47] "Gore, a seasoned debater, is widely expected to have the upper hand when he faces off with Bush, who has gained a reputation for vocabulary flubs and speech stumbles while on the campaign trail," said the UPI.[48] In fact, Bush had participated in debates in both his gubernatorial races and the presidential primary campaign, and in not a single case did he utter a terrible gaffe or acquit himself so poorly as to indicate a lack of debating skill. Gore's performance in debates in which he had participated, on the other hand, was competent but never spectacular. Though he had bested Ross Perot in a debate on Larry King's television show, his performance in the vice-presidential debates of 1992 and 1996 was barely satisfactory, and he was nowhere near as skilled as Bill Clinton.

Like almost all coverage of presidential debates, after the first Bush-Gore debate discussion focused around a single question: how did each candidate's performance relate to the conclusions reporters

[44] Laurie Kellman, "Bush Begins Trip to Boston for Debate," Associated Press, October 2, 2000.

[45] Ken Herman and Scott Shepard, "Bush, Gore Cram for First Showdown," *Austin American-Statesman*, October 1, 2000, p. 1.

[46] Karen Tumulty and John Dickerson, "Debate Mind Games," *Time*, October 2, 2000.

[47] Richard Berke, "Debate Stakes Seen as Critical by Candidates," *New York Times*, October 1, 2000, p. A1.

[48] Mark Kukis, "Bush to Take Campaign Trail to Boston Debate," United Press International, October 2, 2000.

had already made about him? Because Bush was the dumb one, the question was, Did he seem dumb? And because Gore was the liar, the question was, Did he tell any lies?

In searching for a Gore lie, reporters had to dig deep, homing in on a statement he made about school overcrowding. Before the debate, a caterer providing food on Air Force Two gave Gore a letter and newspaper article from the *Sarasota Herald-Tribune* about his daughter having to stand in school because her classroom was so crowded that there were no more desks available. The article included a photo of the girl standing during class. In the debate, Gore related the story just as the article reported it. After the debate reporters extensively checked the story, writing articles in which the principal of the school disputed Gore's version of events. In fact, the only inaccuracy in what Gore said was a matter of verb tense: he claimed that the girl "has" to stand because of overcrowding, although by the time of the debate a chair had been obtained for her, and she was no longer standing.[49]

The other Gore statement in the debate that generated sustained discussion from reporters was equally trivial: Gore claimed he had visited forest fires in Texas with Federal Emergency Management Agency director James Lee Witt, when in fact he had visited the fires with Witt's deputy. Incredibly, these statements were taken as evidence of Gore's dishonesty, while the numerous and consequential lies Bush told during the debates were all but ignored. This was the debate where Bush claimed to have "brought Republicans and Democrats together…to get a patients' bill of rights through," which, as discussed previously, was false—he vetoed the first version of a patients' bill of rights, fought against the second, and when it garnered a veto-proof majority allowed it to become law without his signature. He claimed that Gore had outspent him during the campaign and that Gore's proposals would add twenty thousand new federal employees, neither of which was true. He said he wanted to dedicate "one quarter of the surplus for important projects" and

---

[49] Rick Bragg, "Community Debates Its Role in the Debate," *New York Times*, October 16, 2000, p. A25.

"send one quarter of the surplus back to the people who pay the bills," when in fact his tax cut was more than twice as big as all the new spending he had proposed. He offered the absurdly false claim that "most of the tax reductions [in his plan] go to the people at the bottom end of the economic ladder." Multiple times, he responded to factually accurate criticisms Gore made by simply calling them "fuzzy math," implying that they were untrue. But because reporters thought Gore was the real liar, Bush got away with lying, just as he did over and over during the campaign.

Although the lies George W. Bush told during the 2000 campaign were both more frequent and more consequential than Al Gore's fibs, only Gore was branded a liar. The reason is that reporters just didn't like him. On the other hand, since Bush was the friendly, authentic one whose lies don't feel like lies, they'd never call him a liar as they did Gore. Bush managed to build up a reservoir of goodwill with reporters that made them not only forgive his failures but ignore it when he lied right to their faces and to the American people.

HITTING THE GROUND RUNNING

Within days of taking office, Bush administration officials, particularly former press secretary Ari Fleischer (who may have been the most dishonest person to ever occupy that position, no small feat),[50] subtly propagated false rumors that departing Clinton staffers had "trashed" the White House and pillaged Air Force One. Bush advisers gave off-the-record comments suggesting that the Clintonites had rampaged through the White House, ripping phone cords out of walls, gluing drawers closed, destroying locks on doors, stealing whatever wasn't bolted down, and in a final insult, taking the "W" keys from some computer keyboards (the only allegation that turned out to be true).

Reporters eager to give Clinton one last kick on his way out the door ate the story up with a spoon, giving breathless accounts of the "vandalism." When asked about it, Fleischer implicitly confirmed the rumors by saying the White House was "cataloguing that which

---

[50] For a detailed deconstruction of Fleischer's particular talent for dishonesty, see Jonathan Chait, "Defense Secretary: The Peculiar Duplicity of Ari Fleischer," *New Republic*, June 10, 2002.

took place." When asked to describe what exactly did take place, Fleischer said, "I choose not to. I choose not to describe what acts were done that we found upon arrival because I think that's part of changing the tone in Washington." Actually changing the tone might have meant simply stating the truth, which was that the rumors were false. But that would have failed to keep the story going. Fleischer later said he had tried to "knock down" the rumors, an absurdly false claim.[51]

A juicy but false part of the story was that on their last ride on Air Force One, Clinton staffers stole everything they could get their hands on. Conservative pundits leapt on the rumor and exaggerated it as far as they could. The plane, Kate O'Beirne said, had been "stripped bare," while Brit Hume described it as a "raid that was conducted aboard that Air Force plane, the presidential plane."[52] Sean Hannity said, "Look at the way Clinton goes out...they trash the place. Then they strip Air Force One of the china and everything else that wasn't bolted down."[53] But it turned out that *nothing* was taken from Air Force One, as President Bush himself later admitted.

At the urging of Republican Congressman Bob Barr, the General Accounting Office spent $200,000 investigating the charges of White House vandalism. What did they find? Among the horrors they found were "many offices that were messy, disheveled, or contained excessive trash or personal items" and "numerous prank signs, printed materials, stickers, and written messages that were left behind, some of which contained derogatory and offensive statements about the president." In the end, the GAO concluded that the mess left by departing Clinton staffers was probably no different from the mess left when previous administrations had vacated their offices (although some Bush Sr. staffers had apparently carved their initials into their desks, something that no one in the Clinton administration had done). The

---

[51] Salon.com did the most complete debunking of these stories (Kerry Lauerman and Alicia Montgomery, "The White House Vandal Scandal That Wasn't," May 23, 2001).

[52] O'Beirne and Hume quotes from Jake Tapper, "President Bush, Clinton Defender," Salon.com, February 14, 2001.

[53] Howard Kurtz, "Doing Something Right," *Washington Post*, February 5, 2001, p. C1.

idea that there had been less than a capital crime committed so enraged the Bush White House that they wrote a seventy-page rebuttal to the GAO report, insisting that pranks like the removal of the W key from some computer keyboards or the leaving of a T-shirt with a picture of a tongue sticking out draped over a chair were really, really serious. They labored to describe the normal wear and tear on office furniture as vandalism, a phone sitting on a table (i.e., not plugged in) as mischievous, missing television remote controls as theft. The grand total to fix the "damage"? Less than $20,000. Not exactly a huge amount, given that we're talking about 395 offices vacated after eight years, or around $50 in repairs per office. But reporters loved the White House vandalism story, just as they did the false rumors that the Clintons were showered with gifts just before they left office and that Hillary had set up a bridal-like registry at a fancy store.[54]

Clinton's last-minute pardon of fugitive financier Marc Rich, while hardly defensible, was treated by the press as though it should be placed alongside the Cambodian genocide and the rape of Nanking in the annals of history. No presidential pardon since Richard Nixon's got as much news as the Rich pardon. As a point of reference, consider how it compares to the press's reaction when George Bush Sr. gave a last-minute pardon to six officials implicated in the Iran-Contra scandal (along with some other unsavory characters, including terrorists and drug dealers). The most notable pardon was given to former Secretary of Defense Caspar Weinberger, who was about to go on trial for lying to Congress in connection with the Iran-Contra affair. Was Bush's pardon simply a humanitarian act? Probably not, considering that among the items that would have been introduced into evidence in the trial were Weinberger's notes, which showed that, as vice president, Bush had been an active participant in a number of meetings in which the arms-for-hostages scheme was discussed. If the trial had proceeded, what many had suspected—that Bush had been lying to the American public for years about his involvement in the scandal—would have been proven

---

[54] Eric Boehlert, "Hillary's Mysterious Bridal Registry," Salon.com, February 9, 2001.

beyond a shadow of a doubt. Bush wrote in his own diaries when the scandal broke, "I'm one of the few people that know fully the details....This is one operation that has been held very, very tight, and I hope it will not leak."[55] He would later lie repeatedly about his knowledge, claiming to be "out of the loop."

On the scale of sleazy pardons, one would think this one would rank pretty high. Bush Sr. used the power of the presidency to save his own skin, eluding responsibility for both his role in the scandal and his subsequent and repeated lies about it. Did the pardon provoke outrage, Congressional hearings, calls for post-facto impeachment? Where was the so-called "liberal media"? The *New York Times* mentioned the Weinberger pardon in sixteen articles in the first two months of 1993. By comparison, the pardon of Marc Rich was mentioned in no fewer than 176 *Times* articles in the first two months of 2001. And that doesn't begin to cover CNN, MSNBC, Fox News, etc. In the space of just over two months, Chris Matthews did no fewer than thirty-three episodes of *Hardball* about Marc Rich.[56]

CHANGING THE TONE

Of course, the press was not nearly so hard on the new administration, which was assumed to have only the highest ethical standards. But unlike the strategy of friendliness Bush himself had pursued on the campaign trail, the Bush White House handled the press with a combination of threats, punishment, and hostility.

Reporters who cover government are to a great extent captives of their sources, which has the inevitable consequence of muting criticism. For instance, a reporter assigned to the Defense Department knows that if she writes a story too critical of the Secretary of Defense, the Secretary can choose to retaliate and make it virtually impossible for her to do her job. Without the willingness of officials in the Pentagon to provide her with information, she will be unable

---

[55] Walter Pincus and George Lardner Jr., "Diary Says Bush Knew 'Details' of Iran Arms Deal," *Washington Post*, January 16, 1993, p. A1; David Corn, "Iran/Contra Rehab," *The Nation*, March 11, 2002.

[56] Matthews first discussed the Rich pardon on January 23, 2001. This count of thirty-three stops at the end of March, although Matthews continued to discuss the Rich pardon.

to write her stories. One Pentagon reporter found this out when he inquired why he had been excluded from a group of journalists allowed to cover a special-forces operation in Afghanistan. "We don't like your stories," a press-affairs officer told him, "and we don't like the questions you've been asking."[57]

Nowhere is this more true than in the White House itself. While the White House beat may be the most glamorous because of reporters' proximity to the center of power, it is in reality a rather dull assignment with extremely circumscribed opportunities for enterprising reporting. White House reporters spend a great deal of time waiting around for officials to feed news to them.

So when the Bush team took office, they decided they would handle the press with an iron fist. One White House correspondent, speaking on the condition of anonymity, told the *American Prospect* about the White House's system of settling scores: "There seems to be a system within the White House of retribution. Basically, if you write something [negative], it's like at the communication meeting with [Bush senior adviser] Karen Hughes the message goes out that so-and-so's on the blacklist—in some cases for that day, in some cases for that week."[58] When Bennett Roth, a reporter for the *Houston Chronicle*, asked Ari Fleischer a question about Jenna Bush's arrest for under age drinking, Fleischer called Roth to warn him ominously that his impertinence had been "noted in the building."[59] After ABC News ran a story in July 2003 detailing declining morale among reporters being shot at in Iraq, a Bush aide called Internet gossip Matt Drudge to encourage him to trumpet on his website the fact that the ABC reporter who did the story was not only gay, but Canadian as well.[60] Again, the theory being that a frightened press is a compliant press.

---

[57] Nicholas Confessore, "Beat the Press: Does the White House Have a Media Blacklist?" *American Prospect*, March 11, 2002, p. 12.

[58] Nicholas Confessore, "Beat the Press: Does the White House Have a Media Blacklist?" *American Prospect*, March 11, 2002, p. 12.

[59] Al Kamen, "Roundabout to the Oval Office," *Washington Post*, May 14, 2001, p. A19.

[60] According to Drudge, it was "someone from the White House communications shop" who tipped him to the reporter's personal background. Lloyd Grove, "The Reliable Source," *Washington Post*, July 18, 2003, p. C3.

The one prominent reporter who has been willing to give straightforward accounts of Bush deceptions is the *Washington Post's* Dana Milbank. When Milbank was assigned to the White House, Karl Rove reportedly called his editors at the *Post* to get them to send him somewhere else.[61] But in the face of the White House's threats and intimidation, few other reporters have found the wherewithal to consistently ask the tough questions and demand truthful answers.

This is not to say, of course, that no note of criticism ever emerges from the White House press corps. But that criticism is inevitably muted by both the fear of retribution and the White House's extraordinary achievements in leak containment and message control. Nonetheless, whatever criticism there was from the Fourth Estate vanished on September 11, 2001.

When America was attacked by terrorists on that day, President Bush's initial performance was lacking. Bush had an important appointment that morning, reading to elementary-school children in a school in Sarasota, Florida. The first plane hit the World Trade Center just before Bush entered the classroom; he was informed of the event by his aides but went into the classroom to begin the photo-op. After being informed of the crash of the second plane—and thus that there was no doubt that America was under attack—instead of saying, "I'm sorry children; I have to go," Bush obeyed the command scrawled in block letters on a pad by press secretary Ari Fleischer, "DON'T SAY ANYTHING YET."[62] Bush then stayed in the classroom for ten more minutes, reading a book called *Pet Goat* with the second-graders.[63]

When he got around to speaking to the nation, Bush could muster only some awkward statements, promising to "conduct a full-scale investigation to hunt down and to find those folks who committed this act," when of course the "folks" who hijacked the

---

[61] Nicholas Confessore, "Beat the Press: Does the White House Have a Media Blacklist?" *American Prospect*, March 11, 2002, p. 12.

[62] Bill Sammon, "Suddenly, a Time to Lead," *Washington Times*, October 7, 2002, p. A1.

[63] A minute-by-minute chronology of the September 11 events may be found at http://www.cooperativeresearch.org/timeline/main/dayof911.html.

planes were already dead. He then spent the rest of the day hop-scotching around the country, seemingly too afraid to return to Washington. Only days later, when his speechwriters had had time to carefully compose statements for Bush to read, was he able to take on the appearance of a president.

In his first press conference after the attacks, which came a month later, Bush's rhetorical dexterity was pretty much the same as it had always been. Keeping the focus on consumption, he said, "We cannot let the terrorists achieve the objective of frightening our nation to the point where we don't conduct business or people don't shop." In describing the different nature of the current war, Bush offered this little history lesson: "The greatest generation was used to storming beachheads. Baby boomers such as myself was used to getting caught in a quagmire of Vietnam where politics made decisions more than the military sometimes. Generation X was able to watch technology right in front of their TV screens, you know, burrow into concrete bunkers in Iraq and blow them up."

Yes, Bush certainly did get caught in the quagmire of Vietnam, what with the stress and strain of defending Corpus Christi from the Vietcong. When asked what sort of sacrifices he might be ask-ing the American people to make, Bush responded, "Well, you know, I think the American people are sacrificing now. I think they're waiting in airport lines longer than they've ever had before."

Many who watched it were no doubt amazed on opening the next morning's *New York Times* to read this description of the press conference:

Mr. Bush made a confident entrance to the formal setting of the East Room down a long red carpet, mounted his podium and delivered his opening statement in the somber tones of a leader in the midst of war. During 45 minutes of questioning, he made no verbal slip of any signifi-cance, resorted to humor at times, and otherwise conveyed the seriousness of the moment through a new gravitas—seeming grayer, graver and more comfortable in the role.[64]

Just as it had ever since he arrived on the national scene, the press kept the bar for Bush extraordinarily low. The fact that he "made no verbal slip of any significance"—the slips he made were all insignificant—was a triumph. Was this a Republican party press release? No, this was a *news* article from the leading publication of the "liberal media." On their editorial page, the praise was only slightly more ebullient. Under the title "Mr. Bush's New Gravitas," they wrote,

> He seemed more confident, determined, and sure of his purpose and was in full command of the complex array of political and military challenges that he faces in the wake of the terrible terrorist attacks of Sept. 11. It was for the most part a reassuring performance that gave comfort to an uneasy nation. In the weeks ahead, Mr. Bush should return to this and similar venues to talk to the American people. He's better at it than he and his aides think.[65]

USA Today agreed:

> Bush prefers jeans to suits and conversation to public grilling by reporters, but he marched into the historic room on a regal red carpet and seemed comfortable beneath the crystal chandeliers. There was little of the verbal fumbling that often marked his late-in-the-day speeches during the campaign. He spoke with the passion and authority that used to be evident only when he talked of favorite issues such as education.[66]

In the wake of September 11, the press also graciously avoided printing any of Bush's misstatements, as any mention of the

[64] Patrick Tyler and Elisabeth Bumiller, "Bush Offers Taliban '2nd Chance' to Yield," *New York Times*, October 12, 2001, p. A1.
[65] — "Mr. Bush's New Gravitas," *New York Times*, October 12, 2001, p. A24.
[66] Judy Keen, "President Soothes, Warns in Remarks," *USA Today*, October 12, 2001, p. 3A.

"Bushisms" in which they had previously delighted was banished. Consider this passage, from a speech at the CIA on September 27:

> It's also a war that declares a new declaration that says if you harbor a ter-rorist, you're just as guilty as the terrorist....And in order to make sure that we're able to conduct a winning victory, we've got to have the best intelligence we can possibly have....[We must] make sure that we run down every threat, take serious every incident....The folks who conducted the act on our country on September 11th made a big mistake....They mis-underestimated the fact that we love a neighbor in need. They underesti-mated the compassion of our country. I think they misunderestimated the will and determination of the commander-in-chief, too.

Less than Churchillian, shall we say—in these seven sentences Bush manages four grammatical errors, two "misunderestima-tions," and one puzzling non sequitur about loving a neighbor in need. But no matter. Reporters were unanimous in their admira-tion of Bush's new clothes. He had been "transformed" by Sep-tember 11, as we were told over and over. Bush was "transformed by the unimaginable catastrophe of Sept. 11," said the *Dallas Morning News*.[67] "Almost everyone agrees that George W. Bush is a different president than he was two months ago," said *Fortune* magazine.[68] The *New York Times* said, "President Bush has seemed transformed from a casually educated son of privilege into a mature leader of a nation at war."[69] Bush was compared to Lin-coln and Moses. Even the estimable Anthony Lewis would later write mistakenly, "the mangled syntax, the sense of being unpre-pared and uninformed fell away as he presented himself as a 'war president.'"[70] But in truth, Bush was no more eloquent or

[67] David Jackson, "From Florida to Afghanistan, a Year of Making History for Bush," *Dallas Morning News*, December 13, 2001, p. 10A.
[68] Jeffrey Birnbaum, "The Making of a President, 2001," *Fortune*, November 12, 2001.
[69] Elisabeth Bumiller, "Seeing Is Believing: America Reflected in Its Leader," *New York Times*, January 6, 2002, p. A1.
[70] Anthony Lewis, "On the West Wing," *New York Review of Books*, February 13, 2003, p. 6.

informed than he had been before. The difference was in the version of Bush the press decided it was important for Americans to see. For the media, September 11 created an atmosphere of nationalism that did not allow for the questioning of the commander-in-chief. After all, journalists are Americans, too. They saw their country attacked and responded by temporarily putting aside the conventions of their profession. As Dan Rather said a week after the attacks, "George Bush is the president, he makes the decisions, and, you know, as just one American, he wants me to line up, just tell me where."[71] George Bush may not have been transformed by September 11, but the news media—already less than critical of the new president—certainly was.

In December of 2001, *Newsweek* ran a cover story on the Bushes, entitled "Where We Get Our Strength." Reading more like a profile in *Tiger Beat* than the product of a national newsweekly, the article by Howard Fineman and Martha Brandt included the following tidbits: "He has been a model of unblinking, eyes-on-the-prize decisiveness....He has been eloquent in public, commanding in private....Bush would rather look forward than backward....Where does this optimism, the defiant confidence, come from? His family, to begin with...Another source of strength is physical conditioning. For Bush it's a concern bordering on obsession, and it's paid off in self-confidence....He feels destined to win—and to serve."[72]

As his first year in office came to a close on January 20, 2002, CBS News gave Bush a "report card" that sounded as if it had been produced in the Republican National Committee studios. As Bush took office, anchor John Roberts said, America had "unsettled feelings about its new president." Then, the story went on, September 11 happened, and, as political scientist Alan Lichtman (the only person quoted in the story) testified, "History has found the right man." Lichtman went on to compare Bush to

---

[71] *Late Show with David Letterman*, September 18, 2001.
[72] Howard Fineman and Martha Brandt, "'This Is Our Life Now,'" *Newsweek*, December 3, 2001, p. 22.

Abraham Lincoln, a comparison Roberts seconded by saying, "Lincoln triumphed, in part because he struck a chord with many Americans who themselves had already decided the Union had to be saved. On the issues of terrorism and homeland security, at least, Mr. Bush may have succeeded in striking that same deep connection."[73]

Coverage of Bush after September 11 was not simply devoid of criticism over what some might consider trivial matters like his struggles with syntax. Reporters went much further, offering glowing tributes to his strength of character, his commanding leadership, and his pure heart. They treated every word out of his mouth as a message of great import all citizens should heed. According to an analysis by *Salon,* during the first fifteen months of the Bush administration, CNN cut into its regular programming to broadcast Bush speeches live no fewer than 150 times. As a point of contrast, in Bill Clinton's final fifteen months in office, CNN broadcast live remarks by the president eighteen times—an eight-fold difference. While some of the Bush speeches in the middle of this period concerned the war on terrorism, plenty were simply political appearances—speeches before a partisan crowd, with no questions, for the purpose of supporting a Republican candidate for Senate, House, or governor. Of the 150 speeches CNN carried live, 106 had nothing to do with the war on terrorism.[74]

Presented with the image of the commanding warrior fighting terrorists, many Americans might say that though Bush has largely failed on the domestic front, he has demonstrated superb leadership in the war on terrorism. So it may be the ultimate heresy to suggest that Bush's post–September 11 performance was less than commanding. Although some have gingerly questioned his actions on the day of the attacks—making a few awkward statements, then hopping around the country instead of returning to the nation's capital—few would dare imply that he had made a misstep in the war on terrorism. Even his Democratic opponents are careful to point

---

[73] *CBS Evening News,* January 20, 2002.
[74] Eric Boehlert, "All Bush, All the Time," Salon.com, April 18, 2002.

out, as they criticize him on domestic issues, that they support Bush in the war on terrorism and admire his performance.

But what is the substance of the extraordinary leadership that Bush supposedly provided? That he demonstrated it is stated as a fact but never detailed. What is it that he did that any other president would not have done in his place? He gave a good speech before Congress, it's true—but of course, the words were written by others; Bush read his teleprompter competently, hardly the stuff of which legends are made. So what exactly did he do to win such praise? New York mayor Rudy Giuliani, who managed without the benefit of a script to convey a moving combination of grief, compassion, and resolve, opined that "there was some divine guidance in the president being elected."[75] Like others who saw the Almighty's hand at work on November 7, 2000, Giuliani neglected to explain why God would have allowed more people to vote for Al Gore, as Joe Conason pointed out.[76]

The idea that God chose George W. Bush to lead America is quite common among evangelicals, including Bush himself. "I've heard the call," he said during the 2000 campaign. "I believe God wants me to run for president."[77] This was no doubt an unintentional slip affording a view into the interior of Bush's head. Such a statement belies the carefully crafted Bush persona of the regular guy. An ordinary fella, modest and unpretentious, would never say that God had chosen him to run for president. But apparently, God has been a regular policy advisor to Bush, weighing in on matters large and small; the Israeli newspaper *Ha'aretz* reported in June 2003 that Bush told former Palestinian leader Mahmoud Abbas, "God told me to strike at al-Qaeda and I struck them, and then he instructed me to strike at Saddam, which I did, and now I am determined to solve the problem in the Middle East."[78] One should keep

---

[75] *Meet the Press*, December 23, 2001.

[76] Joe Conason, "Is George W. Bush God's President?" *New York Observer*, January 14, 2002, p. 5.

[77] Aaron Latham, "How George W. Found God," *George*, September 2000.

[78] Arnon Regular, "'Road Map Is a Life Saver For Us,' PM Abbas Tells Hamas," *Ha'aretz*, June 26, 2003.

in mind that the report was first related by Abbas in Arabic, then translated into Hebrew for the *Ha'aretz* report, then translated for their English edition, so the wording may not be precise. But if Bush truly believes, as he said after September 11, that he can "rid the world of evil"[79] through the force of arms, then the scope of his ambition is truly terrifying.

WHAT LEGITIMACY PROBLEM?

While the worshipful coverage the press gave George W. Bush after September 11 often went to extremes that embarrassed their profession, no gift journalists gave to Bush was of more value than their whitewashing of the events that brought him into office in the first place. Once the election was over, a consortium of news organizations including the *New York Times,* the *Washington Post,* the *Wall Street Journal,* and the Associated Press hired the highly respected National Opinion Research Center at the University of Chicago to conduct a complete count of all the ballots cast in the 2000 presidential election in Florida. The results of the count were released to the news organizations two months after September 11. What ensued was one of the most appalling media distortions in memory: a unified effort on the part of reporters and editors, even at supposedly liberal publications like the *Times* and the *Post,* to twist the facts toward a predetermined conclusion—one that was utterly false.

Before we examine what the consortium results actually showed, we should see what the press said about them. The judgment was almost unanimous: George W. Bush would have won Florida under almost any scenario. "Bush Still Had Votes to Win in a Recount, Study Finds,"[80] said the *Los Angeles Times.* "A Review of Controversial Election Shows Bush Winning a Recount of Florida Ballots," said the *Wall Street Journal.*[81] From the *Washington Post:* "Florida Recounts Would Have Favored Bush."[82] The

---

[79] Speech at the National Cathedral, September 14, 2001.
[80] Doyle McManus, Bob Drogin, Richard O'Reilly, November 12, 2001, p. 1.
[81] Jackie Calmes and Edward Foldessy, November 12, 2001.
[82] Dan Keating and Dan Balz, November 12, 2001, p. A1.

New York Times said, "Study of Disputed Florida Ballots Finds Justices Did Not Cast the Deciding Vote."[83] The *St. Petersburg Times* headline said simply, "Recount: Bush."[84] While a few papers went with headlines emphasizing the ambiguity of the results *(Newsday's* story was headlined "Media's Own Recount in Florida Is Inconclusive"[85]), the overwhelming majority proclaimed a vindication of the Bush win.

The story was the same on television. On the *Today* show, Matt Lauer said, "A yearlong study by a consortium of news organizations has concluded that the Supreme Court did not cast the deciding vote in the presidential election. The winner is, and was, George W. Bush."[86] Like many others, *Good Morning America's* Antonio Mora managed to make it seem as though the consortium had produced many scenarios resulting in a Bush win but only one with a Gore win: "Finally, a comprehensive media review of last year's presidential election in Florida indicates that under all recount scenarios but one, the results probably would not have changed. The review shows that Al Gore might have won only if he had asked for a statewide recount, a request he did not make."[87] Like Mora and many others, Brit Hume of Fox News took pains to point out that Bush "would" have won, while Gore "might" have won, despite the fact that both occurrences were based on the same data and were equally hypothetical.[88] Bush's victory was discussed in terms denoting certainty, while Gore's victory was described using words that made it seem unlikely.

On CNN, Paula Zahn said, "Well, now a comprehensive review of the Florida outcome shows that if the U.S. Supreme Court had allowed a hand recount, a statewide recount, George W. Bush would still have won the presidency." She then interviewed Jeffrey Toobin, author of a book about the events in Florida, and asked him whether he held to his book's contention that the wrong man emerged

---

[83] Ford Fessenden and John Broder, November 12, 2001, p. A1.
[84] Tim Nickens, November 12, 2001, p. 1X.
[85] John Riley, November 12, 2001, p. A8.
[86] *Today*, NBC, November 12, 2001.
[87] *Good Morning America*, ABC, November 12, 2001.
[88] *Special Report with Brit Hume*, Fox News, November 12, 2001.

victorious. When Toobin responded in the affirmative, arguing that the most important question was whom more Floridians intended to vote for, Zahn asked him incredulously, "Jeffrey, how can you say that? How can you say that given the conclusion of this analysis...?"[89] Obviously, Zahn was not familiar with the analysis, but as far as she knew, any interpretation other than that Bush had won was ridiculous.

But the truth was another story. The NORC researchers actually reported forty-four different results, covering eleven different scenarios, each one producing four results based on different standards of agreement between the coders examining the ballots. Had you seen all this coverage, you probably would have concluded that there were forty-three results that showed Bush winning and one that showed Gore winning. In fact, this was not the case. As befitted the 2000 election, there were twenty-two results that showed Bush ahead and twenty-two that showed Gore ahead. Most of the scenarios that had Bush ahead came from counts that included undervotes—ballots that the machines read as having no vote indicated—but not overvotes, ballots that the machines read as having votes for more than one candidate. There were thousands of overvotes on which the voter's intent was more than clear—for instance, many voters filled in the circle next to a candidate's name and also wrote his name in the write-in space. In other words, if *all* the Florida votes were counted, Gore would have won.[90]

Well, Bush partisans might argue, that wasn't going to happen—the overvotes were not going to be counted. However, the *Orlando Sentinel* reported that Terry Lewis, the judge who would have overseen the recount had the Supreme Court allowed it to go forward, would have ordered the counting of overvotes as well as undervotes, which was confirmed by communications between Lewis and the canvassing boards before the Supreme Court shut the counting down. "Logically, if you can look at a ballot and see, this is a vote for Bush or this is a vote for Gore," Lewis said, "then you would have to count it."[91]

[89] *CNN Live at Daybreak*, November 12, 2001.
[90] Data from the NORC study may be obtained at http://www.umich.edu/~nes/florida2000/index.htm.
[91] Michael Isikoff, "The Final Word?" *Newsweek* Web exclusive, November 19, 2001.

But the press bent over backward to make sure no one would know not only that the consortium results showed that Gore was as likely the victor as Bush, but that had all the votes been counted Gore would almost certainly have won. The press's perspective was summed up by a story on the consortium results on CNN, reported by Candy Crowley. "Maybe the best thing of all," Crowley said at the end of the story, "is that the messy feelings at the Florida ballot box have really only proven the strength of democracy." We then see the Sergeant-at-Arms on the floor of the House of Representatives, announcing in a booming voice, "Mr. Speaker, the President of the United States!" as Bush enters to applause. He is president and democracy is strong, as evidenced by his role in the ceremonial rituals of power. The electoral system has been vindicated.[92]

But does this story really prove the strength of democracy? Hardly. It shows that the world's oldest democracy is actually not particularly strong at all. It is open to manipulation by those with power and the willingness to use it ruthlessly. When the five conservative justices on the Supreme Court went against the fundamental principle that had guided their jurisprudence for years (federalism), embraced an argument to which they had shown little but hostility in previous cases (equal protection), then proclaimed their own dishonesty by writing, "Our consideration is limited to the present circumstances, for the problem of equal protection in election processes generally presents many complexities"—in other words, we are using this twisted logic here to arrive at the outcome we want, but don't even think about using it as precedent—Americans knew that their democracy could be hijacked.

The fact that Bush took office with barely a peep over his legitimacy from those representatives of the left permitted to speak in mainstream media is particularly striking. Imagine for a moment how Al Gore would have been treated by the likes of Rush Limbaugh, the *Wall Street Journal* editorial page, Fox News, and Republicans in Congress had the situation been reversed. Many on the

---

THE EMPEROR'S FASHION CRITICS   129

right never accepted Bill Clinton's legitimacy despite the fact that he was elected twice without any question about who got the most votes. They simply could not come to terms with the fact that the American people had elected a Democrat to the office their party had held for twenty of the twenty-four previous years. House Majority Leader Dick Armey refused to acknowledge that Clinton was president of the entire United States, referring to him in conversation with Democrats as "your president."[93] Bob Dole admitted that "We had a pretty hard-right group in the party who were just never going to accept him."[94] The Christian Coalition called Clinton's inauguration "a repudiation of our forefathers' covenant with God," while conservative activist Paul Weyrich announced, "The nation deserves the hatred of God under Clinton."[95] North Carolina Senator Jesse Helms said that if the commander in chief came to the Tar Heel state, he had "better watch out if he comes down here. He better have a bodyguard."[96] Although threatening the president is a federal crime, the Justice Department showed no interest in prosecuting Helms.

Try to imagine, then, what the result would have been had this been the sequence of events: Bush wins half a million more votes than Gore nationally. The electoral vote is determined by a single state. In this state, Gore's brother happens to be governor. The chief election official, who will render the ultimate judgment on who won, happens to be the cochair of the state's Gore campaign. Before the election, she hires a private firm to purge the state's voter rolls of people with felony convictions; this company decides to take it a couple of steps farther and remove not only people whose convictions happened in other states (and are thus eligible to vote in Florida) but also "possible" felons, most of whom are in a demographic category that in Florida will give over

[93] John Harris, "Mr. Bush Catches a Washington Break," *Washington Post*, May 6, 2001, p. B1.
[94] Joe Klein, *The Natural: The Misunderstood Presidency of Bill Clinton*. New York: Doubleday, 2002, p. 86.
[95] David Brock, *Blinded by the Right*. New York: Crown, 2002, p. 135.
[96] *Inside Politics*, CNN, November 22, 1994.

90 percent of its votes to Bush, but who have the misfortune of having a similar name, age, and race as someone who has committed a crime. Thousands of these men show up to vote on election day, only to find that their names have been removed from the voter rolls. In one county, thousands of Republican voters mistakenly vote for Ralph Nader because of a confusing ballot. It becomes clear that the least reliable voting machines—those most prone to throwing out legitimate votes—were overwhelmingly used in Republican precincts. The Gore cochair takes steps to cut off hand counts in heavily Republican counties and certify the state for Gore, issuing ruling after ruling that benefits the Tennessean. It is later revealed that, despite her denials, she and her staff were in constant contact with the Gore campaign during the recount process.[97] In one majority Republican county, a mob organized by Democratic congressional staffers and spurred on by DNC phone banks and Democratic radio talk-show hosts stages a riot, intimidating election officials into halting their vote count, after a Democratic congressman issues an order over the phone to "Shut it down!" Instead of castigating the brownshirts for their tactics and pledging his support for democratic principles, Gore pays for a party, complete with entertainment provided by Wayne Newton, to celebrate their success in shutting down the vote counting; he and his running mate make a congratulatory phone call to the revelers and joke about the riot.[98] The Gore cochair finally certifies a Gore victory by a margin of less than one one-hundredth of one percent. The challenge to the result reaches the Supreme Court, where the liberal majority first issues a stay halting the counting of votes, citing as its justification saving Gore from political harm should the count reveal that he actually lost. It then turns its back on the most fundamental principle which

[97] Jeffrey Toobin, *Too Close to Call.* New York: Random House, 2001; David Barstow, "Data Permanently Erased From Florida Computers," *New York Times*, August 8, 2001, p. A10.
[98] Nicholas Kulish and Jim Vandehei, "Protest in Miami-Dade Is a Well-Organized GOP Effort: Bush Campaign Pays Tab for Capitol Hill Aides Flown In for Rallies," *Wall Street Journal*, November 27, 2000, p. A40.

had guided its jurisprudence in order to award Gore the victory. In an unprecedented remark, the Court admits that its decision has no legitimate basis by warning future appellants that the decision may not be used as precedent. IRS documents later reveal that Gore spent four times as much money as Bush fighting for Florida.[99] Months later, a reexamination of the ballots reveals that more people voted for Bush than for Gore.

On reflection, this scenario seems farcical, but if you take the previous paragraph and change "Gore" to "Bush" and vice-versa, it is exactly what happened. Now take this scenario and add in what you know about the Republican party and its supporters in the media. How would they have treated such a President Gore? Would someone have introduced a bill in the House to impeach Gore the day after his inauguration? After all, a bill was introduced in the House to impeach President Clinton long before anyone had heard the name Lewinsky. How many elected Republicans would refuse to acknowledge President Gore? How many congressional committees would launch investigations of the voting in Florida? How long would it have taken for Republicans to call for indictments of the congressman and congressional staffers who coordinated the brownshirt riot in Miami? Would articles of impeachment be introduced to remove the partisan Supreme Court justices from office? What terms would the right-wing media devise to refer to Gore to avoid using the word "president"? How quickly would a constitutional amendment abolishing the electoral college move through the Congress? How many books would right-wing publisher Regnery rush into print challenging the results of the election? Would the right ever, for a single day of his presidency, cease challenging President Gore's legitimacy?

The analogous reaction to the actual events could be found only on those parts of the left that the "mainstream" media dismisses as, well, out of the mainstream. Not among liberal members of Congress,

---

[99] Bush spent $13.8 million on the Florida recount, compared to Gore's $3.2 million. Thomas Edsall, "Bush Far Outspent Gore on Recount," *Washington Post*, July 27, 2002, p. A4.

not on the Sunday talk shows, not on the op-ed pages of newspapers, not in news magazines. In these outlets, Bush's ascension was "controversial," not a coup or a theft or a betrayal of democracy. September 11 was not needed to make questions about Bush's legitimacy out of bounds—they had already been declared so.

My point here is not to prove that the election in Florida was stolen. The argument is hardly worth having, since what polls revealed at the time remains true today: if you voted for Gore you think Gore won Florida; if you voted for Bush you think Bush won Florida; and nothing will convince you otherwise. When the National Annenberg Election Survey asked voters what the outcome would have been if there were a perfect recount in Florida, 91 percent of those who voted for Bush said Bush would win while 87 percent of those who voted for Gore said Gore would win.[100] But what should be apparent to anyone, regardless of their party affiliation, is that Democrats' quiescence in the face of Bush's assumption of power is striking in its contrast to what would have ensued had the situation been reversed. And the allegedly liberal media raised no questions about Bush's legitimacy.

THE POST–SEPTEMBER 11 PRESS

We can see the same contrast at work in the post–September 11 events. To his credit, Bush waited a full month before launching an attack on Afghanistan, taking time to prepare militarily and assemble an international coalition. During this time, Democrats remained united behind Bush, not daring to utter a critical word in public. Would the Republicans have been as patient with Gore as Democrats were with Bush? The notion strains credulity. How many days without retaliation would Congressional Republicans have waited before calling Gore a gutless coward? And what about the conservative media? As Bill Clinton said in an April 2002 interview, "One of my friends called me the other day and said, if we had a Democrat in there, they would have had a 'Bin Laden watch' every day. They

---

[100] Information on the National Annenberg Election Survey may be found at www.naes2004.org.

would have been up there for the last three months just marking off the days [when he hadn't yet been caught]."[101] Yet the Democrats barely uttered a peep over the fact that Bush first defined Bin Laden as "The Evil One," and said he wanted him "dead or alive," then when Bin Laden got away changed his tune and said Bin Laden had been "marginalized." "I truly am not that concerned about him," Bush said after it became likely Bin Laden wouldn't be caught after all.[102] Bush's communications director actually said, "I don't know if finding Bin Laden is one of our objectives."[103] When Bush changed his mind about who America's No. 1 enemy was, the press went happily along.

If the paeans to the glory of President Bush emanated only from the right-wing media, then they might have had a limited effect. But long after September 11, the mainstream press continued to act as though the "war" on terrorism necessitated rally-round-the-flag cheerleading for our brave and wise president (and conveniently enough for Bush, the war on terrorism has no foreseeable end). In December of 2002, a *Time* magazine article proclaimed, "It has been President Bush's role from the earliest days to handle our hopes, reacquaint us with our resilience and remind our allies of our resolve....Together [Bush and Cheney] are leading us along a rough road with sharp curves, and while we may argue about where we're heading, we have no choice but to follow, because a nation fights as one....People trust Bush because his easy candor makes him seem more authentic than the average politician...However anxious they may be, most Americans are inclined to give Bush the benefit of the doubt; they trust his motives and approve of his performance."[104] Again, repeating these mantras makes them seem true. This was at a time when *Time*'s own polling showed his approval had fallen 35 percentage points from its post–September 11 high to 55 percent.[105]

[101] Jonathan Alter, "Life Is Fleeting, Man," *Newsweek*, April 8, 2002, p. 42.
[102] Mark Sandalow, "Bush Says Bin Laden No Threat," *San Francisco Chronicle*, March 14, 2002, p. A1.
[103] Anne Kornblut, "Some See Political Risk in Bush's Lofty Goals," *Boston Globe*, July 1, 2002.
[104] Nancy Gibbs, "Double-Edged Sword," *Time*, December 30, 2002.
[105] "Bush's Approval Comes Down to Earth," *Time*, December 30, 2002.

Their timidity reached its apotheosis on March 6, 2003, when the White House press corps assembled for a press conference just in advance of the Iraq war. Reporters quickly realized that Bush had before him a list of reporters his aides had determined would have their questions answered; indeed, Bush admitted as much. "This is a scripted..." he said before stopping himself. The reporters chuckled, but went on playing their part, raising their hands as though he might actually call on them. The reporters Bush did call on asked tough questions, like "How is your faith guiding you?" One commentator called the press conference "a mini-Alamo for American journalism, a final announcement that the press no longer performs anything akin to a real function."[106]

Just as Ronald Reagan's aides told reporters of decisions he had made to prove that he was more than a puppet (when he took over the chief of staff job during the Iran-Contra scandal, Howard Baker Jr. felt the need to assure reporters that Reagan was "more than fully engaged" with the activities of his own administration),[107] Bush aides give breathless accounts of questions Bush has asked or books he has read. In this, journalists are happy accomplices. After Bush produced a decision on the question of federal funding of stem-cell research, Bush aide Karen Hughes appeared before reporters and held aloft for the cameras a book—an actual book!—she claimed Bush had read before making his decision. Reporters neglected to point out that Bush's decision to allow federal funding for research with existing stem-cell lines but forbid the creation of further lines was 1) unjustifiable by the principles he claimed to hold, 2) centered on a false contention that there were "more than 60" stem-cell lines available for research, when the actual number was 9,[108] and 3) perfectly calibrated to minimize political danger. Yet the decision was hailed as the product of wise and considered reflection.

---

[106] This was written by Matt Taibbi of the *New York Press*, quoted in Rachel Smolkin, "Are the News Media Soft on Bush?" *American Journalism Review*, August/September 2003.
[107] Terence Hunt, "Washington Dateline," Associated Press, March 3, 1987.
[108] Stephen Hall, "Bush's Political Science," *New York Times*, June 12, 2003, p. A35.

In the early days of his presidency, Bush faced his first foreign crisis when an American spy plane was forced to land in China and the Chinese government held the plane's crew prisoner. Once the American soldiers were returned, the *Washington Post* ran a story constructed almost entirely from White House staffers' accounts of the president's commanding presence during the crisis, entitled "Behind the Scenes, Bush Played Vigorous Role." The centerpiece was an account of how, on returning to the White House one day, Bush stepped off the helicopter and in a show of awe-inspiring command, immediately said to an aide, "Get me Condi."[109] Of course, none dared portray the conclusion of the crisis, in which the United States offered groveling apologies to China, as a humiliation or a defeat. Later, the *Post* ran a multipart series on the administration's actions in the immediate aftermath of September 11, again relying almost exclusively on the admiring descriptions offered by loyal Bush aides.

Offering interviews for the behind-the-scenes exclusive is a technique the administration perfected, safe in the knowledge that with no sources other than administration officials strictly on message, the resulting reports will be full of fluff like this, from the *New York Times*'s story describing the view of the Iraq war from the White House: "He also met privately with the families of some of the marines who had died, hearing their stories, going through family pictures, talking to children whose fathers would never return. 'It broke his heart,' said one aide who was there. 'It's the hardest moment of the job.'"[110] One can only hope that conversations with the families of those who died might offer some perspective to the man who pumped his fist in glee and announced, "Feels good" upon starting the war.

Just as his father had, Bush produced a war the press could not resist. The tactic of "embedding" reporters with military units—while a reversal of press policy in the first Gulf War, in which

---

[109] Dana Milbank and Dan Balz, "Behind the Scenes, Bush Played Vigorous Role," *Washington Post*, April 12, 2001, p. A1.
[110] Elisabeth Bumiller, David Sanger, and Richard Stevenson, "How 3 Weeks of War in Iraq Looked from the Oval Office," *New York Times*, April 13, 2003, p. A1.

reporters were largely kept from the battlefield and force-fed news by the military—was no less effective in getting the administration's preferred message to dominate the news. Embedded reporters, particularly those working for television, delivered a combination of breathless, night-vision-goggled accounts of units rumbling through the desert and *People* magazine–worthy portraits of the soldiers, just as the administration knew they would. The reports produced by the embeds were kinetic and at times even beautiful, with far-off explosions and vehicles rumbling through the dusty desert. What was missing? Context, perspective, and any view of the death and suffering that is the essence of this and every war. In the words of one general, the military "achieve[d] information dominance."[111]

As is always the case in war, objectivity stopped at the water's edge. Once the bullets began to fly, all press discussion about the war's wisdom was banished. The shifting rationales of the administration for war were accepted without question, as "weapons of mass destruction" were forgotten, to be replaced in the blink of an eye by "the liberation of the Iraqi people." All the networks refrained from showing too much of the actual human cost of war on either side because, as CNBC put it on April 1, "some of the pictures are too distressing to show you."[112] Lest the fragile American public become distressed, the media voluntarily served us much the same sanitized vision of the second Iraq war that the Pentagon had forced them to deliver twelve years before by keeping them from the battlefield.

George W. Bush and his advisers are nothing if not adept at manipulating the press. But for all their skill, the unceasingly positive coverage Bush has received could not have been accomplished were reporters not so willing to accept and pass on the daily stream of propaganda emanating from Pennsylvania Avenue. When he ran for president, nothing helped Bush so much as the press corps' contempt for his opponent. But the man who campaigned by acting friendly so reporters would praise him as "comfortable in his own skin" quickly

---

[111] John Cook, "Military, Media Meet Off Battlefield to Debate War Coverage," *Chicago Tribune*, August 18, 2003.
[112] *The News with Brian Williams*, CNBC, April 1, 2003.

turned on them once he was elected. The Bush administration treats them with barely disguised contempt, lies to them regularly, is characterized by an obsessive secrecy (Bush has "run the White House that is most closed of any presidency I've covered," said *USA Today*'s Washington bureau chief),[113] and gets its way through a combination of threats, bullying, and numbing message discipline. But few reporters have found the wherewithal to offer the American public a truthful picture of Bush and his administration. To be too critical of the man they lauded after September 11 as a leader for the ages would be to risk the charge of "liberal bias" and incur the wrath of a vindictive White House and a thousand Limbaugh listeners. So they nod their heads, faithfully record the administration's spin, and don't make waves. The only loser is the American people on whose behalf journalists are supposed to labor, comforting the afflicted and afflicting the comfortable, as the old saying goes.

---

[113] Samantha Nelson, "*USA Today* Editor: Bush Can't Rely on War in 2004," *Daily Northwestern*, April 29, 2003.

5.

Working the "Liberal" Media

How to Make the Press Fear You

In January of 2002, George W. Bush walked past reporters and photographers ostentatiously toting a copy of Bernard Goldberg's book *Bias: A CBS Insider Exposes How the Media Distort the News* as he boarded Marine One. Anyone who saw a picture of Bush with Goldberg's shrill, vindictive, and poorly argued book got the message: the president is a believer in the conservative belief of the "liberal media."

Bush's photo-op endorsement of *Bias* was hardly accidental. Those on the right, from Bush on down, no doubt genuinely believe that the media are biased against them. But they also understand that the more they complain about liberal media bias, browbeating reporters over slights real and imagined, the more favorable coverage they'll receive. So the other essential part of the fraud is to ensure that the friendly press never turn unfriendly by intimidating them with the charge of liberal bias. Perhaps more importantly, the strategy serves to blunt potential anti-elite feelings whose natural target is the Republican party. In this, the liberal-media charge serves as a handmaiden to Republican efforts on everything from taxes to the environment, keeping the press so fearful of being perceived as liberal that they fail to expose the truth.

THE TRUTH ABOUT THE "PROOF"

One can hear complaints about the liberal media from the likes of Fred Barnes, Michael Barone, Tony Blankley, Brent Bozell, Pat Buchanan, William F. Buckley Jr., Mona Charen, Linda Chavez, Ann Coulter, Jonah Goldberg, Sean Hannity, Brit Hume, Laura Ingraham, John Kasich, Alan Keyes, Mort Kondracke, Charles Krauthammer, Larry Kudlow, John Leo, G. Gordon Liddy, David Limbaugh, Rush Limbaugh, Rich Lowry, Michelle Malkin, John McLaughlin, Michael Medved, Oliver North, Robert Novak, Bill O'Reilly, Michael Reagan, Michael Savage, Joe Scarborough, Tony Snow, Thomas Sowell, Andrew Sullivan, Cal Thomas, R. Emmett Tyrrell, and George Will, to name just a few. The allegedly liberal media overflow with conservative voices, while one would strain to assemble a roster of liberals even half as long.

Nonetheless, it is probably true that there are more liberal reporters than conservative reporters, particularly in Washington.[1] But this imbalance is far less substantial than conservatives would have Americans believe. In the most authoritative survey of reporters, Indiana University journalism professor David Weaver and his colleagues found in 2003 that 37 percent of reporters were Democrats, just barely above the proportion of Democrats in the general population. A smaller number, 19 percent, said they were Republicans, with the rest affiliating with neither party.[2] It is the fact that Democratic reporters outnumber Republican reporters—and nothing about the actual content of news—that allows those on the right to argue unceasingly that the news itself is biased.

---

[1] The source most often cited for evidence of the liberal makeup of the journalistic class is a 1995 survey showing that 89 percent of Washington-based journalists voted for Bill Clinton in 1992 (Kenneth Dautrich and Jennifer Necci Dineen, "Media Bias: What Journalists and the Public Say about It," *Public Perspective*, October/November 1996, pp. 7-14). While this particular survey's methodological flaws are substantial enough to make its findings virtually worthless, few doubt that the majority of Washington-based journalists vote Democratic.
[2] David Weaver et al, "The Face and Mind of the American Journalist," 2003. Results of this study may be viewed at www.poynter.org.

But the idea that the fact that more journalists vote Democratic constitutes "proof" that liberal bias exists is specious logic for a number of reasons. First, it assumes that the way a journalist votes is the only factor determining how he or she covers politics, when in fact professional biases (such as the bias toward conflict, the bias toward official sources, or the bias toward information that can be obtained quickly) exert a far greater influence. Second, it assumes that how a journalist votes is the only factor that makes a difference in their political outlook. While it is true that as a group reporters are liberal on social issues such as abortion and gay rights, on economic issues they are far more conservative than the public at large.[3]

If their combination of social liberalism and economic conservatism determined the slant of their reporting, then Bill Clinton would have gotten better press than any president in history, something no reasonable person would contend. Even Republican strategist and former Christian Coalition head Ralph Reed admitted in 1996, "I think if you look at the way Clinton's been treated for example, I think you'd be hard-pressed to say that the personal liberal ideological views of most reporters...have somehow led to a free ride for Bill Clinton."[4] Years later, ABC News Political Director Mark Halperin admitted, "Any objective person would say that in some ways Clinton was covered too aggressively, and Bush is not covered aggressively enough."[5]

One might think the argument that journalists are particularly critical of Republicans would have become increasingly difficult to sustain given the reverential coverage President Bush continues to receive. But the right tends to substitute anecdote for evidence when arguing about bias, claiming that any unfavorable statement about any Republican official or conservative idea offers *prima facie* proof of liberal bias. Of course, there is a great deal of difference between coverage that is

[3] David Croteau, "Examining the 'Liberal Media' Claim: Journalists' Views on Politics, Economic Policy and Media Coverage," Fairness & Accuracy in Reporting.
[4] Eleanor Randolph, "GOP Finds That Media-Bashing Is the Right Path," *Los Angeles Times*, July 22, 1996, p. A12.
[5] Rachel Smolkin, "Are the News Media Soft on Bush?" *American Journalism Review*, August/September 2003.

favorable or unfavorable and coverage that is biased. To cite just one example, conservatives love to cite coverage of the 1992 and 1996 presidential elections as cases of liberal bias, but somehow fail to mention the three elections that preceded them, not to mention the 2000 election. Because so much of campaign coverage centers on the horse race, whichever candidate is ahead, be he a Democrat or Republican, inevitably receives coverage praising his successful campaign. Such coverage has a bias but not an ideological one. Examine the coverage of 2000, and it becomes obvious that Al Gore received better coverage in only one period—from his convention in mid-August to the third week of September—when he was surging and ultimately leading in the polls. When Bush led in the polls, he got more favorable coverage[6] (although one study of CNN's coverage across the campaign showed that when they reported on their poll results, they described Bush's gains and leads in more favorable terms than Gore's gains and leads).[7] And if the media are liberal, it's odd that in election after presidential election the Republican presidential candidate gets more newspaper endorsements than the Democrat. In fact, the only Republicans who failed to get more endorsements than their opponents were Barry Goldwater in 1964 and George Bush Sr. in 1992. In 2000, George W. Bush got the endorsement of 61 percent of the papers that responded to a survey by *Editor & Publisher* magazine.[8] A recent meta-analysis surveying fifty-nine scholarly studies on the topic of media bias concluded, "On the whole, no significant biases were found for the newspaper industry. Biases in newsmagazines were virtually zero as well….studies of television network news showed small, measurable, but probably insubstantial…biases."[9]

---

[6] Richard Johnston, Michael Hagen, and Kathleen Hall Jamieson, *The Presidential Election of 2000 and the Foundations of Party Politics*. New York: Cambridge University Press, forthcoming.

[7] Alex Slater, *Bias and the Media's Reporting on Polls: CNN's Coverage of the CNN/USA Today/Gallup Tracking Poll During the Presidential Election of 2000*. University of Pennsylvania master's thesis, 2003.

[8] Greg Mitchell, "Bird in the Hand for Bush?" *Editor & Publisher*, November 6, 2000, pp. 24–27.

[9] Dave D'Alessio and Mike Allen, "Media Bias in Presidential Elections: A Meta-Analysis," *Journal of Communication* 50(4):133–56 (2000).

Once in a great while, a conservative admits what Rich Bond, then the chairman of the Republican National Committee, said in 1992, "There is some strategy to it. I'm a coach of kids' basketball and Little League teams. If you watch any great coach, what they try to do is 'work the refs.' Maybe the ref will cut you a little slack on the next one."[10] At its most effective, working the ref can lead news organizations to do things like bring on Rush Limbaugh to give election-night "analysis," as NBC did in 2002 (if you missed Noam Chomsky following up Limbaugh, that's because there were no leftists brought on). "The conservative press is self-consciously conservative and self-consciously part of the team," conservative strategist Grover Norquist told the *Washington Monthly*. "The liberal press is much larger, but at the same time it sees itself as the establishment press. So it's conflicted. Sometimes it thinks it needs to be critical of both sides, to be nonpartisan."[11] As Eric Alterman wrote in his comprehensive critique of the subject, *What Liberal Media?*, "Working the refs works."[12]

THE CONSERVATIVE PRESS

What conservatives now have that they didn't ten years ago, at least in as mature a form, is an entire alternative media devoted to advancing the conservative cause—"part of the team," in Norquist's phrase. As Al Gore described it, "Something will start at the RNC…and it will explode the next day on the right-wing talk-show network and on Fox News.…And then they'll create a little echo chamber, and pretty soon they'll start baiting the mainstream media for allegedly ignoring the story they've pushed into the *zeitgeist*. And then pretty soon the mainstream media goes out and disingenuously takes a so-called objective sampling, and lo and behold, these Republican National Committee talking points are woven into the fabric of the *zeitgeist*."[13] Along with newspapers like the

[10] Lloyd Grove, "Media to the Left! Media to the Right! The GOP, Shooting the Messengers," *Washington Post*, August 20, 1992, p. C1.
[11] Paul Glastris, "Why Can't the Democrats Get Tough?" *Washington Monthly*, March 2002.
[12] Eric Alterman, *What Liberal Media? The Truth about Bias and the News*. New York: Basic Books, 2003, p. 267.
[13] Josh Benson, "Gore's TV War: He Lobs Salvo at Fox News," *New York Observer*, December 2, 2002, p. 1.

Washington Times and the *New York Post,* not to mention Fox News, nominally "objective" sources are filled with aggressively conservative voices that have no liberal counterpart. The *Wall Street Journal* editorial board was given its own show on CNBC, where its members chewed the fat on the issues of the day, both economic and political. Imagine what the right would say if one of the cable networks gave a show to, say, the *Washington Post* editorial board—which is not a tenth as far to the left as the *Journal* editorial board is to the right. As conservative writer and later Bush speechwriter David Frum put it in 1997, "What happens with the liberal press is that there are loyalties to causes. With conservatives, I suspect there is much more of a loyalty to people."[14] Little wonder, then, that when Michael Tomasky analyzed the editorials of major conservative and liberal newspapers, he found that while the liberal papers criticized Bill Clinton as often as they praised him, the conservative papers almost never uttered a word of reproach to George W. Bush.[15] To the conservative papers, the interests of the Republican party will usually trump devotion to principle.

In few places is this more clear than on the pages of the *Washington Times,* widely noted as Ronald Reagan's favorite newspaper. Cult leader Reverend Sun Myung Moon started the paper in 1982 "in response to Heaven's direction."[16] In July of 2002, Moon reported that at a heavenly meeting attended by Muhammad, Confucius, and Buddha on the previous Christmas, Jesus proclaimed Moon to be the Messiah, and all present agreed. According to Moon, God himself was too busy to make the meeting, but sent a letter giving a big thumbs-up.[17]

Although the activities of Moon's cult seem mostly harmless— mass marriages, not mass suicides—one would think that

[14] Timothy Noah, "Obedience on the Right?" *U.S.News & World Report,* June 30, 1997, p. 30.
[15] Michael Tomasky, "Whispers and Screams: The Partisan Nature of Editorial Pages," Joan Shorenstein Center on the Press, Politics and Public Policy, Research Paper R-25, July 2003.
[16] Roxanne Roberts, "Moon Eclipses Birthday Bash for *Times,*" *Washington Post,* May 22, 2002, p. C1.
[17] Felicity Barringer, "Decisions Differ on Religious Ad," *New York Times,* July 22, 2002, p. C7.

respectable politicians and activists would be hesitant about associating with such a person. So how do our president and his conservative friends view Moon's paper? As a shameful rag, to be avoided at all costs? Well, no. At their twentieth anniversary gala in 2002 attended by legions of Republican officials, Bush sent a message praising the *Times* as a "distinguished source of information and opinion," and said the paper was "a credit to journalism."[18] His father, speaking in 1996 at the inauguration of a Moon paper in Argentina (one of many times he has been a paid speaker at Moon-sponsored events), proclaimed, "I want to salute Reverend Moon."[19] And a group with close ties to Moon's Unification Church received $475,280 in taxpayer funds from the Bush administration to promote abstinence.[20]

Along with groups such as Accuracy in Media and the Media Research Center that relentlessly press the case for liberal bias, the conservative media repeat the "liberal media" charge as an argument that may be tacked to the beginning or end of any substantive discussion: "What the liberal media doesn't want you to know is..." And at least some reporters believe it works. "The press responds to critics on the right by bending over backward not to look liberal," former *Washington Post* ombudsman Geneva Overholser told Eric Boehlert in *Rolling Stone*. "The cumulative effect is the opposite: They're tougher on Democrats."[21] News organizations bend over backwards in a hundred different ways; for instance, when just before the Iraq war an intern at the *Columbia Journalism Review* called the *Nashville Tennessean* to ask how many of their letters to the editor opposed the war, he was told that the figure was 70 percent, but the paper was printing as many pro-war letters as possible to avoid being charged with liberal bias.[22]

---

[18] Ellen Sorokin, "Glasses Raised High for *Times*' 20th," *Washington Times*, May 22, 2002.

[19] Robert Parry, "The Bush-Kim-Moon Triangle of Money," March 10, 2001, consortiumnews.com.

[20] John Gorenfeld, "Bad Moon on the Rise," Salon.com, September 24, 2003.

[21] Eric Boehlert, "The Press vs. Al Gore," *Rolling Stone*, December 6–13, 2001.

[22] Brent Cunningham, "Rethinking Objectivity," *Columbia Journalism Review*, July/August 2003.

The charge has other benefits as well; for instance, it is used as an effective fundraising tool as Republicans argue that because all of the media are arrayed against them, donors must contribute in order to allow them to compete. In a fundraising letter for a group that trains future conservative activists, J.C. Watts wrote of the media, "Their constant attacks on conservative principles reveal just how much they hate the idea of traditional American ideals."[23] And it offers a convenient scapegoat for Republicans to deflect criticism for their own faults. When then–House Majority Leader Dick Armey referred publicly to openly gay Congressman Barney Frank as "Barney Fag," he tried to deflect responsibility by attacking the press for reporting his slur. "To have my five children or anybody else's five children turn on their TV today and see a transcript of a mispronunciation on the air as if I had no sense of decency, cordiality, or even good manners is unacceptable and is an act in itself that is indecent," he said.[24] Using a similar tactic, President Bush tried to argue that economic uncertainty was not produced by his war but by the fact that the media had reported his war. "Remember on our TV screens—I'm not suggesting which network did this," Bush said, "but it said, 'March to War,' every day from last summer until the spring—'March to War, March to War.' That's not a very conducive environment for people to take risk, when they hear, 'March to War' all the time."[25] The fact that Bush's government was, in fact, marching to war—and arguing daily how necessary the war was—must not have had anything to do with it.

But as a rhetorical strategy, these considerations are secondary. The liberal bias charge has its greatest use in allowing Republicans to divert attention from their own power and the consequences of their agenda.

After he wrote an editorial for the *Wall Street Journal* accusing his CBS colleagues of being unprofessional (since so many reporters equate objectivity with professionalism), Bernard Goldberg was shocked to find them displeased with him. "It's as if there were two

---

[23] Blaine Harden, "In Virginia, Young Conservatives Learn How to Develop and Use Their Political Voices," *New York Times*, June 11, 2001, p. A10.
[24] Molly Ivins, "The Masters of Mean," *Mother Jones*, March/April 2002.
[25] Press conference at the White House, July 30, 2003.

Americas," he wrote, "or at least two American cultures: the media-elite America, which was shunning me, and the other America—the one between Manhattan and Malibu—which was thanking and congratulating me for saying publicly what they had been thinking for years."[26] Although he claims to be a liberal, Goldberg defines the communication environment in precisely the way many conservatives do: a small cabal of liberals, who are not true Americans, has seized control of the media. Barely anyone supports their agenda of abortion rights and government regulation of business, which is why they have to be so sneaky.

This critique enables the right to package an argument about class as an argument about the media. The right knows that it doesn't have to work to maintain the support of the business community or the wealthiest Americans who are the beneficiaries of its policies. But convincing those of modest means to vote against their own interests (or not to vote at all, a result half as good) requires fooling them about who it is who is fooling them.

The conservative-media critique claims not simply that the news is shaped by liberals but that it is shaped by liberal "elitists" (search Lexis/Nexis for "liberal media elite" and you get more than three hundred articles; "liberal elitist" and "elitist liberal" gets you just under one thousand). This notion helps advance the larger Republican project of convincing the public that those who vote Republican are "real" Americans and those who vote Democratic are something else. And it defines conservatives—despite their extraordinary hold on all three branches of government—as underdogs struggling against those who hold the real power.

ATTACKING WITH CLASS

George W. Bush is in many ways the perfect president to complement the use of "liberal bias" as the underpinning of conservative argumentation. Bush has labored long and hard to construct a persona as divorced as possible from the extraordinary advantages of

---

[26] Bernard Goldberg, *Bias: A CBS Insider Exposes How the Media Distort the News*. Washington: Regnery, 2002, p. 45.

money, power, and connections that he enjoyed in life. The son of a president and grandson of a senator, educated at Andover and Yale and Harvard, managed to convince Americans that he is just a plain-speakin', cowboy-boot wearin', baseball-lovin' regular guy. Just as his father charged that his two presidential opponents—both self-made sons of poor parents—were members of the "liberal elite," Bush defines the suspect, powerful elite as the intellectual class.

The complaint about media bias is a contemporary manifestation of what Richard Hofstadter described as the "paranoid style" in American politics. Found usually but not exclusively on the right, adherents of the paranoid style see forces both malevolent and powerful arrayed against them, holding the nation in their grip as they advance their sinister goals. "The enemy is clearly delineated," Hofstadter wrote in 1964. "He is a perfect model of malice, a kind of amoral superman—sinister, ubiquitous, powerful, cruel, sensual, luxury-loving. Unlike the rest of us, the enemy is not caught in the toils of the vast mechanism of history, himself a victim of his past, his desires, his limitations. He wills, indeed he manufactures, the mechanism of history, or tries to deflect the normal course of history in an evil way."[27] This would not be an inaccurate description of the way many on the right see Dan Rather.

Contemporary Republicans have gone beyond anti-intellectualism to construct an ideology defining anything with which they disagree as the work of "liberal elitists." If one feels unconstrained by the dictates of logic, the charge that a liberal position is elitist can be applied to just about anything. For example, Republican power broker Ed Gillespie said that by arguing that the country should think about using less energy, Democrats were a bunch of rich elitists shoving austerity down the throats of ordinary Americans. "The Democratic party and its leadership," he said, "is dominated by elitists who believe that the rest of us should carpool, while they drive their Chevy Suburbans to the lake house for the weekend."[28] The

---

[27] Richard Hofstadter, "The Paranoid Style in American Politics," *Harper's*, November 1964, pp. 77–86.
[28] Thomas Edsall, "A Broker of Power, Able to Wear Many Professional Hats," *Washington Post*, June 24, 2002, p. A17.

clients on whose behalf Gillespie was arguing were hardscrabble folks like Enron and DaimlerChrysler.

One suspects that Gillespie, whose boutique lobbying and public-relations firm made $25 million in its first two years of existence,[29] won't be squeezing into his neighbor's Geo Prizm to get down to K Street any time soon (Gillespie temporarily put aside his lobbying to become chairman of the Republican party, a perfect metaphor for the degree to which the Republicans serve corporate interests). But occasionally one hears a Republican, almost by mistake, trip over into an anti-elite message attacking wealth. Just as Gillespie argued that liberals concerned about energy consumption must be rich SUV-drivers, the National Republican Senatorial Committee aired an ad in 2002 feigning outrage at the size of Democratic Senator Mary Landrieu's house. "A mansion that's a symbol of elitism," the ad said. "Mary Landrieu's cushy in her million-dollar Washington mansion."[30] How many nanoseconds would it have taken the very same NRCC to cry "class warfare!" if their counterparts on the Democratic side had produced such an ad?

Given ever-increasing income inequality and the government's inability to solve basic problems like the lack of health insurance, it is no wonder that many people, upon being told that the nation's politics are manipulated by a powerful elite hostile to their well-being, would nod their heads in agreement. The reason so many believe it is liberals doing the manipulation is that only one side is making that case.

This is not to say that rank-and-file conservatives don't actually believe the news media are biased in favor of liberals and liberal views. But their perception is less a product of clear-eyed analysis than a manifestation of what communication researchers call the "hostile-media effect," the tendency to perceive news coverage—regardless of its actual skew—as biased against one's point of view. Since many of us tend to see reports favorable to our point of view as factual and accurate and those unfavorable to our side as biased

---

[29] Thomas Edsall, "A Broker of Power, Able to Wear Many Professional Hats," *Washington Post*, June 24, 2002, p. A17.
[30] This ad, along with the other political ads mentioned in this book, are available to *National Journal* subscribers at http://nationaljournal.com.

and distorted, even scrupulously even-handed reports will seem like a mix of truth and egregious lies. One study of the hostile-media effect in the 1992 election found, "People with strong attachments to the Republican party were more likely to see their paper as leaning toward Clinton, independent of the paper's actual coverage. Similarly, people with strong Democratic identifications were likely to see their newspaper as leaning toward Bush. This holds even when individuals were judging the same newspaper."[31]

But if we were all suffering from the incorrect perception of a hostile media, the belief in a biased media would be as common among liberals as it is among conservatives, which it is not. While news coverage has, if anything, grown more conservative in recent years, more and more people have become convinced that the news is liberal. Researchers have found that perceptions of bias are fueled not by political coverage but by coverage of bias itself: the more media discussion there is of media bias, the more people believe that the media are biased.[32] Thus, the ubiquity of the liberal-bias charge *creates* the belief. While there are some on the left who chronicle and protest what they see as conservative bias, most notably Fairness and Accuracy in Reporting (FAIR), there are few if any voices in the media consistently railing against conservative bias.

The charge of liberal bias has been given new life by the ascension of Fox News, which now draws more viewers than CNN or MSNBC. Fox's particular stance, as Michael Wolff wrote, is "about having a chip on your shoulder; it's about us versus them, insiders versus outsiders, phonies versus nonphonies, and, in a clever piece of postmodernism, established media against insurgent media."[33] The network certainly has its own distinctive style. Instead of "Fair

[31] Russell Dalton, Paul Beck, and Robert Huckfeldt, "Partisan Cues and the Media: Information Flows in the 1992 Presidential Election," *American Political Science Review* 92:111–26 (1998).

[32] Mark Watts et al, "Elite Cues and Media Bias in Presidential Campaigns: Explaining Public Perceptions of a Liberal Press," *Communication Research* 26:144–75 (1999).

[33] Michael Wolff, "One Nation under Fox," *New York Magazine*, December 9, 2002, p. 23.

and Balanced," their motto ought to be "Often Wrong, But Never in Doubt"—they are all action and attitude, triumphalism and testosterone, with hosts who collectively adhere to the philosophy that if you say everything with absolute certainty and a tone implying that anyone who disagrees must be immoral or an idiot (or both), people will conclude that you know what you're talking about. One study of public knowledge about Iraq found that heavy viewers of Fox News were more likely to think that weapons of mass destruction had been found in Iraq, and that citizens of most other countries supported the Iraq war—beliefs based not on the world as it is but the world as they would like it to be.[34]

But a good part of Fox's popularity can be explained by the fact that it gives its largely conservative viewership not only validation of their political views but validation of their suspicion that the media have a liberal bias—and the opportunity to feel like noble underdogs. No other news network spends as much airtime complaining about other networks' coverage.

The charge of liberal bias is Fox's stated *raison d'etre* and an all-purpose retort to criticism. Since the rest of the news media is so hopelessly liberal, they argue, Fox only seems conservative in comparison. Their twin mottos, "Fair and Balanced" and "We Report, You Decide," are themselves preemptive strikes against the charge of conservative bias and posed as counterpoint to the alleged bias of the rest of the media. As the *Weekly Standard*'s Matt Labash said when asked about the conservative media, "We've created this cottage industry in which it pays to be unobjective. It pays to be subjective as much as possible. It's a great way to have your cake and eat it too. Criticize other people for not being objective. Be as subjective as you want. It's a great little racket. I'm glad we found it actually."[35]

At times, Fox's assertion of neutrality must be hard even for the network itself to actually believe. When asked about his network prominently displaying the American flag on screen after

---

[34] Lori Robertson, "Baghdad Urban Legends," *American Journalism Review*, August/September 2003.
[35] Interview with Journalismjobs.com, May 20, 2003.

the September 11 attacks, Fox News Senior Vice President John Moody responded bizarrely, "I'd sure prefer that to a hammer and sickle, I'll tell you that."[36] It was unclear whether anyone had actually proposed that Fox used the communist symbol instead, but the American flags stayed on the screen and on Fox personalities' lapels. And "cheerleading" would not begin to describe the coverage Fox gave to the Iraq war, beginning with its inspiring graphic of a fighter plane flying across the screen, firing its guns, then morphing into a bald eagle. While the other networks found their own labels for the war, from "Target: Iraq" to "America at War," Fox helpfully went with the administration's "Operation Iraqi Freedom." In their quest to appeal to Fox's conservative audience, MSNBC followed suit. And Fox was the only prominent news organization (other than the *New York Post*, which is also owned by Rupert Murdoch) to go along with the Bush administration's attempt to rename "suicide bombings" into the nonsensical "homicide bombings," something most journalists rejected.[37]

Fox's principal anchor, Brit Hume, had some interesting things to say about the nature of objectivity thirty years ago, when he was a mere reporter. "These guys on the [campaign] plane claim they're trying to be objective," he told Timothy Crouse for his 1972 book *The Boys on the Bus*. "They shouldn't try to be objective, they should try to be honest. And they're *not* being honest. Their so-called objectivity is just a guise for superficiality. They report what one candidate said, then they go and report what the other candidate said with equal credibility. They never get around to finding out if the guy is

---

[36] Jim Rutenberg and Bill Carter, "Draping Newscasts with the Flag," *New York Times*, September 20, 2001, p. C8.
[37] Of course, every bombing that kills someone is a homicide bombing; what makes a suicide bombing distinctive is that the bomber kills him or herself in the process. Explaining the administration's semantic shift, Press Secretary Ari Fleischer said, "The reason I started to use that term is because it's a more accurate description. These are not suicide bombings. These are not people who just kill themselves. These are people who deliberately go to murder others, with no regard to the values of their own life. These are murderers. The president has said that in the Rose Garden. And I think that is just a more accurate description of what these people are doing. It's not suicide, it's murder." (White House press briefing, April 12, 2002).

telling the truth. They just pass the speeches along without trying to confirm the substance of what the candidates are saying. What they pass off as objectivity is just a mindless kind of neutrality."[38] While Hume's description still describes the establishment media quite well, he has evidently decided to cast off such neutrality, as he alternates between anchoring a news broadcast and offering his conservative opinions on Fox chat shows. Many liberals (myself included) believe that there is nothing wrong with the ideological bent of Fox News—they only wish there was a counterpart as devoted to disseminating the liberal message as Fox is to the conservative one.

EXPLOITING THE "LIBERAL BIAS"

For years, Republicans have been more effective at communication strategies than Democrats, shaping news coverage in subtle but important ways. To take a small example, reporters routinely refer to tax cuts as "tax relief," an ideologically weighted term that started as a Republican characterization and became common parlance. While a similar effort to make the deceptive term "death tax" the preferred appellation for the estate tax has met with only limited success, recent years have seen a spate of successful Republican language projects, from "partial-birth abortion" to "faith-based" groups. These efforts are successful because everyone on the Republican side, from government officials to lobbyists to pundits, agrees upon the preferred terminology and sticks to it relentlessly. As Republican consultant Frank Luntz told his compatriots, "We can only succeed when we work together and talk together and stick together as a team. Only through a movement-wide effort and constant repetition can our voices unite in perfect harmony."[39] They follow this advice to the letter.

Republicans see the browbeating of the media over alleged bias, like the efforts to change the terms reporters use to describe policies, as a long-term project. There is no balance of voices or tone of

---

[38] Timothy Crouse, *The Boys on the Bus*. New York: Ballantine, 1972, p. 323.
[39] Deborah Tannen, "Let Them Eat Words," *American Prospect*, September 2003, p. 31.

coverage that will satisfy them because getting fair treatment is not the point. After all, the worshipful coverage President Bush continues to receive in the mainstream press should have convinced them that the battle over media bias has been decisively won.

Rather, the point is to convince Americans that the elite is not those on whose behalf the Republican party toils, shaping national policy to enhance the power of the powerful, the influence of the influential, and the wealth of the wealthy. No, it is university professors and Hollywood actors whom ordinary people should resent and fear. When the Bush administration trots out yet another round of tax cuts aimed at millionaires, conservative media voices argue that those who object must be elitists. That the right has convinced so many that such a thing could be true is no small feat indeed.

The media environment in contemporary America is unbalanced, but not in the way the conservatives would have us believe. On one side are aggressive, partisan, conservative outlets, spewing bile at liberals and reciting Republican National Committee talking points; on the other are establishment news outlets devoted to the ideal of objectivity and working endlessly to prove that they have no bias. Conservative columnists who never hesitate to resort to the most vicious attacks on Democrats are pitted against nominally liberal columnists who (with but a few notable exceptions) balance timid criticisms of President Bush with compliments to his integrity. Radio airwaves and cable news channels overflow with the hate-mongering and rantings of conservatives like Ann Coulter and Michael Savage, while no liberal nearly as far to the ideological fringe is anywhere to be found. When was the last time you turned on your television and heard a liberal advocate the murder of those with whom she disagrees, as Coulter does routinely? Coulter wrote about Bill Clinton that the most appropriate debate would be "whether to impeach or assassinate"; said that Al Gore's and Gray Davis's status as Vietnam veterans made for "the only compelling argument yet in favor of friendly fire"; said after the Oklahoma City bombing that, "My only regret with Timothy McVeigh is he did not go to the *New York Times* building"; and said about "American Taliban" John Walker Lindh, "We need to execute people like John Walker in order to physically intimidate liberals, by making them realize that they can be killed too. Otherwise they will turn out to be outright traitors."[40] (That Lindh, who joined the most reactionary conservative government on earth, could be considered a liberal is beyond bizarre.)

While Coulter has too many bookings to handle and a new conservative seems to get his own cable show each month, journalists get fired for attending antiwar rallies; radio networks ban music by artists who criticize the president; and Phil Donahue, the lone liberal with his own television show, is cancelled by MSNBC for opposing the Iraq war, despite the fact that his show was the highest-rated program on the network.[41] Consultants hired by NBC told the executives that Donahue made for a "difficult public face for NBC in a time of war...He seems to delight in presenting guests who are antiwar, anti-Bush and skeptical of the administration's motives." Their report warned of the possibility that Donahue's show could become "a home for the liberal antiwar agenda at the same time that our competitors are waving the flag at every opportunity."[42] Donahue was soon shown the door; in the same week MSNBC announced that ultra-right radio tantrum stylist Michael Savage had been added to its lineup. MSNBC president Erik Sorenson described Savage as "brash, passionate, and smart." He must not have been referring to Savage's statements on "turd world nations," the "Million Dyke March," and "ghetto slime"; his opinion that Latino immigration is "part of the grand plan, to push homosexuality to cut down on the white race"; or perhaps his suggestion that teenagers distributing

---

[40] *High Crimes and Misdemeanors*, Regnery, 1998; "California: The Democrats' Laboratory," *FrontPage Magazine*, August 14, 2003; George Gurley, "Coultergeist," *New York Observer*, August 26, 2002, p. 1; Jay Bookman, "Liberals, Report to Re-Education," *Atlanta Journal and Constitution*, February 14, 2002, p. 18A.

[41] Allison Romano, "All the Right Moves," *Broadcasting & Cable*, March 3, 2003, p. 1.

[42] This memo was leaked to Rick Ellis of allyourtv.com.

food to the homeless "like the excitement of it. There's always the thrill and possibility they'll be raped in a dumpster while giving out a turkey sandwich."[43] But Savage's formula didn't translate well to television, and his show got mediocre ratings. He was finally fired by MSNBC after he told a caller to "get AIDS and die."

Situated underneath the conservative-dominated pundit universe is an establishment press whose professional standards can be easily manipulated in the service of deception. If there is one thing George W. Bush understands about contemporary American journalism, it is that objectivity, supposedly the guarantor of truth, can in practice become its enemy. Bush appreciates that the even-handed, "both sides" operationalism of objectivity has a post-modern perspective on the truth. It posits all arguments, as long as they are made by those deemed *a priori* to be "part of the debate" (and no one is more central to the debate than the president), to be of equal value—none inherently more true than any other. Every debate is described as "the Republicans say this, and the Democrats say that," with little effort made to guide citizens toward the truth. Consequently, Bush knows that he is free to lie, distort, and contradict himself, and the wry stenographers of the fourth estate will faithfully pass on his palaver to the public. Because they long ago decided he is honest, he will never be called a liar, no matter how many lies he tells.

Despite what Bush and his allies say, the notion that the main-stream news media evince a liberal bias does not stand up to scrutiny. Even though nearly every Republican presidential candidate garners the lion's share of newspaper endorsements, though the pundit uni-verse is dominated by conservatives, though huge corporations con-trol the levers of communication, though Bush's coverage has ranged from the mildly laudatory to the sycophantic, the right continues to play the "liberal bias" card. The press can be intimidated into what Brit Hume called "a mindless kind of neutrality," even when the facts are far from neutral, and the fraud continues unabated. Working the refs does work.

---

[43] These statements are collected and sourced at www.fair.org/activism/msnbc-savage.html.

6.

Putting the Con in Compassionate Conservative

Bush's Ideological Two-Step

To make George W. Bush palatable to the American public, he and his handlers had to create the impression that ideologically, Bush is not some hard-hearted, punitive, far-right ideologue who cares only about the wealthy. Rather, we were told that he is something else entirely, "a different kind of Republican," someone who combines the best of both parties into a new political animal, the "compassionate conservative." But despite what he, his supporters, and much of the press corps have been telling us from the moment he decided to run for president, George W. Bush is *not* a different kind of Republican. He may not be as stern as Bob Dole or as publicly vicious as Newt Gingrich, but when the rubber hits the road Bush is as ideologically conservative as any president of the last hundred years. The Bush fraud thus depends on reactionary policies being disguised in a cloud of compassionate words and pictures. And nobody knows this better than the hardest of hard-right Republicans themselves. The hard-core conservatives weren't fooled by all the talk of "compassion"—they knew from the first moment that Bush was their guy. "This administration is shaping up to be the best," gushed veteran conservative activist Paul Weyrich two months into Bush's tenure.[1]

---

[1] Dana Milbank and Ellen Nakashima, "Bush Team Has 'Right' Credentials," *Washington Post*, March 25, 2001, p. A1.

In contrast, Bill Clinton actually was a different kind of Democrat, and genuine liberals always felt ambivalent about him. On one hand, he pursued a number of policies—punitive welfare reform, expansion of the death penalty, a punishment-based approach to the problem of drugs, signing the Defense of Marriage Act—that liberals disagreed with vehemently. On the other hand, he had a way of not only arousing conservatives' ire but defeating them that liberals found irresistible. But the hard-core conservatives are George W. Bush's most enthusiastic supporters. They know that the walks in the woods, the talk about helping the poor, and the hugging of children are just for show. (Bush is a great advocate of the power of hugging—asked about sending troops into harm's way, he said, "There's only one person who hugs the mothers and the widows, the wives and the kids upon the death of their loved one. Others hug, but having committed the troops, I've got an additional responsibility to hug and that's me and I know what it's like."[2]) As Bush himself said, "I don't care what anyone says, politics is all about perception."[3] He understood that he could create the perception of compassion without giving up any of his conservatism.

Behind the Strategy
The Bush ideological strategy had two prongs. First, find a friendly catchphrase that makes you seem different from the hard-hearted Republicans of the past. Presto: "compassionate conservatism." Second, pose for a lot of pictures with blacks and Hispanics, regardless of the effects your policies might have on them. After all, it's a big country—you can always find someone willing to let the president give them a hug while the cameras click away. On the first version of the Bush 2004 campaign website, a photo of Laura reading to Hispanic children was accompanied by a caption helpfully noting, "This week's photo is of the First Lady reading to Hispanic children." A link offered the opportunity to "See more Hispanic photos." Though those less-than-subtle captions were soon taken

[2] 20/20, ABC, December 13, 2002.
[3] Bill Minutaglio, *First Son: George W. Bush and the Bush Dynasty*. New York: Three Rivers Press, 2001, p. 330.

down, the site later featured a "Compassion Photo Album." Of the twenty photos in the album, one featured Bush alone in front of an American flag, one showed him alone in front of a sign that read "The Corporate Council on Africa," and one showed him in front of a sign reading "National Urban League." Every one of the other seventeen photos showed Bush and/or Laura with blacks and Hispanics, mostly children.[4]

For someone as far to the right as Bush is, the creation of misconception about his policy agenda is the *sine qua non* of national victory and a strategy that has been used before. When they analyzed the 1988 election, political scientists Michael Delli Carpini and Scott Keeter discovered that significant numbers of people who voted for George Bush Sr. were in effect fooled into doing so: they believed that the Reagan/Bush administration had increased funding for causes they supported, such as the environment, schools, and aid to the poor, when in fact the opposite was true.[5] Although it seems unlikely that George W. Bush is familiar with this research, there is little doubt he understands what it reveals: a sunny disposition and some kind words can deceive people into thinking that if you're a nice guy, your policies must be nice, too.

To see how this works, we can examine a few of the things Bush said during his 2000 debates with Al Gore, which turned around his slide in the polls and as much as any other campaign event were responsible for him becoming president. Asked a question about the price of oil in the first debate, Bush said, "First and foremost, we got to make sure we fully fund LIHEAP, which is a way to help low-income folks, particularly here in the east, to pay for their high fuel bills." The Low Income Home Energy Assistance Program, which helps poor Americans with their heating bills to make sure no one freezes to death in the winter, is an extremely popular program that conservatives like Bush don't much like. But while a more honest politician would come out and say he was opposed to it and try to

---

[4] http://www.georgewbush.com.
[5] Michael Delli Carpini and Scott Keeter, *What Americans Know about Politics and Why It Matters*. New Haven, CT: Yale University Press, 1996.

make a case for why, Bush's impulse is to tell Americans what they want to hear, pledging support for the popular liberal program, then take a chainsaw to it when nobody's looking. When it came time to actually do what he had promised, Bush was not quite so sympathetic to those low-income folks; his 2003 budget proposed cutting LIHEAP by $300 million.[6]

An even clearer example of the Bush modus operandi emerged in their next debate, when Al Gore observed that under Bush's leadership, Texas ranked forty-ninth out of fifty states in the percent of children with health insurance, forty-ninth in the percentage of women with health insurance, and dead last in the percentage of families with health insurance. This was Bush's response:

> We spend $4.7 billion a year on the uninsured in the state of Texas. Our rate of uninsured, the percentage of uninsured in Texas has gone down, while the percentage of uninsured in America has gone up. Our CHIPS program got a late start because our government meets only four months out of every two years, Mr. Vice President. It may come for a shock for somebody who's been in Washington for so long, but actually, limited government can work in the second largest state in the union. And therefore, Congress passes the bill after our session in 1997 ended. We passed the enabling legislation in '99. We've signed up over 110,000 children to the CHIPS program. For comparable states our size, we're signing them up fast as any other state. And I — you can quote all the numbers you want, but I'm telling you, we care about our people in Texas.

I should clarify that CHIP is the federal Children's Health Insurance Program administered by the states that provides insurance for poor children. CHiPs, on the other hand, was a 1970s television show in which intrepid motorcycle cops Ponch and John zoomed around the Los Angeles freeways after bad guys. That

---

[6] "Out in the Cold," *Boston Globe*, January 23, 2003, p. A10.

aside, Bush's answer is an interesting one when you look at the facts. First, he lies about spending on the uninsured in Texas, claiming $4.7 billion as what the Texas government spends on health care for the uninsured, when in fact you get that total only if you add Texas government spending to that of every private charity and nonprofit group in the state—the actual figure for the Texas government was around $1.2 billion.[7] Then, Bush acknowledges that because of the part-time Texas legislature, thousands of children went without health insurance for longer than they should have, yet he somehow believes that such a failure shows that "limited government can work." Finally, he says that the facts don't really matter—what's important is whether or not he cares: "you can quote all the numbers you want, but I'm telling you, we care about our people in Texas." When Gore responded with more factual evidence of his failure to provide health insurance for the citizens of his state, Bush said, "If he's trying to allege that I'm a hard-hearted person and I don't care about children, he's absolutely wrong." If you were one of the thousands of parents who couldn't get health care for their kids because of the Texas government's stinginess, the fact that Governor Bush claimed to really, really care deep in his heart about you was probably cold comfort. But Bush would have Americans believe that what matters is the content of his heart, not the consequences of his actions.

The story of Bush's performance in Texas on the question of health insurance for poor children, which was laid out in detail by Molly Ivins and Lou Dubose in their book *Shrub: The Short But Happy Political Life of George W. Bush,* is so despicable that it bears repeating. Under CHIP, which was passed by Congress and signed by President Clinton in 1997, the federal government gives states around $3 for every dollar they spend to provide insurance for poor children. The states decide exactly who gets it, but most states have set the ceiling at 200 percent of the poverty level (although some states set it higher). When the Texas legislature took up the issue, Bush lobbied to keep the

---

[7] Yvonne Abraham and Glen Johnson, "Campaigns Wage a Turf War," *Boston Globe,* October 17, 2000, p. A27.

ceiling at 150 percent of the poverty level. At the time, 150 percent of the poverty level for a family of four was a yearly income of $25,050. So Bush felt that two parents, each making the princely sum of $12,526 a year, were so well-off that they didn't deserve any help with health insurance for their children. By setting the ceiling at 150 percent of the poverty level instead of 200 percent, Bush kept two hundred thousand children from getting health insurance.

In addition, he backed a move to require that families apply separately for CHIP and for Medicaid. The concern was that too many poor families would apply for CHIP and find out that they were eligible for Medicaid, meaning that the whole family, not just the children, could be insured. If you made them apply separately, then the extra burden of red tape would keep many from following through. With the presidential race approaching, Bush's people were reportedly concerned that if too many poor families were given health insurance, his presidential-primary opponents would charge that he wasn't successful in reducing the rolls of all forms of public assistance.

All politicians are faced with choices between doing the right thing and maximizing their own political advantage. The choice that Bush made—leaving a couple of hundred thousand poor families without health insurance for the sake of heading off a hypothetical attack in a primary debate—was particularly coldhearted. At the same time that he was trying to limit the number of children covered under CHIP, however, Bush pushed a piece of "emergency" legislation giving a $45 million tax break to owners of low-producing oil wells in Texas, most of which were held by Exxon. "There's a lot of people hurting," Bush said sympathetically.[8]

These episodes offer clues to the contrast between Bush's rhetoric and the ideology apparent in his deeds. He is not particularly fond of government programs that provide services like health insurance and home-heating assistance, but rather than simply opposing them, he pledges his support in public but works to undermine them in private. He stands before America and issues an inspiring plea to expand

---

[8] Molly Ivins and Lou Dubose, *Shrub: The Short But Happy Political Life of George W. Bush*. New York: Vintage, 2000, p. 101.

the AmeriCorps service program, then allows congressional Republicans to slash the program with his tacit approval. He gets an education bill passed, then stands by while it, too, is underfunded. He proclaims "National Family Caregivers Month," then moves to cut funding for the National Family Caregivers Support Program.[9] Time passes, cuts appear in the fine print, the memories of citizens and reporters fade, and the myth of "compassion" can be maintained without anything compassionate actually taking place.

CONSERVATIVE CONSERVATISM

The party Bush leads contains adherents of two distinct ideologies: economic conservatism and social conservatism. There is little reason why these should necessarily go together, why opposition to both abortion and comprehensive regulation of business, for instance, are sides of the same coin. True libertarians who believe in minimal government involvement in both the economy and in personal decisions involving such matters as sexuality and drug use have a much more coherent view of the role of government than those who are both socially and economically conservative. But many of those whose primary interest is in the economic realm have simply left discussion of social issues to the religious wing of their party; in return, the social conservatives have embraced laissez-faire economics. As Marshall Wittman, himself a Republican (albeit a McCain supporter), has written, "Social conservatism is what Republicans talk about at church on Sundays. Corporate conservatism is what many Washington Republicans practice during the week."[10]

The compromise between the two wings of the Republican party evolved as the realignment begun in the 1960s matured. After Lyndon Johnson signed the Civil Rights Act in 1964, he told his aide Bill Moyers, "I think we have just delivered the South to the Republican party for a long time to come."[11] Although the process took a few

---

[9] Matthew Yglesias, "Turkeys Take Note," *American Prospect*, December 2003, p. 9.

[10] Marshall Wittman, "Under the Corporate Influence," *Blueprint Magazine*, May 21, 2002.

[11] This oft-cited quote can be found in Robert Dallek, *Flawed Giant: Lyndon Johnson and His Times, 1961–1973*. New York: Oxford University Press, 1998.

decades, Johnson was right. While the South had been a one-party region, once Democrats became associated with civil rights, conservative Southern whites began to flee to the Republican party. As hard as it may be to conceive of it today, such arch-conservatives as Strom Thurmond and Phil Gramm were first elected to office as Democrats.

As this realignment proceeded, the GOP took on more and more of a Southern cast. In recent years, nearly all of the national Republican leaders—George W. Bush, Newt Gingrich, Dick Armey, Tom DeLay, Trent Lott, Bill Frist—hail from the South. As the party's center of gravity moved from the Eastern establishment to the old Confederacy, it became more fundamentalist Christian as well. Nowhere is this movement more clear than in the contrast between George Herbert Walker Bush—scion of the Connecticut elite, friend of Wall Street, trained to be so modest that he can hardly bear to speak in the first person—and George Walker Bush, he of the exaggerated drawl and enormous belt buckles. While the father hardly ever spoke of his religion, the son believes and proclaims that God guides his every move.

Though the Southern constituency of the new Republican party may be motivated largely by issues like prayer in school and gay marriage, the GOP leadership didn't move away from the traditional Republican ideas about economics. To the contrary, they elevated laissez-faire to the level of a religious mandate. Forget about that eye of the needle stuff—to today's GOP, cutting taxes, particularly on the wealthy, is practically a command from God.

Democratic presidents like FDR and LBJ wanted government to be a loving patriarch, providing for the people's needs from cradle to grave. In this vision, government would make sure you had enough to eat, that you were educated, that you had a place to live, that you had a job, that you didn't retire in poverty. Bush, on the other hand, would have government be an absent, abusive father. Most of the time it just isn't around to help you with your problems. When it does show up, it smacks you across the face and tells you to shape up or else.[12] While Bush talks a lot about compassion, when you examine his actual policies you see that all the compassionate stuff is supposed to be done by someone other than the government, most notably religious organizations. In Bush's vision, what government does is punish people.

At times, this can lead to policies that seem on their face to contradict the libertarian philosophy to which Bush claims a certain degree of commitment. Take Total Information Awareness, an Orwellian initiative that would be absurd were it not so frightening. The project (later renamed "Terrorist Information Awareness" to shift the focus) would collect data on every American from every source it could, then compile that data to keep tabs on who is being naughty and who is being nice. The idea that government bureaucrats would be examining your credit card bill might strike those who vote Republican in order to get government off their backs as something of a betrayal. But it is in fact quite compatible with Bush's punitive vision of government, since it treats every citizen like a criminal suspect.

The moral vision that drives Bush's beliefs says that the way to order society is through punishment and the threat of punishment. That's how you raise kids; that's how you keep people in line. In fact, there is a fairly strong relationship between views on child-rearing and political views; for instance, conservatives are substantially more likely to support spanking of children than liberals.[13] Look at a map of where the law allows public school personnel to use physical violence against children as a disciplinary tool and it looks remarkably like the red-blue electoral map of the 2000 election: corporal

---

[12] Parental metaphors for government have been used before. Commentator Chris Matthews refers to the Republicans as the "daddy party" and Democrats as the "mommy party"; in a related vein, linguist George Lakoff argues that conservatives are guided by "strict father morality" while liberals are guided by "nurturant parent morality" (George Lakoff, *Moral Politics: What Conservatives Know That Liberals Don't*. Chicago: University of Chicago Press, 1996.) My analysis in this section draws on Lakoff's insights.

[13] In the 2000 General Social Survey, 42 percent of conservatives said they "strongly agreed" with the statement, "It is sometimes necessary to discipline a child with a good, hard spanking," compared to only 27 percent of liberals.

punishment in public schools is forbidden in the Northeast, upper Midwest, and West, but allowed in the South and lower Midwest. Corporal punishment is most strongly supported by those who believe that the Bible is the inerrant word of God, that people are essentially corrupt, and that sin must be punished.[14]

When you apply this worldview to an issue such as crime, for instance, practical questions like prevention become irrelevant. If you commit a crime, you must be punished. So let's say the question is whether inmates should be given drug treatment, psychological counseling, or job training. The liberal says yes—not only might this individual be personally redeemed, but when he gets out, as most inmates eventually do, he will be much less likely to commit more crimes, instead having a good chance at becoming a contributing member of society. That protects everyone—you don't have to have sympathy for the inmate to see that it's the most practical thing to do.

A conservative like George W. Bush, on the other hand, considers things like drug treatment and job training to be doing the inmate a favor. Since he committed a crime, he is unworthy of any such benefits and instead should simply be punished in the most unpleasant way possible. The efficacy of treatment and training in preventing recidivism is simply irrelevant. This is why, despite the common belief that liberals are starry-eyed idealists, liberals are often much more practical than conservatives. Liberals are willing to examine causes and effects and weigh them in making policy decisions. Conservatives are much more likely to divide the world into good people and bad people. Bad people—whether pot smokers, fornicators, or welfare recipients—deserve only public disgrace and scorn.

It should be noted that the American public generally favors treatment over incarceration for those with drug problems, and sensibly so; a study by the Rand Corporation showed that every dollar spent on treatment reduces drug use by the same amount as seven dollars spent on law enforcement, ten dollars spent on interdiction, and

---

[14] Based on analyses of General Social Survey data.

twenty-three dollars spent on attacking drugs at their source.[15] In another study, treatment was found to reduce ten times as much crime as enforcement and fifteen times as much crime as mandatory-minimum sentences.[16] So when the Bush administration realized their continued belief in tough-but-dumb policies didn't jibe with public opinion, they employed some Enron-style accounting to their drug budget (like counting federally funded alcohol-treatment programs, which the Office of National Drug Control Policy has absolutely nothing to do with, and not counting the cost of incarcerating nonviolent drug offenders in federal prisons) in order to create the illusion that they were spending almost as much on treatment as they were on interdiction and incarceration. Without making any meaningful changes in spending priorities, they claimed that the percentage of the drug budget spent on treatment went from 33 percent to 47 percent.[17]

But while the Bush administration's rhetoric may play to Americans' reasonable assessment of what works and what doesn't, his punishment-first philosophy can be found in the realities of policy. When Bush proposed a punitive revision to welfare regulations—requiring recipients to work forty hours a week (and proposing that they could be paid less than minimum wage) and refusing to count education toward their work requirement, Democrats responded with their own bill that would allow recipients to go to college. Bush apparently believed that a college education was less likely to help someone get ahead in life than working at McDonald's. "Now that's not my view of helping people become independent," he said about counting education toward satisfying the work requirement. "And it's certainly not my view of understanding the importance of work and helping people achieve the dignity necessary so they can live a free life, free from government control."[18] Later, Bush proposed making it harder for kids to obtain free school lunches, when it was

[15] Michael Massing, "Drugs: Missing the Story," *Columbia Journalism Review*, November/December 1998, p. 43.
[16] Jonathan Alter, "The Buzz on Drugs," *Newsweek*, September 6, 1999, p. 24.
[17] "'Fuzzy Math' in New ONDCP Report," Drug Policy Alliance, February 12, 2003.
[18] Elisabeth Bumiller, "Bush Sharply Criticizes Senate Version of Welfare Bill," *New York Times*, July 30, 2002.

revealed that some ineligible children were probably receiving them.[19] This proposal shines a light on Bush's ideological perspective. The idea that someone might be getting a free lunch seems to trouble him more than the idea that a child might go hungry.

When Bush is described as a "different kind of Republican," Exhibit A is usually his interest in the issue of education. In the 2000 campaign, Bush successfully mitigated the traditional Democratic advantage on the issue by airing a series of ads showing him with smiling schoolchildren. Offering substance-free bromides like, "Reading is the new civil right, because if you can't read you can't access the American dream,"[20] Bush convinced people that, as one radio-show caller said, "Bush is for education,"[21] though they didn't have much of an idea about what that might constitute. The repetition makes it seem true. While Bush may be unlike previous Republicans who wanted to abolish the Department of Education, Bush's approach to the issue, like his approach to many issues, is based on punishment. Providing resources has ranked lower on the list—to take one example, while his 2004 budget spent almost as much on the military as every other country on Earth combined, Bush proposed to cut $172 million from schools that serve the children of military personnel.[22]

Bush's creative thinking about education begins and ends with high-stakes testing. As he said during the 2000 campaign, "Laura and I really don't realize how bright our children is sometimes until we get an objective analysis."[23] The idea here is that the only thing that will motivate children and teachers to perform well is fear. If children in a school are having problems, it's not because the school doesn't have enough resources, or the children aren't getting enough parental

---

[19] Jennifer Toomer-Cook, "Free-Lunch Plan May Backfire," *Deseret News*, April 9, 2003, p. B1.
[20] Bush campaign ad, cited in Kathleen Hall Jamieson and Paul Waldman (eds.), *Electing the President 2000: The Insiders' View*. Philadelphia: University of Pennsylvania Press, 2001, p. 151.
[21] Deborah Tannen, "Let Them Eat Words," *American Prospect*, September 2003, p. 29.
[22] Brian Faler, "Educators Angry over Proposed Cut in Aid," *Washington Post*, March 19, 2003, p. A29.
[23] *Tim Russert*, CNBC, April 15, 2000.

support, or any of a host of other reasons—it's because they're just not trying. If you threaten the kids with being left back and threaten the school with getting funds taken away, they'll shape up.

This kind of thinking is on full display in Bush's Texas, where they do a test long called the Texas Assessment of Academic Skills, or TAAS.[24] Every year, the schools literally discard all their regular educational agenda for months—teaching, learning, etc.—to engage in an orgy of test-prep drills known colloquially as "Taasmania." Many schools have simply stopped teaching the subjects that aren't on the TAAS. One of the economic benefits of TAAS and other high-stakes tests is that they have spawned an industry of test-prep materials. Since schools lose funding if they don't improve scores every year, many spend thousands of dollars on these materials, instead of, say, books.[25]

When he ran for president, Bush called increasing test scores in his state "the Texas miracle." "In Texas," his ads said, "George Bush raised standards, and test scores soared. Now Texas leads the nation in academic improvement." It was only later that a somewhat-less-miraculous picture emerged. What are the facts? Not too surprisingly, high-stakes testing gave a powerful incentive for schools to cook the books. Some schools exempted most of their special education students from the TAAS, then saw their average scores shoot up.[26] A lawsuit charged that schools intentionally held back ninth graders who were ready to move to the next grade, but whom the schools feared would not perform well on the tenth-grade test.[27] Principals were under intense pressure to meet dropout goals, which many apparently did by simply calling dropouts something else; in inner-city Houston, schools were reporting zero dropouts.[28]

---

[24] The test was recently renamed, but the idea is the same.
[25] Peter Schrag, "Too Good to Be True," *American Prospect*, January 3, 2000, p. 46.
[26] Michele Kurtz, "Texas Sees Increase in Test Scores and Student Exemptions," Cox News Service, November 3, 2000.
[27] Jim Yardley, "Critics Say a Focus on Test Scores Is Overshadowing Education in Texas," *New York Times*, October 30, 2000, p. A14.
[28] Michael Winerip, "The 'Zero Dropout' Miracle: Alas! Alack! A Texas Tall Tale," *New York Times*, August 13, 2003, p. B7.

One of Bush's only legislative achievements in his first term was the No Child Left Behind Act, which requires every public school in America to institute high-stakes testing or lose federal funds. After it passed the Senate, Bush said, "These historic reforms will improve our public schools by creating an environment where every child can learn through real accountability, unprecedented flexibility for states and school districts, greater local control, more options for parents, and more funding for what works."[29] Once again, Bush lies in order to make his policy seem to accord with a popular ideal. Regardless of the merit of federally imposed testing requirements, they certainly represent the very opposite of "unprecedented flexibility" and "greater local control." Unsurprisingly, Bush's 2004 budget failed to fully fund the No Child Left Behind Act, and it proposed cutting child care assistance, literacy programs for children, dropout prevention programs, and after-school programs.[30]

Faced with criticism of his lack of funding for schools, Bush threw some false numbers at a crowd in Nashville, saying, "The budget for next year boosts funding for elementary and secondary education to $53.1 billion. That's a 26-percent increase since I took office. In other words, we understand that resources need to flow to help solve the problems." But his proposed elementary- and secondary-education budget was actually $34.9 billion, not $53.1 billion—the $53.1 billion was the administration's entire education budget. And the $34.9 billion was a cut, not a "boost," from its level the previous year.[31]

When commentators are looking for evidence of Bush's compassion, the No Child Left Behind Act is usually mentioned, despite the fact that there's nothing compassionate about it. What often follows are facile comparisons to Bill Clinton, equating his

---

[29] Diana Jean Schemo, "Senate Approves Bill to Expand Federal Role in Public Education," *New York Times*, December 19, 2001.
[30] Information on the effects of Bush's budgets on children can be found at the website of the Children's Defense Fund, www.childrensdefense.org.
[31] David Corn, "Capital Games: The Latest Bush Gang Whoppers," thenation.com, September 15, 2003.

policy-based centrism with Bush's photo-op illusion of centrism. And in his rhetoric, Bush testifies to a bleeding heart, while obscuring the realities of his policies. Standing on the stage of the First Union Center in Philadelphia to accept his party's nomination for the presidency, he told this moving tale:

> Couple of years ago, I visited a juvenile jail in Marlin, Texas, and talked with a group of young inmates. They were angry, wary kids. All had committed grown-up crimes.
>
> Yet when I looked in their eyes, I realized some of them were still little boys.
>
> Toward the end of conversation, one young man, about fifteen years old, raised his hand and asked a haunting question: "What do you think of me?"
>
> He seemed to be asking, like many Americans who struggle, "Is there hope for me? Do I have a chance?" And, frankly, "Do you, a white man in a suit, really care what happens to me?"
>
> A small voice, but it speaks for so many: single moms struggling to feed the kids and pay the rent; immigrants starting a hard life in a new world; children without fathers in neighborhoods where gangs seem like friendship, where drugs promise peace, and where sex sadly seems like the closest thing to belonging. We are their country, too.
>
> And each of us must share in its promise, or the promise is diminished for all.
>
> If that boy in Marlin believes he's trapped and worthless and hopeless, if he believes his life has no value, then other lives have no value to him, and we are all diminished.

Bush's use of this story to demonstrate his "compassion" is so appalling that it borders on the obscene. Based on the realities of Bush's policies, this passage, which is meant to be moving, is fundamentally misleading. Bush won the Texas governorship in no small part by stoking public fears of a fictitious epidemic of juvenile crime; the issue was one of the pillars of his campaign. If there was one clear message in Bush's policies on crime and punishment, it was that once a person commits a crime, his life has no value. In Bush's Texas, a fourteen-year-old who committed a crime could be tried as an adult, and sixteen-year-olds could be housed with adult convicts, where they would be trained for a lifetime of crime. Bush campaigned against drug treatment for prisoners and favored the execution of the mentally retarded. Asked about rehabilitation programs for drug offenders, he said "Incarceration is rehabilitation."[32] Bush's standard response when asked about the death penalty was that he had two standards for signing a death warrant: was the person guilty, and did they have full access to the courts. Yet he vetoed a bill that would have required that an indigent defendant be given a lawyer within twenty days of being tossed in jail. That's what Bush likes to call "full access to the courts."

Yet the policy decisions that actually affect people's lives are noticed only by a few, while the insincere rhetorical prose of compassion is broadcast throughout the land. Over time, the Bush image is what people come to understand as the "real" Bush. But the reality is not the words. It is in Bush's policies and their implementation. Who among us is keeping track of those?

THE WAR ON GOVERNMENT

In navigating the tension that exists in all political systems between freedom and equality (complete freedom usually leads to unequal outcomes, while insuring equality usually involves restricting the freedom of at least some), conservatives tend to favor greater freedom while liberals tend to favor greater equality. Both make arguments about the greater good, but in attempting to persuade, the liberals usually aim at people's altruistic feelings while the conservatives aim at their self-interested feelings. The key for conservatives is to convince people that if we set up a system with winners and losers, you will be one of the winners. Sure, if we privatize Social Security some people will

---

[32] Robert Bryce, "Louder Than Words," Salon.com, August 24, 1999.

wind up eating cat food in their declining years, but *you* won't be one of them—you'll probably stumble onto the next Microsoft and get rich! There is certainly fertile ground in the American psyche to sow these seeds. After all, millions of people are hopeful enough to buy lottery tickets week after week in the face of not only the laws of probability but repeated evidence that they are not going to hit the jackpot.

Bush has seen openings for the advancement of core conservative goals in what appear on the surface to be movements toward the center, which he often describes as expanding liberty while pretending that his plans involve no costs and will not exacerbate inequality. In order to satisfy public demands to add a prescription-drug benefit to Medicare, he came up with a plan that looks compassionate—helping seniors to get drugs—but did so by forcing them to choose between staying in Medicare and getting drug coverage. The plan was designed in part to wear away at their reliance and loyalty to Medicare and thus the very idea that government is responsible for providing health care. His Social Security plan has a similar intent—by "letting you invest," it moves to break the bond between citizens and government, cementing the notion that if you find yourself at eighty with no money it's because you made bad decisions. Democratic focus groups during the 2000 campaign found that men loved the idea because, as one consultant put it, they all thought they were going to be Donald Trump. Women, on the other hand, tended to express a lot more concern about their husbands investing in the market.[33]

The "that might apply to you one day" fantasy that the men in these focus groups believed is what makes things like Social Security privatization seem reasonable. Like many Republican policies, it's all about the winners. When Republicans argued against health-care reform by repeating over and over that "we've got the best health-care system in the world," what they meant was that if you've got gold-plated coverage, we've got the best health-care system in the world. And if you've got a great financial advisor, you might do better in the stock market than you will with Social Security. But Social Security

[33] Kathleen Hall Jamieson and Paul Waldman (eds.), *Electing the President 2000: The Insiders' View*. Philadelphia: University of Pennsylvania Press, p. 173.

is about security, not getting rich. It was created to alleviate poverty among seniors. The idea was that no American after a lifetime of work should be forced to live in squalor. It's an insurance policy, not a wealth-accumulation program.

But Bush and his party understand that Social Security is the keystone around which public support for federal programs is built and sustained. While the government does many things whose benefits are universally enjoyed—national defense, clean air, and public parks, to name a few—Social Security is the only one that, eventually, sends a monthly check to every citizen of the country. That check your grandmother gets is a constant reminder that the government has and meets an obligation to care for its citizens. The fact that the system is pay-as-you-go—meaning that current workers put in money not for themselves but for current retirees, with the understanding that when we retire our children and grandchildren's generations will pay for us—maintains the idea of mutual obligation. Instead of paying taxes only for our own gain, we collectively contribute to a system from which we all benefit. Consequently, the most far-reaching threat of privatization is not the enormous debt it will create or the individuals who will lose out when their stock picks or timing aren't quite right, but the renunciation of the notion of mutual obligation that it represents.

Ronald Reagan and Newt Gingrich tried mightily to dismantle the legacy of the New Deal and the Great Society. With a little help from Bill Clinton, they succeeded in part. But they barely tried to touch Social Security and Medicare, both of which Bush hopes to privatize. He admitted as much during a visit to a factory in May of 2000, where in response to a question he said, "It's going to take a while to transition to a system where personal savings accounts are the predominant part of the investment vehicle. This [his plan to divert part of Social Security funds to private accounts] is a step toward a completely different world, and an important step."[34]

---

[34] James Dao and Alison Mitchell, "Gore Denounces Bush Social Security Plan as Too Risky," *New York Times*, May 17, 2000, p. A20.

IDEOLOGICAL CROSS-DRESSING

While there are any number of issues on which George W. Bush attempts to mask his true agenda, examining one of them in detail can illuminate the various techniques by which Bush's actual ideology is finessed. Bush's 2000 convention speech included this passage: "My generation tested limits—and our country, in some ways, is better for it. Women are now treated more equally. Racial progress has been steady, if still too slow. We are learning to protect the natural world around us. We will continue this progress, and we will not turn back."

Bush cited the accomplishments of liberal endeavors—the women's rights, civil rights, and environmental movements—to show how compassionate he is, and he took credit for them, along with the rest of his generation. He was right—in America today women are treated more equally, racial progress has been made, and the natural world is more protected than it had been. But these improvements in American life didn't happen because of people like Bush—just the opposite, in fact. They happened because liberals overcame the determined, bitter opposition of conservatives. Had Bush been thirty years older, would he have been a supporter of civil rights in their most critical hour? Would he have supported measures to eliminate job discrimination against women? We can't say for sure, but the idea that he would have broken with his ideological soulmates strains credulity. We do know that protecting the natural world, like so many other liberal goals that Bush finds personally repugnant but that are widely embraced by the public, is something to which he has pledged support but worked hard to undermine.

In early 2003, Republican pollster Frank Luntz distributed a memo advising Republicans on how to deal with their environmental problem. "The first (and most important) step to neutralizing the problem and eventually bringing people around to your point of view on environmental issues," the memo said, "is to convince them of your 'sincerity' and 'concern.'"[35] The key is in the quotation

---

[35] Terry McCarthy, "How Bush Gets His Way on the Environment," *Time*, January 20, 2003.

marks: actually being sincere and concerned is beside the point; instead, it is only necessary to convince people that you "are."

This is a fairly good encapsulation of the environmental efforts of the Bush administration. There may be no administration in American history that has moved as aggressively to roll back environmental regulations. But when any such moves come to light, the Bush administration comes up with a friendly-sounding name to attach to the effort, making it seem as though they are gentle stewards of the land. This is a lesson he learned from his Republican forebearers. Think the MX Missile sounds sinister? Rename it the Peacekeeper Missile, as Ronald Reagan did. Don't want your war on the poor to come off sounding mean? Call your punitive welfare bill the Personal Responsibility and Work Opportunity Act, as Newt Gingrich did. Want to hand national forests over to timber companies? Call it the Healthy Forests initiative, as Bush does. Want to free polluters from regulations on air quality? Call it the Clear Skies initiative. Most will hear the name but never learn of the reality. It was only fitting that Bush went to the Detroit Edison plant in Michigan to demonstrate the wonder of "Clear Skies." Under the plan, the power plant, one the nation's dirtiest, would be freed from any requirement to reduce the toxic stew of emissions it spews into the air for the next seventeen years.[36]

In February 2002, Eric Schaeffer, a top Environmental Protection Agency official originally appointed by Bush's father, quit the agency in disgust, saying he had grown tired of "fighting a White House that seems determined to weaken the rules we are trying to enforce."[37] In both of his first two budgets, Bush proposed cutting the EPA. An analysis of EPA enforcement showed that the average fine levied against polluters dropped by 64 percent once Bush's people took over.[38]

---

[36] Dana Milbank, "Bush Lauds Michigan Power Plant as Model of Clean Air Policy; But Opponents Say It's a Polluter Excused by 'Clear Skies' Plan," *Washington Post*, September 16, 2003, p. A3.
[37] Katherine Seelye, "Top EPA Official Quits, Criticizing Bush's Policies," *New York Times*, March 1, 2002.
[38] Seth Borenstein, "EPA Is Forcing Fewer Fines," *Tallahassee Democrat*, November 5, 2002.

Bush's modus operandi on the environment should have come as no surprise. When he was governor and Texas regulators considered imposing restrictions on polluters, Bush leapt into action. He told the polluters to go ahead and draft up some voluntary measures freeing them from the threat of actual enforcement or consequences for violations, which he would then push through the legislature (of course, Bush felt no input from environmentalists was needed). The companies that drafted the law expressed their thanks with almost $1 million in contributions to his presidential campaign. Yet Bush tried to argue that he had been an environmental achiever: "You've got to ask the question," he said, "'Is the air cleaner since I became governor?' And the answer is yes." But what are the facts? Of course, the actual answer was "no"—during his tenure Houston passed Los Angeles to become America's smog capital, and Dallas-Ft. Worth was downgraded by the EPA from "moderate" to "serious" levels of ozone. Bush also convinced the legislature to overturn the law that mandated emissions tests for cars and appointed only industry representatives to the state's environmental regulatory commission. [39]

During his second debate with Al Gore, Bush touted his environmental record. "We need to make sure that if we decontrol our plants that there's mandatory—that the plants must conform to clean-air standards, the grandfathered plants. That's what we did in Texas. No excuses. I mean, you must conform." This was completely false, giving the impression that Bush was a tough environmental regulator when the opposite was true. The 1997 change in Texas law Bush cited did not require the grandfathered plants to conform to clean-air standards, it merely *requested* that they do so voluntarily. If they went on polluting, there were no legal consequences. [40]

In the same vein, in February 2002 Bush announced a new plan to "cut" greenhouse gas emissions. Just as he had in Texas, Bush proposed a voluntary plan, asking polluters if, please, they might consider not poisoning Americans' air and water. And to measure

---

[39] Jim Yardley, "Bush Approach to Pollution: Preference for Self-Policing," *New York Times*, November 9, 1999, p. A1.

[40] Jim Yardley, "Bush Approach to Pollution: Preference for Self-Policing," *New York Times*, November 9, 1999, p. A1.

progress on decreasing greenhouse gas emissions, what did Bush propose? Certainly not actually measuring greenhouse gas emissions—that might show that his voluntary plan wasn't working. Instead, the administration invented a new measure for the sole purpose of allowing them to claim that an increase in emissions was actually a decrease.

This magical number, "emissions intensity," would measure the change in emissions divided by the change in national economic output. In other words, if the economy grew at 4 percent a year, and greenhouse gas emissions increased by 3 percent a year, Bush would be able to claim that he had *reduced* emissions, since 3 percent is less than 4 percent. On the same day he unveiled his new emissions measure, the administration also revealed that it would roll back pollution rules for power plants, allowing more emissions of mercury, sulfur, and nitrogen oxide.[41]

The creation of "emissions intensity" is emblematic of the Bush administration's approach. As far as they are concerned, the truth is not absolute; rather, it is like clay, ready to be molded and shaped to suit the agenda. In this, Bush has created a kind of postmodern presidency in which antiquated notions like "facts" and "truth" lose all meaning and an increase in pollution can be hailed as a successful decrease in pollution.

At one point, Bush's EPA, having been safely purged of anyone who might contemplate protecting the environment, proceeded to argue that *toxic sludge is actually good for fish*. The issue was the fact that the Army Corps of Engineers dumps two hundred thousand tons of sludge into the Potomac River each year, in violation of the Clean Water Act. Upon having the toxic sludge dumped on them, the agency argued, fish would flee upstream, serendipitously avoiding the fishermen trying to catch them.[42] This sounds like a joke, but it's actually true: the agency charged with protecting the environment, arguing in favor of dumping toxic sludge.

---

[41] "A Global Warming Nonplan," *Buffalo News*, February 18, 2002, p. B6.
[42] Audrey Hudson, "EPA Says Toxic Sludge Is Good for Fish," *Washington Times*, June 19, 2002.

Over the objection of many of its conservative supporters, the Bush administration acknowledged in an EPA report submitted to the United Nations in June 2002 that global warming does in fact exist, and humans are partly to blame. When Bush himself was asked about the EPA report, he said dismissively, "I read the report put out by the bureaucracy."[43] This assertion was a little hard to believe—given that Bush once, when asked to name something he wasn't good at, responded "Sitting down and reading a five-hundred-page book on public policy or philosophy or something"[44]—but in any case put the blame on a sinister, faceless force, not his own appointees. He then sent Ari Fleischer out to reiterate that there is "considerable uncertainty" as to the causes of global warming. Later, Fleischer admitted that Bush had not actually read the 268-page report, saying, "Whenever presidents say they read it, you can read that to be he was briefed."[45] In other words, Bush lied about having read the report—not a particularly consequential lie, but a lie nonetheless.

In September 2002, the Environmental Protection Agency, under pressure from the White House, decided to delete the section on global warming from its annual report on pollution. "Some people at pretty high levels in my organization were saying, 'Take it out,'" said an EPA official.[46] Nine months later, when EPA staffers mentioned global warming in another report on the state of the environment, the White House ordered the section deleted.[47]

On the issue of global warming, the corporate conservatives have managed to propagate a world-class deception on the American people. Through an aggressive PR campaign, oil companies and their allies managed to convince many people that the existence of global

---

[43] "Bush Withholds Backing of EPA Report on Warming," *Washington Post*, June 5, 2002, p. A2.

[44] Tucker Carlson, "Devil May Care," *Talk*, September 1999.

[45] "Bush Withholds Backing of EPA Report on Warming," *Washington Post*, June 5, 2002, p. A2.

[46] Andrew Revkin, "With White House Approval, EPA Pollution Report Omits Global Warming Section," *New York Times*, September 15, 2002.

[47] Andrew Revkin and Katherine Seelye, "Report by EPA Leaves Out Data on Climate Change," *New York Times*, June 19, 2003, p. A1.

warming was a matter of scientific controversy, when in fact there are virtually no reputable scientists not on the oil companies' payroll who believe that it does not exist. Unsurprisingly, George W. adopts the oil companies' position—we just don't know whether global warming exists, so we'd better not do anything about it—as his own.

But it isn't only on global warming that the Bush administration works to cover up inconvenient facts. When the EPA's Office of Children's Health Protection concluded that large numbers of women had elevated levels of mercury in their blood, which can cause birth defects, and that smokestack emissions were partially to blame, the White House suppressed the data for months until the information was leaked to the *Wall Street Journal*.[48] When the EPA was about to issue a warning to millions of homeowners that the Zonolite insulation in their homes contained deadly asbestos, the White House squashed the warning. "It was like a gut shot," said one EPA staffer. "It wasn't that they ordered us not to make the declaration, they just really, really strongly suggested against it. Really strongly. There was no choice left."[49]

As *Mother Jones* reported in mid-2003, Bush's appointments seem to be guided by the principle that only foxes should be allowed to guard the nation's environmental henhouse. Consider the following list:

- Steven Griles, a lobbyist for oil and mining companies, was appointed Deputy Secretary of the Interior where he oversees public lands.
- Mark Rey, a timber lobbyist, was appointed Undersecretary for Natural Resources and the Environment in the Department of Agriculture where he oversees public forests.
- James Connaughton, a power-company lobbyist, was appointed Chairman of the Council on Environmental Quality.

---

[48] Tim Dickinson, "Where the Sun Don't Shine," *Mother Jones*, September/October 2003, p. 19.
[49] Andrew Schneider, "White House Office Blocked EPA's Asbestos Cleanup Plan," *St. Louis Post-Dispatch*, December 29, 2002, p. A1.

- Jeffrey Holmstead, a chemical-company lobbyist, was appointed Assistant Administrator for Air and Radiation at the EPA.
- Bennett Raley, a "property rights" lobbyist, was appointed Assistant Secretary for Water and Science at the Department of the Interior.
- William Myers, a ranching- and mining-company lobbyist, was appointed as the Interior Department's chief lawyer.
- Thomas Sansonetti, a coal-company lawyer, was appointed Assistant Attorney General for Environment and Natural Resources, where together with Myers he is in charge of enforcing environmental laws.
- David Bernhardt, a lobbyist for oil, mining, and chemical companies, was appointed Director of Congressional and Legislative Affairs for the Department of the Interior.[50]

These are just a few of the hundreds of actions that the Bush administration has taken that have demonstrably harmed the environment, from opening up public lands all over the country for oil drilling, to weakening federal oversight of efforts to clean up waterways, to resisting efforts to increase automobile-fuel efficiency, to moving to increase logging in national forests, to dragging its heels on Superfund cleanup of toxic sites, to shifting responsibility for paying for those cleanups from polluters to taxpayers, to moving to weaken the Clean Water Act and Clean Air Act, to supporting devastating "mountaintop removal" coal mining, to breaking his promise to reduce carbon-dioxide emissions, to limiting protections for endangered species, to increasing allowable levels of arsenic in drinking water, to moving to exempt power plants from pollution regulations, to opening up old-growth forests in Alaska to logging, to pressuring the EPA to falsely claim that the air at Ground Zero was safe to breathe immediately after September 11, to freeing utilities from the requirement to install pollution-control devices when they

---

[50] "Behind the Curtain," *Mother Jones*, September/October 2003, p. 51.

upgrade their plants then dropping investigations into dozens of power plants for violating the Clean Air Act, to proposing to end testing for salmonella in beef served to public school students, and on and on in an endless assault on our environment and public health.[51] Fortunately for him and unfortunately for the rest of us these moves have gone largely unnoticed by the American people.

One can recite a similar list on any number of issues. On the rights of working people, for instance, Bush:

- blocked a rule requiring that federal contracts be given only to companies without extensive criminal records on workplace violations;
- required government contractors to post notices discouraging workers from joining unions;
- sought "paycheck protection" rules to undermine the political power of unions;
- killed OSHA workplace ergonomic rules more than ten years in the making;
- revoked grants to study workplace safety and health;
- rescinded a rule requiring labor-relations consultants and attorneys to report their union-busting activities to the Department of Labor;
- cut funding for job training (he appointed Eugene Scalia, whose professional work centered on fighting workplace-safety rules on behalf of large corporations, to be the Labor Department's chief lawyer);
- cut enforcement positions in OSHA and the Mine Safety and Health Administration;
- proposed paying welfare recipients sub-minimum wage;
- proposed banning 170,000 federal employees in the Department of Homeland Security from collective bargaining and exempting them from whistleblower protections;
- blocked the release of funds to monitor the health of rescue

---

[51] A number of environmental groups, including the Natural Resources Defense Council, have taken on the arduous task of cataloging this litany; see www.nrdc.org/bushrecord.

workers at Ground Zero in New York;

- booted a fire chief from the federal Medal of Valor Commission because he was affiliated with the International Association of Fire Fighters (which had criticized Bush);
- proposed privatizing 850,000 federal jobs;
- eliminated Labor Department reporting of mass layoffs and plant closings;
- stacked government advisory committees on trade and workplace issues with corporate representatives while shutting labor representatives out;
- imposed onerous expense-reporting requirements on unions, forcing them to itemize for the government nearly everything they spend on organizing, lobbying, and political activities;
- proposed expanding the red tape required of low-income workers looking to receive the Earned Income Tax Credit; and
- proposed changing overtime laws in a way that would deprive as many as 8 million people of overtime pay.[52]

These are just a few ways Bush has waged war on working people. Here as on the environment and a host of other issues, Bush is well aware that a single photo opportunity can be worth more in the public mind than a hundred retrograde policy actions. It is not merely an accident that the image and the reality are not aligned; rather, the image is constructed for the very purpose of obscuring the reality.

BUSH AGAINST THE GOVERNMENT
Even what are claimed to be fundamental principles of political philosophy can be easily discarded. The Bush administration's actions on issues like medical-marijuana clubs and assisted suicide, in which they sought by fiat to overrule state-government policies enacted by voters, give the lie to conservatives' alleged devotion to federalism, the notion

---

[52] Information on the moves listed here, among many others, can be found at www.aflcio.org/issuespolitics/bushwatch/.

that state power is always preferable to federal power. When he was inaugurated as governor of Texas, Bush proclaimed, "I will use every resource at my disposal to make the federal government in Washington heed this simple truth: Texans can run Texas."[53] But when he became president he was quite pleased to have the federal government assert power over the states as long as it did so in service of a conservative goal. In contrast, liberals never argued that there was something inherently superior about the federal government. They took the side of the federal government over the states in the significant clashes of the past because those conflicts found the federal government attempting to accomplish liberal goals. So when the federal government moved to force desegregation in the South, liberals argued that desegregation was the right thing to do, while conservatives tried to hide their support of segregation behind the canard of "states' rights."

But prominent Republicans love to argue that the government, particularly the federal government, is incapable of providing services efficiently, causes nothing but destruction when it attempts to regulate, and restricts individual freedom with its every step. Few sound this note louder than George W. Bush, who campaigned for office by repeating endlessly that his opponent "trusts the government," while "I trust the people."

The antigovernment mantra has the rhetorical advantage of simple-mindedness. Liberals are going to continue to lose the argument on the role of government until they decide to *make* the argument instead of running away from it, engaging the other side and calling them on their ridiculous, simplistic rhetoric. When former House Majority Leader Dick Armey says, as he often does, "The market is rational; the government is dumb,"[54] someone should ask him who built the road on which he drove to work that morning.

When government does what it is supposed to, Republicans offer praise to the triumph of the human spirit and American values while ignoring the role played by the state. For example, when nine coal

---

[53] R.G. Ratcliffe and Clay Robison, "Inauguration Inspires Vows of Cooperation," *Houston Chronicle*, January 18, 1995, p. A1.

[54] Julie Mason, "Armey's Going, But Not Quietly," *Houston Chronicle*, December 7, 2002, p. A10.

miners were rescued after being trapped in a mine in Pennsylvania, Bush was quick to capitalize on their inspiring story, rushing to have his picture taken alongside the men. Had they been in possession of accurate mine maps and their employer taken appropriate safety precautions, the accident would never have occurred in the first place, but this didn't seem to bother Bush, who not too long before had moved to cut the budget for the Mine Safety and Health Administration.[55]

Bush neglected to mention that the successful rescue of the miners was yet another example of the critical role of government. When you're trapped in a mine shaft, you don't wait for the invisible hand of the market to come down and fish you out—you call the government. They don't ask whether you have insurance before they come get you; they just do it, because government is there to serve its citizens. Every one of the police officers and firefighters hailed as the heroes of September 11 was a government employee doing his or her job.

At the 1996 Republican convention, Newt Gingrich found himself on stage with an Olympic beach volleyball athlete. Gingrich was so moved that he offered this tribute: "A mere forty years ago, beach volleyball was just beginning. Now it is not only a sport in the Olympics...there's a whole new world of opportunity opening up that didn't even exist thirty years ago or forty years ago, and no bureaucrat would have invented it. And that's what freedom is all about."[56]

Newt's argument that "freedom is all about" bureaucrats not inventing beach volleyball, which got some well-deserved ridicule, shows the absurdities the reflexive antigovernment pose ends up devolving into. Something similar happened to George W. Bush on the stump just before the 2000 election, when he took his "they trust the government; I trust the people" argument to its illogical conclusion, saying, "They want the government controlling the

[55] Steven Greenhouse, "Rise in Mining Deaths Prompts Political Sparring," *New York Times*, July 26, 2002, p. A14.
[56] Associated Press, August 14, 1996.

Social Security, like it's some kind of federal program."[57] The point is not that Bush was actually under the impression that Social Security is something other than a federal program, but that when you instinctively throw antigovernment rhetoric at anything and everything, you wind up saying some pretty idiotic things. Even when Bush signed the most pork-laden farm bill in history, a $180 billion behemoth by which the government shields farmers from the cruel realities of the market by larding subsidies and setting prices, he incredibly said, "It will allow farmers and ranchers to plan and operate based on market realities, not government dictates."[58]

One of the things the farm bill showed is that while Republican officeholders pose as small-government fiscal conservatives, in fact they are just as friendly toward government as Democrats—as long as government benefits them and their agenda. When the Associated Press studied patterns of spending under Democratic and Republican control of Congress, they found what you might expect—when the Democrats ran the show, districts represented by Democrats got more government spending than Republicans, and when the Republicans took over, they sent more money to their own districts. But there was a difference in the difference: in the last budget before the Gingrich revolution, Democratic districts got an average of $35 million more than Republican ones, while in the 2001 budget, Republican districts averaged $612 million more than Democratic ones. But it wasn't just pork projects. Rather, "the change was driven mostly by Republican policies that moved spending from poor rural and urban areas to the more affluent suburbs and GOP-leaning farm country."[59] That was $612 million.

In addition to leading one down the road to absurdity, reflexive antigovernment rhetoric can also slip into outright falsehood. Dick Cheney got away with one of the most amazing whoppers of the

[57] Dan Balz and Mike Allen, "Gore, Bush Hit Illinois and Other Key States," *Washington Post*, November 3, 2000, p. A1.
[58] "Cringe for Mr. Bush," *Washington Post*, May 14, 2002, p. A20.
[59] David Pace, "Billions in Federal Spending Shifted to GOP Districts after 1994," Associated Press, August 5, 2002.

2000 campaign during his debate with Joe Lieberman. Lieberman said that people were better off than they had been eight years before and that from what he had read, Cheney was much better off than eight years before, too. (Cheney made $36 million in 2000 from his golden parachute from Halliburton.)[60] Cheney's witty response was, "And I can tell you, Joe, the government had absolutely nothing to do with it." Everyone laughed.

As lies go, this one was truly spectacular. Did the company make Cheney its CEO because of his business experience? No, when he got there he had no business experience—he had spent his life working in government. It was Cheney's government experience and government contacts they were after. And it paid off—after Cheney's arrival, the company almost doubled its business from the government, reaping $2.3 billion in government contracts. Halliburton also got fifteen times the government-backed loans in Cheney's five years at the helm as it did the five years before, for a total of $1.5 billion.[61] In short, the government had *everything* to do with the money Cheney made.

But most papers and television news programs used the quote to show how clever and sharp Cheney was, not to show that he was a hypocrite and a liar. The Associated Press called it a "quick-witted comeback,"[62] while the *Hartford Courant* noted that "the audience roared."[63] "Cheney's quick wit was at its best" in the exchange, said the *San Francisco Chronicle*,[64] while ABC News said it "showed both men have a sense of timing and of humor"[65] and NPR said, "Cheney got the last laugh."[66] Columnist Lars-Erik Nelson was one of the few to point out the facts.[67]

---

[60] Scott Lindlaw, "Bush Family Reports $894,880 in Income for 2000; Cheneys $36 Million," Associated Press, April 13, 2001.

[61] Knut Royce and Nathaniel Heller, "Cheney Led Halliburton to Feast at Federal Trough," Center for Public Integrity, August 2, 2000.

[62] "Both Sides Claim Victory over Veep Debate in Wyoming," Associated Press, October 6, 2000.

[63] David Lightman, "Lieberman, Cheney Feature Fact—Not Flak—In Low-Key Forum," *Hartford Courant*, October 6, 2000, p. A1.

[64] "Election Watch No. 6," *San Francisco Chronicle*, October 6, 2000, p. A18.

[65] ABC *World News Now*, October 6, 2000.

[66] *Morning Edition*, National Public Radio, October 6, 2000.

[67] Lars-Erik Nelson, "Cheney's Missed Opportunity," *New York Daily News*, October 6, 2000, p. 4.

In the debate Cheney also said, "I've been out in the private sector building a business, hiring people, creating jobs." After Cheney completed the merger of Halliburton with Dresser Industries—his signal accomplishment as CEO, which everyone involved now acknowledges had the effect of practically running the company into the ground—Cheney proceeded to lay off more than nine thousand workers.[68] (He also cut retirees' medical benefits to squeeze out more profit.)[69]

Now think about this for a moment. Imagine nine thousand families all in one place—let's say Madison Square Garden. At 2 parents and 2.5 kids, that's more than forty thousand people. Think about a crowd that size, and consider how every one of them had their lives turned upside down and in many cases ruined completely by Dick Cheney's visionary business leadership. Cheney's $36 million golden parachute adds up to $4,000 for every one of those families he sent to the unemployment line.

While at Halliburton, Cheney also approved the overseas reincorporation of no fewer than thirty-five Halliburton subsidiaries in an effort to avoid paying U.S. taxes.[70] "Reincorporation" is the euphemism for a kind of economic treason, the practice of setting up a dummy company, often nothing more than a mail drop, in a country like the Cayman Islands that doesn't make foreign corporations pay taxes. The corporation then attributes its profits to the dummy company so it doesn't have to pay American taxes. Before the 2002 election, Republicans reluctantly condemned the practice (except for the reliable Texas Senator Phil Gramm, who described attempts to prevent companies from evading taxes in this way as "right out of Nazi Germany").[71] But once the election was over and they had control of Congress, the Republicans showed their true colors, inserting into the Homeland Security bill a provision

[68] Edward Walsh and Amy Goldstein, "Cheney's Style: Cool, Methodical, and Conservative," *Washington Post*, July 26, 2000, p. A1.
[69] Diana Henriques, "Cheney Is Said to Be Receiving $20 Million Retirement Package," *New York Times*, August 12, 2000, p. A1.
[70] Peter Beinart, "Eight Days," *New Republic*, December 2, 2002.
[71] Paul Krugman, "Springtime for Hitler," *New York Times*, October 18, 2002, p. A31.

authorizing companies that had evaded U.S. taxes by reincorporating to receive Homeland Security contracts.[72]

At Halliburton, Cheney also happily did business with a number of terror-sponsoring regimes, including Libya, Iran, and Iraq. When during the campaign he was asked whether Halliburton had any contracts in Iraq, Cheney said, "I had a firm policy that we wouldn't do anything in Iraq, even arrangements that were supposedly legal. We've not done any business in Iraq since UN sanctions were imposed on Iraq in 1990, and I had a standing policy that I wouldn't do that." But as the *Washington Post* discovered in June of 2001, Halliburton actually had $73 million worth of contracts to provide Saddam Hussein's government with oil-production equipment and spare parts through a subsidiary when Cheney was CEO. Cheney then sent out an aide to claim he didn't know anything about it.[73]

The particular brand of capitalism embraced by Bush, Cheney, and their allies on the right asks Americans to pay for huge tax cuts for corporations and the "corporate welfare" Cheney was so adept at securing, but demands that no strictures be put on the corporations' own behavior. Most Americans, on the other hand, would probably ask that corporations live by the same standards as ordinary citizens. Corporations should have the freedom to succeed and grow, but the price of that freedom is the responsibility not to harm others—their employees, their shareholders, the communities and natural environments in which they operate. When they fail to live up to those responsibilities, they should be held accountable. This is the same standard all of us live by every day. If I drop a sewage line from my house into my neighbor's living room or sideswipe his car on my way to work, we all understand that I must take responsibility and accept the consequences. But the contemporary Republican party wants corporations to have freedom without responsibility or accountability. What most Americans understand, however, is that freedom is impossible without responsibility and accountability. And freedom is likewise impossible without government.

---

[72] Peter Beinart, "Eight Days," *New Republic*, December 2, 2002.
[73] Colum Lynch, "Firm's Iraq Deals Greater Than Cheney Has Said," *Washington Post*, June 23, 2001, p. A1.

While many conservatives try to paint government as the enemy of freedom, government is in actuality the guarantor of freedom. By reining in people's worst tendencies and preventing the unscrupulous from harming the innocent, government allows freedom to flourish. This is no less true in commerce than in any other sphere of human activity—indeed, maybe more so, since without government to enforce economic contracts both formal and informal, the market itself would cease to function.

The problem with the antigovernment pose is that it assumes that if one can locate any government inefficiency, one has proved that government itself is incapable of acting efficiently. No one would argue that there are no areas in which government is inefficient. But it would be no less reasonable to argue that because the market fails to provide an optimal delivery of certain goods (health care, for instance) that markets are useless and must be constrained anywhere and everywhere possible. As historian Gary Wills has written, "Even the best of governments will show on occasion most of the faults that governments are accused of—becoming wasteful, inefficient, impersonal, rigid, secretive, oppressive. But when marriages fail, we do not think it is because marriage is an evil in itself. Government is a necessary good, not a necessary evil; and what is evil in it cannot be identified and eliminated from the good if the very existence of the good is being denied at every level."[74]

There is no doubt that there are ways government could improve much of what it does. But Bush and his allies are not particularly interested in improving government. They have little desire to make the delivery of services more efficient or more accountable. In fact, they are only too happy when government operates inefficiently, because that serves their ultimate goal of stopping the delivery of services altogether or at least to the greatest extent possible. While Republicans fought tooth and nail against the establishment of Medicare, for instance, they eventually

---

[74] Gary Wills, *A Necessary Evil: A History of American Distrust of Government.* New York: Simon & Schuster, 1999, p. 297.

realized that killing the program was politically impossible. So their current tack is to try to privatize it, proposing to give senior citizens vouchers with which they can beg private insurers to give them coverage. (Bush's latest plan as of this writing is to force seniors to choose between staying in Medicare with grossly inadequate prescription-drug coverage or dropping out of Medicare and going to an HMO to get drug coverage.) The stated justification is that if it is forced to compete, Medicare will operate more efficiently. But the truth is that Medicare already operates far more efficiently than private insurers—for instance, while private insurers spend around 9.5 percent of their expenses on administrative costs (not to mention what must be carved out for profits), Medicare spends only 2 percent to 3 percent.[75] In addition, Medicare recipients are more satisfied with their insurance and have an easier time obtaining care than those covered by private insurance.[76] To most Americans who receive a steady diet of denunciations of government waste and abuse, the idea that a government program works far better than its private counterparts would no doubt be surprising.

But there are many things that government does well, and there are many more that *only* government can do. Legal segregation and the disenfranchisement of African-Americans in the South didn't end because people looked into their hearts; it ended because the federal government stopped it. The interstate highway system and the Internet weren't built by entrepreneurs; they were built by the government. Private industry didn't bring electricity to America's rural areas; the government did. Before Social Security, old age was synonymous with abject poverty; it isn't any longer, thanks to the government. A generation of young men who served their country in World War II got to go to college, thanks to the government. All of these things happened despite the opposition of conservatives issuing dire warnings about the heavy hand of government interfering in our lives.

---

[75] "Medicare Reform: A Century Foundation Guide to the Issues," New York: Century Foundation Press, 2001.
[76] Karen Davis et al, "Medicare Versus Private Insurance: Rhetoric and Reality," *Health Affairs*, October 2002.

Watch What I Say, Not What I Do

It has been said that conservatives are often kind in person and cruel in policy. George W. Bush has elevated this contradiction to a political strategy, attempting to substitute good will for good works as he assures us that all we need to be concerned with is the purity of his heart. Bush is fond of saying, "I wish I knew the law that I could sign that would say we would love each other,"[77] his way of saying that though he isn't going to lift a finger to do anything about the problem being discussed, he feels real bad about it. When asked in the second of his 2000 debates with Al Gore whether he would support the Employment Non-Discrimination Act, which would protect gays and lesbians from discrimination in housing and unemployment, he said, "I'm the kind of person—I don't hire or fire somebody based upon their sexual orientation. As a matter of fact, I'd like to take the issue a little farther. I don't really think it's any of my—you know, any of my concerns what—how you conduct your sex life....I'll tolerate people." The fact that I'm a nice guy, in other words, means you don't need protection from other powerful people who might not be so nice.

Bush proclaims himself an opponent of discrimination when it comes to the personal: if you come to him for a job, he won't care whether you're gay. And presumably, he supports the laws that prevent job discrimination based on race, religion, sex, and national origin. But for whatever reason—fear of angering his most conservative backers is the likely suspect—he doesn't have the courage to put what he claims are his personal beliefs into law. If the same person whom he would be willing to hire tried to get a job at the bank down the street and was told, "You're the most qualified applicant, but we don't hire queers," Bush's response would be, "Too bad." He offers no defense of this position because he can't do so without contradicting what he claims to be his personal beliefs. In answer to the question, "Do you oppose discrimination?" an ordinary person may reasonably reply, "I don't discriminate." But for a president, it is simply not enough.

---

[77] Speech at Zephyr Field, New Orleans, LA, April 25, 2001.

Once again, we must return to the question of what matters to us as citizens. If we support the principle that people shouldn't be discriminated against in housing or employment because of their sexual orientation, who Bush hires and why is utterly meaningless. He is the president; the question is what policies he supports or opposes and what laws he would enact or change. Those are the things that affect people's lives. The millions of gay Americans couldn't care less whether Bush has a few gay staff members; what they're worried about is getting fired or evicted from their homes because they're gay. When he was governor, Bush once pulled aside Glen Maxey, a Texas state representative who is gay, to tell him, "I value you as a person and I value you as a human being, and I want you to know, Glen, that what I say publicly about gay people doesn't pertain to you."[78] Maxey was justifiably flabbergasted. Bush was trying to tell him that his heart was in the right place and that deep down he isn't really a bigot despite the winks and nods he might give in public to those who are and his support of policies like bans on gays adopting children. This represents a particularly vulgar hypocrisy.

Bush has played this card many a time, sometimes with the active cooperation of people who ought to know better. At a press conference in July 2002, a reporter asked Bush about criticisms of his administration's civil-rights record. He responded, "Let's see. There I was sitting around the leader—the table with foreign leaders looking at Colin Powell and Condi Rice."[79] Having satisfactorily established that some of his best friends are black, Bush asked for the next question.

Whether Bush's comment made Rice and Powell cringe with embarrassment or seethe with anger, we'll never know. But for her part, Condoleezza Rice uttered one of the most ridiculous statements of the 2000 campaign when during her speech at the Republican convention she said that she was proud to be a member of a party that saw her not as a member of a group, but as an individual. The fact that for the first time in memory a candidate's foreign-policy

---

[78] John Judis, "Bush's Year of Living Immoderately," *New Republic*, September 25, 2000.
[79] White House press conference, July 8, 2002.

advisor got a prime-time speaking slot at a party convention couldn't have had anything to do with her being a black woman.

The point about Rice is not that Bush appointed her because of her race—she's certainly qualified to be National Security Adviser—but that the appointment is taken to be so significant and such clear proof of Bush's open-mindedness and how far his party has come. Many African-Americans are no doubt pleased to see two of their own in such high-profile positions in the Bush administration, but they are, after all, only two people.

Rice wasn't the only African-American prominently featured at Bush's convention in Philadelphia. In fact, most of the couple dozen African-Americans in attendance were seen in front of the television cameras at one point or another, the better to demonstrate the GOP's inclusiveness. Candidates for obscure offices were given speaking slots if they happened to be black or Hispanic. Conservative commentator David Brooks compared the convention to a Utah Jazz game—a virtually all-white audience in the stands, watching the minority performers on stage.[80]

In fact, whenever African-Americans meet Bush, they run the risk of being shoved in front of the television cameras to provide a tableau of inclusiveness. When the Supreme Court authorized vouchers for religious schools, Bush gave a speech in Cleveland praising the decision. One reporter at the scene noticed that while the audience was 95 percent white, for some reason things were a little different on stage, where the program featured an all-black gospel choir and a nearly all-black high school choir, and two-thirds of the people standing behind Bush in camera view were black.[81]

But African-Americans certainly weren't fooled by Bush's act during 2000—he garnered a pathetic 8 percent of the African-

[80] David Brooks, "Report from Philly: Why the GOP Is Playing Nice," *Newsweek*, August 3, 2000, p. 10. Author's note: I attended a couple of nights of the GOP convention, and I noticed that the delegates seemed to have a genuine desire, albeit a somewhat condescending one, to have as many African-Americans as possible in their party. Whenever I saw a black person, he or she would be surrounded by a group of smiling white people, a spinning circle of self-congratulation.
[81] Doug Oplinger, "Bush Takes Up Education, Compassionate Conservatism," *Akron Beacon-Journal*, July 2, 2002.

American vote, lower than any presidential candidate since segregation supporter Barry Goldwater in 1964. They understood that when it comes to a president, the personal is insufficiently political. What matters is not the content of his heart, not his good will, not his words, but his actions. African-Americans in Texas, who presumably knew Bush best, were unimpressed with their governor's performance: 91 percent of them voted for Al Gore. [82]

Bush knew that he wouldn't do too well among African-Americans, but plucking a few of them out of a crowd to be paraded before the cameras is a strategy not aimed at African-Americans at all. Instead, its target is moderate voters, who are intended to see Bush embracing people of all races and say, "Gee, he seems like a nice, moderate guy." This was a strategy Bush adviser Karl Rove had been using successfully for years; in a 1986 memo to his client Bill Clements, a former Texas governor running to recapture his governorship, Rove wrote, "emphasizing your appointments of women and minorities will not win you the support of feminists and the leaders of the minority community; but it will bolster your support among Republican primary voters and urban independents." [83] Like all of Bush's efforts at moderation, his courting of minorities is about creating images that will lead to false conclusions about his policies.

This kind of deception is distressingly easy to accomplish. One of the unfortunate facts of American political life is that when it comes to politics, most people know next to nothing. This is not because people are stupid. Some simply don't care, some dislike politics, some are cynical, some are disaffected, and some have other priorities for their attention. Let's face it: keeping up with politics takes both interest and time, things many people don't have. With their relentless focus on political tactics, a short attention span for substantive discussion of issues, and an unquenchable need for dramatic visuals, the news media—particularly television—provide little help.

---

[82] David Bositis, "The Black Vote in 2000," Joint Center for Political and Economic Studies.
[83] James Moore and Wayne Slater, *Bush's Brain: How Karl Rove Made George W. Bush Presidential.* Hoboken, NJ: Wiley, 2003, p. 146.

George W. Bush's particular brand of ideological fraud depends not on utter ignorance but on partial ignorance. He understands that people focus on the broadest contours of politics, not on the details. If a phrase—say, "compassionate conservatism"—is repeated often enough, millions will hear it and assimilate its message. Though it may contradict the reality of Bush's plans and policies, only the policy wonks will wade through the analysis of regulatory policy on page A19 of the newspaper and discover the truth. So Bush successfully achieves a kind of transubstantiation of words into reality. He can say again and again, "I'm a uniter, not a divider," or, "I'm compassionate," and people will eventually believe him, despite the lack of evidence in support of the assertion.

The old union song asks, which side are you on? Bush would no doubt protest that such a question divides us. But we might be assured that Bush was not so firmly in the pocket of the wealthy and powerful if once—just once—he had made a decision that advanced the interests of ordinary people at the expense of the wealthiest Americans and large corporations. No matter the policy question, every Bush proposal seems to be constructed first and foremost to protect the interests of the powerful—an energy bill that lards subsidies on oil companies and shields corporate polluters from lawsuits, a prescription drug plan that forbids Medicare from negotiating lower prices for drugs (and thus protects drug industry profits), tax cut after tax cut with feasts for the wealthy and little for the rest.

Bush would rather we didn't ask which side he's on, because the answer doesn't reflect well on him. He has thus far been able to convince people that, though he may work hard for the wealthy and powerful, he nonetheless cares about ordinary folks. But the two are simply not compatible except in a fantasy world in which benefits given to the wealthy really do trickle down to everyone. Since government has finite resources, choices have to be made. Bush would like us to believe that he is not in fact making choices, that his plans and policies benefit everyone equally. But one can predict Bush's support for a program fairly well by measuring the median income of its beneficiaries. Welfare? Poor beneficiaries = strong opposition. The mortgage-interest deduction? Middle-class beneficiaries = steady if unenthusiastic support. Top-rate tax cuts? Wealthy beneficiaries = passionate, unswerving advocacy.

When Trent Lott shot himself in the foot in late 2002 by praising Strom Thurmond's 1948 segregationist run for president, one of the notable things about the ensuing controversy was how often reporters repeated that Lott's remarks were at odds with President Bush's supposed efforts to "reach out to minorities." According to the *San Francisco Chronicle*, "President Bush, who has pushed the party to reach out to minorities, and other GOP leaders feared that the image problem would soon become a permanent stain on the party of Lincoln."[84] The *New York Times* said, "Mr. Lott was undercutting the president's efforts to reach out to minorities in preparation for the 2004 presidential campaign,"[85] so he was replaced with Bill Frist, someone "seen as more in sync with Bush's efforts to reach out to minorities," as the *Los Angeles Times* put it.[86] "Lott's abdication triggered enormous relief from the White House and party leaders," said the *New York Daily News*, "who feared Bush's efforts to reach out to minority groups in the 2004 election could have been crippled with Lott remaining as a party symbol."[87]

Although this idea is repeated many times in the press, Bush mostly "reaches out" to minorities by putting them in front of cameras. This is in the same sense that he "reaches out" to the environment by taking a well-photographed walk around his ranch, while supporting oil drilling in wilderness areas and unrestrained pollution from power plants. He "reaches out" to women by giving a few of them a big hug, then reinstating the gag rule on doctors and

---

[84] Zachary Coile, "Bush Ally Poised to Replace Lott," *San Francisco Chronicle*, December 21, 2002, p. A1.
[85] Elisabeth Bumiller and Carl Hulse, "Lott Vows Fight to Retain His Post as Senate Leader," *New York Times*, December 18, 2002, p. A1.
[86] Janet Hook, "Exit That Could Turn into a Messy Power Play," *Los Angeles Times*, December 18, 2002, p. A24.
[87] Thomas DeFrank, "An Empty Lott in the Senate," *New York Daily News*, December 21, 2002, p. 7.

appointing judges hostile to abortion rights. He "reaches out" to working people by visiting a shop floor, then waging a war on union protections, opposing increases in the minimum wage, and doing nothing to help those without health insurance. But make no mistake, when Bush reaches out to his friends in corporate board rooms and the chamber of commerce, at the country club and the yacht club, it is much more than a photo-op; it's backed up with action, and the beneficiaries have no reason to doubt for a moment that Bush truly has their interests at heart.

The rest of America is given not actions in its interests, but a vision of an imaginary "compassion." We are given "Clear Skies" that are anything but, "Healthy Forests" turned over to timber companies, schools turned to test-taking factories, needed services slashed despite pledges of support, a virtual war on working people, all served up with an endless procession of photo-ops used to fill the "Compassion Photo Album." The rhetoric and the pictures are constructed for the very purpose of obscuring the truth. As George W. Bush said, "Politics is all about perception."

When Bush took office, Fox News anchor Brit Hume told him that Democrats were suggesting that, given the controversial way he took power, he might consider appointing moderates to positions of power and governing in a way that reflected the divided nature of the country. Given Fox's audience, Bush felt he could offer a candid response: "Too bad."[88]

---

[88] *Special Report with Brit Hume*, Fox News, January 18, 2001.

7.

New-Doo Economics

George W. Bush and Taxes

"The apportionment of taxes on the various descriptions of
property is an act which seems to require the most exact impartiality;
yet there is, perhaps, no legislative act in which greater opportunity
and temptation are given to a predominant party to trample on
the rules of justice. Every shilling with which they overburden the
inferior number is a shilling saved to their own pockets."
—*James Madison, Federalist #10*

"I also understand how tender the free enterprise system can be."
—*George W. Bush, July 8, 2002*

George W. Bush tells a variety of lies, some large and some small.
But there is no single issue on which Bush has left a lengthier
trail of deceit than that of taxation. From the moment he emerged
as a presidential candidate to the present day, Bush has consistently
misled the American public about the content of his tax plans and
the very nature of taxes themselves. To understand George W.
Bush—both his passion and his dishonesty—you have to understand the topic of taxes.

This record of deception was made possible by the news media's congenital inability to call a lie a lie, particularly when numbers are involved. Should a president fail to be forthcoming about who shares his bed, reporters will vigorously ferret out the truth and expose any hint of deception. But they have let politicians know that if they lie about the details of their policies, particularly when they involve percentages and projections, revenues and expenditures, well, that's just politics.

Early on, George W. Bush realized that reporters weren't going to call him on his tax deceptions. Some didn't have the time or inclination to delve into the details of his plans and discover whether he was being honest about them. Some simply didn't know enough about the topic to make independent judgments about what was true and what wasn't. But all were hemmed in by the conventions of contemporary American journalism, which frames politics as a game between two opposing sides. The claims of neither of these sides can be evaluated by any objective standard of truth; only their success and failure can be judged. When the two sides argue over facts, as far as reporters are concerned the story is the fact that the two sides are in conflict, not the substance of that conflict. Settling the dispute by saying, "Bush says X, Democrats say Y, and the Democrats are right," has the effect of putting an end to the conflict and thus the story.[1] Journalists prefer to stick to evaluating strategy and tactics, the terrain on which they feel far more comfortable. The vast majority of reporters are experts in politics, not policy. Since politics is what they know, politics is the prism through which they offer judgments.

THE TAX-CUT LIES

Appreciating this context allows us to understand how George W. Bush could offer the American people an extraordinarily lengthy list of dishonest arguments about taxes, each more deceitful than the last, without any evidence of concern that there would be a cost for his deception. It started during the 2000 campaign, when Bush

---

[1] Richard Ericson, "How Journalists Visualize Fact," *Annals of the American Academy of Political and Social Science* 560 (1998), pp. 83–95.

proposed a massive $1.6 trillion tax cut. It may seem like the distant past now, but at the time—thanks in large part to the policies of the Clinton administration and a long period of uninterrupted growth—the government was actually forecasting budget surpluses for years to come. In the flush of good times, with the Congressional Budget Office projecting a surplus of $5.6 trillion over the following ten years when Bush took office, his plan for a huge tax cut didn't seem quite as catastrophic as it turned out to be.[2]

When Ronald Reagan campaigned for the presidency in 1980, he claimed that he could cut taxes, dramatically increase defense spending, and balance the budget. His primary opponent, George Herbert Walker Bush, called it "voodoo economics," but the appeal of the we-can-have-it-all argument was undeniable. Of course, it was a fantasy: Reagan ended up increasing the national debt more than his thirty-nine predecessors combined.[3] Twenty years later, George W. Bush said he could have a huge tax cut, avoid cutting Social Security and Medicare, offer expensive new benefits like prescription drugs for senior citizens, and maintain the budget surplus. Bush's plan was just as impossible as Reagan's.

At first, Bush's people continued to insist that everything with the budget was just rosy. "The surplus has declined from being gigantic to merely immense," said budget director Mitch Daniels.[4] Then Bush tried to argue that a return to red ink was "incredibly positive news," because it would restrain government spending.[5] But by two years after he took office, the CBO said that the entire projected surplus—every last penny of that $5.6 trillion—had disappeared, and Bush submitted a budget with the highest deficits in American history.[6] In all likelihood, it will take at least a generation

[2] Glenn Kessler, "Bigger Surplus Estimate Could Boost Tax Plan," *Washington Post*, January 31, 2001, p. A1.
[3] When Reagan took office, the debt was less than $1 trillion; when he left office it was over $2.6 trillion. Historical data on the national debt are available from the U.S. Treasury Department, http://www.publicdebt.treas.gov.
[4] John Harris and Glenn Kessler, "Who Shrank the Surplus?" *Washington Post* national weekly edition, July 16–22, 2001, p. 6.
[5] David Sanger, "President Asserts Shrunken Surplus May Curb Congress," *New York Times*, August 25, 2001, p. A1.
[6] Data from the Center on Budget and Policy Priorities.

to dig out of Bush's deficit hole, but Bush was shameless enough to proclaim in his 2003 State of the Union address, "We will not pass along our problems to other Congresses, to other presidents, and other generations."

His explanations for those deficits and for the failures of his economic policy are ever shifting; on some days it's Bill Clinton's fault, on some days it's al-Qaeda's fault, on at least one occasion he averred, "It's nobody's fault,"[7] but never does it have anything to do with the administration that has actually presided over the economy. Speaking to defense workers in California in 2003, Bush offered a remarkably dizzying journey of inaccuracy and illogic: "We've got a deficit because we went through a recession....We've got a recession because we went to war and I said to our troops, 'If we're going to commit you into harm's way you deserve the best equipment, the best training, the best possible pay.'[8] So the recession, which Bush was careful to point out started in January 2001 (although it actually began in March 2001),[9] was caused by a war that didn't begin until two years later. That war, though it caused a recession that began two years earlier, was paid for with spending on equipment and training more years back, all causing a deficit that emerged before the war began. If you can follow this, you must be a theoretical physicist; Bush seems to have created the first quantum recession.

Regardless of whether you believe events of the past can be caused by events of the present, the reversal of the last decade has been truly remarkable. While Republicans used to be the party of fiscal discipline, advocating a balanced-budget amendment to the Constitution and forever warning about the economic consequences of budget deficits, it was a Democratic president who finally eliminated the deficit and a Republican who brought it back. In response, congressional Republicans who had been such staunch deficit hawks

---

[7] *Today*, NBC, September 5, 2003.

[8] Speech at United Defense Industries, Mountain View, CÁ, May 2, 2003.

[9] According to the National Bureau of Economic Research (www.nber.org), the governmental body that officially decides such things, the recession began in March 2001 and ended in November 2001.

immediately began proclaiming that deficits were now no problem at all.

It would be worthwhile, therefore, to review a bit of history. In 1993, Bill Clinton pushed through Congress a plan to increase taxes, much to the horror of his opponents. As Paul Krugman has observed, the primary lesson of Clinton's 1993 tax increase and the ensuing years of economic growth is not that the increase caused all of the growth. Rather, the critical lesson lies in what *didn't* happen.[10] When the plan passed by a single vote, with every last GOP member voting against it, the Republicans—legislators, editorial writers, pundits—were unanimous in their conclusion that the sky would surely fall. The deficit would explode, they said; the stock market would crash; the country would plunge into, as Newt Gingrich said, a "job-killing recession."[11] Reading from the same talking points, Gingrich's colleague Bill Archer of Texas called the plan "job-killing poison for the economy."[12] Representative Jim Bunning said, "It won't reduce the deficit, but it will injure the country and decimate the economy. It's a job-killing bill from the word go."[13] The ranking Republican on the Budget Committee, John Kasich, said, "We'll come back next year and try to help you out when this puts the economy in the gutter."[14]

But despite the repeated cries of "job-killing," none of these things happened. The rich didn't curl into a ball, petulantly refusing to invest or save because they had to pick up more of the tax load than those of modest means. (According to the Joint Committee on Taxation, the 1993 plan raised taxes for those with incomes over $200,000 year by an average of 5.4 percent. For all other income groups, the increase was less than 1 percent, and those below

---

[10] Paul Krugman, *The Accidental Theorist and Other Dispatches from the Dismal Science.* New York: W.W. Norton, 1998.

[11] "House OKs Clinton's Budget, 218-216," *St. Louis Post-Dispatch*, August 6, 1993, p. 1A.

[12] David Rosenbaum, "House Passes Budget Plan, Backing Clinton By 218-216 After Hectic Maneuvering," *New York Times*, August 6, 1993, p. A1.

[13] Eric Pianin and David Hilzenrath, "House Passes Clinton Budget Plan by 2 Votes," *Washington Post*, August 6, 1993, p. A1.

[14] Michelle Ruess, "House OKs Tax Hike by Just 2," *Cleveland Plain Dealer*, August 6, 1993, p. 1A.

$20,000 saw their taxes decrease.)[15] Instead, Clinton's policies helped produce the most sustained period of economic growth the country had ever seen, and the deficit was eliminated.

Did the fact that events proved Republican predictions so spectacularly wrong lead Republicans to abandon supply-side economics? Hardly. What George W. Bush and his people realized was not that supply-side economics didn't work. Rather they concluded that in order to succeed in gaining votes among the public and legislators, supply-side had to be gilded, dressed up in populist clothes, and concealed behind a fog of deceptive rhetoric.

Whether supply-side was an effective economic policy was for Bush, like many of his Republican colleagues, not really a question. It was not something that could be tested empirically or subjected to careful analysis. If it were, the experience of the 1990s might have taught them something. Instead, for supply-siders, lowering taxes on the wealthy is simply a matter of moral conviction and religious faith. While they might proclaim that lowering taxes on the CEO is really intended to help the janitor who sweeps out his office, in truth they view it as a moral imperative.

Like his predecessors, Bush wanted desperately to lower taxes for the wealthy. But knowing that such a plan could easily be derided as "trickle-down economics," he devised his tax plan so there was something—no matter how small—for everyone who paid income taxes. Even if someone making $1 million a year would get a tax break of around $55,000 and someone making $20,000 would get less than $400, the fact that the poorer person got something, even a small amount, enabled Bush to claim that in his plan, everyone got tax "relief." When Bush was pushing his tax cut through Congress, he and the Republicans in charge of both houses of Congress decided they would end a practice that had been in place for fifty years: the release of distributional tables to go along with tax legislation, showing how people at various income levels would be affected. Why? Well, they said, allowing people to see the effects of

[15] David Rosenbaum, "House Passes Budget Plan, Backing Clinton By 218-216 After Hectic Maneuvering," New York Times, August 6, 1993, p. A1.

the tax cut "contributed to class warfare."[16] In other words, if Americans saw and understood the skewed nature of the tax cuts, they might resent them.

The Bush tax cut did have one populist element: it sent $300 checks to every person with income-tax liability, essentially a pre-payment of the reduction they would later receive. Although most people may not remember, the idea was actually proposed by congressional Democrats once they realized a tax cut was inevitable.[17] But Bush quickly realized that focusing on the $300 checks could be an effective way of distracting people from the fact that most of the tax cut's benefits went to the wealthy. In his 2002 State of the Union address, Bush said, "Last year, some in this hall thought my tax-relief plan was too small, and some thought it was too big." Republicans in the chamber applauded at "too small," and the Democrats idiotically played their part in Bush's deception by applauding at "too big." "But when those checks arrived in the mail," Bush went on, "most Americans thought tax relief was just right." The $300 checks, of course, had nothing to do with the size of the tax cut; in fact, they made up less than 5 percent of the total package.

But Bush had spent so much time lying about the contents of his tax plan, by the time it passed he may not have known what the truth was. During his second debate with Al Gore, Bush said that with his tax plan, "by far the vast majority of the help goes to the people at the bottom end of the economic ladder." Like much of what Bush says when he talks about taxes, this was simply a lie—not a mistake, not a slip-up, but a lie.

The selling of the Bush tax cut was based on a Big Lie, repeated over and over and over. Bush tried to convince the public—and succeeded enough to get the cut passed—that the tax cut was not tilted toward the rich. There were a number of subsidiary lies to this Big Lie—that those at lower incomes got a huge tax break or that

[16] David Rosenbaum, "Doing the Math on Bush's Tax Cut," *New York Times*, March 4, 2001, p. A22.
[17] Glenn Kessler, "Parties Split on Shape of Tax Relief," *Washington Post*, March 24, 2001, p. A1.

everyone who paid taxes got a tax cut under the plan, for instance. But the central lie was that it was not tilted toward the rich. As Jonathan Chait observed, "Bush's favorite example of who would benefit from his tax cut—repeated countless times over the last 18 months—is a single waitress with two kids who earns around $20,000 per year. 'Under my plan,' he likes to boast, the waitress 'will pay no income tax at all.' That's true. Because the waitress *almost certainly doesn't pay any income taxes to begin with*."[18] To illustrate by looking at the other end, at Dick Cheney's 2000 income of $36 million, the top rate reductions when fully phased in would be worth $1.6 million.

Bush and his aides tried to contend that the wealthiest 1 percent of Americans *only* got 21 percent of the benefits of his tax cut plan, though the real number was almost double that. When Al Gore argued accurately that 42 percent of the benefits of Bush's tax cut went to the wealthiest 1 percent, Bush pulled an Orwellian Misdirection by implying that Gore was lying. "This is a man who's got great numbers. He talks about numbers," Bush said in their first debate. "I'm beginning to think not only did he invent the Internet but he invented the calculator. It's fuzzy math." But there was nothing fuzzy about Gore's claim: it was simply the truth.

Fortunately for Bush, reporters knew exactly how to handle this conflict, as they do most factual disputes between opposing candidates: present both claims but don't say who might be telling the truth. In perhaps the most egregious example of reporters' agnostic abdication of their responsibility to sort out the facts, *Newsweek* wrote it up this way: "Who gains? Gore says that 42 percent of the benefits [of Bush's proposed plan] go to the richest one percent; Bush says the figure is only 21 percent. The truth lies in between; just where, no one knows."[19] In fact, the truth was quite clear: the 42 percent figure covered the entire Bush tax plan; to get the number down to 21 percent Bush just didn't count the most regressive part of his plan, the repeal of the estate tax. In short, Bush was being dishonest, a fact reporters would never dare to point out.

---

[18] Jonathan Chait, "Going for Gold," *New Republic*, May 21, 2001.
[19] David Noonan, "A Voter's Panic Guide," *Newsweek*, November 6, 2000 p. 34.

The net result of the wrangling over just how much of the Bush tax cut went to the wealthiest Americans was sufficiently confusing to throw people off the scent of the plan's true intentions. What is the truth? The best way to illustrate it is with a picture:

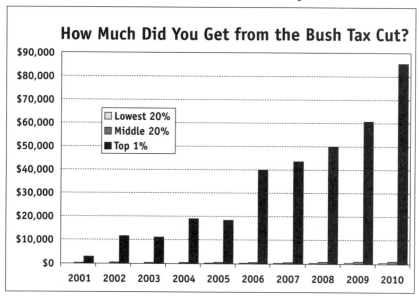

You may be looking at this graph and saying, "Hey, there's something wrong: they left out the middle 20 percent and the lowest 20 percent." But if you look closely, you'll see a tiny set of bars representing the average tax cut given to the middle 20 percent of Americans, those making an average of $34,300 in 2001 and $46,100 in 2010. The tax cut for this group was a princely $403 in 2001, skyrocketing up to $791 by 2010. Unfortunately, the bar for the lowest 20 percent is so small it is invisible on this graph. They got an average of $57 in 2001; by 2010 they'll be raking in $98.[20]

With a Republican Congress, Bush had little trouble passing his plan regardless of how far it was tilted toward the rich. Just to make sure every American got the message, the administration had the IRS send a letter to 91.6 million taxpaying families, proclaiming, "We are pleased to inform you that the United States Congress passed—and

---

[20] Data from analysis by Citizens for Tax Justice.

President George W. Bush signed into law—the Economic Growth and Tax Relief Reconciliation Act of 2001, which provides long-term tax relief for all Americans who pay income taxes."[21] Millions of taxpayer dollars were thus spent on what was in effect an ad for George W. Bush, telling us how lucky we were to have him looking out for us—some of us, anyway.

Bush even went so far as to argue that the deficit created by his tax cut would have been bigger without his tax cut, a position not even the most ardent supply-siders could bring themselves to defend.[22] The theory that cutting taxes raises revenue—another element of what Bush Sr. termed "voodoo economics"—had not been taken seriously by anyone in twenty years. But you can't have it both ways: either your tax cut was meant to return the surplus to the people, in which case it contributed to the deficit by eating up the surplus, or the tax cut didn't bring about the deficit because it increased revenue, in which case you would have sold it as a way to *increase* the surplus. Of course Bush didn't, because had he said that as a candidate he would have been laughed out of town.

THE REAL CLASS WARFARE

Low taxes for the wealthy is such a matter of religious conviction for the Bush administration that it even showed up in its National Security Strategy.[23] The document states that the U.S. will use its military might to force other countries to adopt not only political freedom, but "pro-growth legal and regulatory policies to encourage business investment, innovation, and entrepreneurial activity," and, "Tax policies—particularly lower marginal tax rates—that improve incentives for work and investment." They thus define minimal regulation of business and low marginal tax rates as on par with freedom of expression.

In theory, one could make an argument for giving big tax breaks to the wealthy. For decades the progressive tax system, in which people with higher incomes pay a greater percentage of their income in

---

[21] Philip Shenon, "Dressed as Tooth Fairy, I.R.S. Will Drop a Note to Millions," *New York Times*, June 19, 2001.

[22] Dana Milbank, "This Time a Bush Embraces 'Voodoo Economics' Theory," *Washington Post*, November 14, 2002, p. A7.

[23] The full document may be found at www.whitehouse.gov/nsc/nss.html.

taxes, has irked conservative Republicans, especially the wealthy ones. But until recently, few politicians were willing to explicitly adopt the position that the rich should pay less in taxes.

That isn't to say that Republicans haven't sought to lower taxes on the wealthy, only that they tend to hide their plans with a blizzard of deceptive rhetoric. You will almost never hear a conservative forthrightly proclaim that he does not believe in the principle of progressive taxation, namely that wealthy people should pay more in taxes than those of more modest means. Even those who advocate a flat tax, which embodies the rejection of progressivity, justify it with appeals to "simplicity" and "unleashing entrepreneurial creativity," avoiding the question of fairness. But when the doors are closed, conservatives can always be relied upon to advocate tax changes that lower the share paid by the wealthy. Let a liberal point out the fact that, say, slashing the capital-gains tax benefits only those at the top, and the cry of "class warfare!" will inevitably be heard.

Another principle of this approach to taxes that conservatives will never admit to is that it devalues work. If one believes that capital gains should be taxed at a lower rate than wages, one necessarily believes that money you *work* for should be subject to higher taxes than the money you make when your money makes you more money. The higher you go up the economic ladder, of course, the greater the percentage of income people tend to receive from their investments. For most people, the capital-gains tax might as well be a tariff on imported emu feathers—it has nothing to do with them. For another healthy chunk of the populace, capital gains are a small portion of their income—they wouldn't mind paying less in taxes on them, but if the rate were lowered a few percentage points they'd hardly notice. Only those with substantial investments who in a given year move large amounts of stock feel passionately that justice demands lowering the capital-gains rate (more than three-quarters of all capital gains taxes are paid by the wealthiest 2 percent of Americans).[24] But it is this group of people—not coincidentally, the ones who have the ability to

---

[24] "Who Pays Capital Gains Taxes?" Citizens for Tax Justice, June 26, 1998.

write $2,000 checks to politicians without blinking an eye and have lots of friends they can convince to do the same—who receive a friendly ear from those in Congress and the White House. As George Bernard Shaw said, "A government which robs Peter to pay Paul can always depend on the support of Paul."

But Peter, on the other hand, won't be so pleased. So what's a plutocrat to do? Conservatives tend to devise plans that give huge benefits to the wealthy but sell them by concealing that fact. In 1981, Ronald Reagan's budget director David Stockman admitted that the "supply-side" economics on which Reagan's policies were based "was always a Trojan horse to bring down the top [income tax] rate." "Supply-side" was a term invented to sound like it was based in sound economic theory when it was actually just a renaming of the blunter-sounding "trickle-down"—give all the benefits to the wealthy and eventually they'll trickle down to everyone else. Needless to say, this theory may go over big at the country club, but it's a little hard to swallow if you're the one waiting for the trickle. "It's kind of hard to sell 'trickle down,'" Stockman explained at the time, "so the supply-side formula was the only way to get a tax policy that was really 'trickle down.'"[25]

The tax plan George W. Bush proposed during his 2000 race was the perfect example of this strategy. If you listened to Bush talk, you would have thought that his greatest concern was the taxes paid by waitresses and schoolteachers. In his convention speech, Bush said, "Those in the greatest need should receive the greatest help." But if you looked at the details of Bush's plan, "those in the greatest need" turned out to be people with incomes over $373,000, since that's who got the greatest help from his tax cut. These needy families were earmarked for an average of over $54,000 in tax cuts, or 45 percent of the total value of the package.[26]

Al Gore's plan for taxes, like the man himself, was a bit too complicated to be summed up in a pleasing way. It was an amalgam of

---

[25] William Greider, "The Education of David Stockman," *Atlantic Monthly*, December 1981.
[26] "CTJ Analysis of Bush Plan Updated to 2001 Levels," Citizens for Tax Justice, February 27, 2001.

benefits for this and that—help for putting kids through college, taking care of a sick parent, and so on. This allowed Bush to argue that while Gore wanted to help some people but not others, Bush wanted to help everyone. But there was an important asterisk to this argument, one that most people didn't understand and one that journalists—who are supposed to clear these things up—either failed to grasp or just ignored.

The asterisk is that there are two primary kinds of federal taxes the average person pays: income taxes and payroll taxes. While income taxes fund a variety of government programs, payroll taxes go to fund the Social Security and Medicare systems. All wage earners pay payroll taxes, but people with very low incomes don't pay any federal income taxes. In fact, according to the Congressional Budget Office, 80 percent of Americans pay more in payroll taxes than they do in income taxes.[27]

Bush's plan lowered income-tax rates for everyone who pays income taxes, but didn't touch payroll taxes. This meant that the 26 percent of Americans who pay substantial payroll taxes but no income taxes got no benefits from Bush's plan.[28] For Bush to portray his plan accurately, he would therefore have had to describe it by saying, "If you pay *income* taxes, you get tax relief." To his credit, this is what Bush said. Sometimes.

But dozens upon dozens of other times—including in all three presidential debates and in his television ads—Bush shortened the accurate statement to the more pleasing but false, "If you pay taxes, you get tax relief." Or as he said in his acceptance speech at the 2000 Republican convention, "We will reduce tax rates for everyone, in every bracket." But when the tax cut eventually passed, thirty-four million Americans didn't get those $300 checks the Democrats forced Bush to include (and for which he naturally took credit)—they got no check and no tax cut.[29]

[27] Paul Krugman, *Fuzzy Math: The Essential Guide to the Bush Tax Plan*. New York: W.W. Norton, 2001.
[28] "51 Million Taxpayers Won't Get Full Rebates from 2001 Tax Bill," Citizens for Tax Justice, June 1, 2001.
[29] David Rosenbaum, "Tax Rebate Will Bypass Many, Study Finds," *New York Times*, June 12, 2001.

The difference between income taxes and payroll taxes is not some arcane fact of tax law buried in a dusty book in the bowels of the IRS. Anyone who participates in public debate, George W. Bush included, knows full well that these are two separate and very different taxes. Conservatives who talk about the amount of income taxes paid by the wealthy while leaving out payroll taxes—or those who conflate the two, saying things like, "only [the rich] pay significant taxes," as George Will did—are being knowingly disingenuous.[30]

But those kinds of statements are intended to fool people into believing that the wealthy labor under a terribly unfair burden of taxation, pulling the national cart while the rest of us sit comfortably inside. A close look at the taxes Americans pay—federal, state, and local—shows that this picture is entirely false. The wealthiest 1 percent of Americans earned 18 percent of total pretax income in 2001 and paid 25 percent of federal taxes. When it comes to other taxes, the rich get off easy: the average state and local tax rate (including sales, income, and property taxes) for the wealthiest 1 percent of Americans is 5.2 percent. The middle 20 percent of families pay 9.6 percent of their income in state and local taxes while the poorest 20 percent pay 11.4 percent, more than twice as much as the richest.[31] What it all adds up to is that in America we have something that looks remarkably like a flat tax: the poorest fifth of Americans pay 18 percent of their income in taxes, the richest fifth pay 19 percent, and those in the middle pay from 14 percent to 17 percent.[32]

But when you hear conservatives talk about taxes, they virtually never mention payroll or sales taxes, concentrating only on progressive federal income taxes and hoping that their listeners will be fooled into thinking those are the only taxes worth talking about. One prime example is the *Wall Street Journal*'s editorial page, which

[30] George Will, "The Long and Short of the 'Stimulus Package,'" *Washington Post*, January 8, 2003, p. A19.

[31] Robert McIntyre et al, "Who Pays? A Distributional Analysis of the Tax Systems in All 50 States," Washington, DC: Institute on Taxation and Economic Policy, January 2003.

[32] Daniel Altman, "Doubling Up of Taxation Isn't Limited to Dividends," *New York Times*, January 21, 2003.

doesn't bother to hide its advocacy of the interests of the wealthy behind any assurances that they really want what's best for everyone. They want what's best for the rich, and they're proud to say it. In November of 2002, a *Journal* editorial that read like a clever satire actually complained that people who earn less than $12,000 a year were getting off easy when it came to taxes. "Who are these lucky duckies?"[33] they asked, in dismay that those with gross incomes of a princely $1,000 a month are sitting pretty while millionaires struggle under the burden of progressive taxation.

When the Enron scandal broke, the *Journal* put the blame squarely on—who else—Bill Clinton: "We'd say it's also impossible to understand Enron outside of the moral climate in which it flourished. Those were the roaring '90s, when all of America reveled in the economic boom. They were also the Clinton years, when we learned that 'everybody does it.'"[34] Longtime *Journal* editor Robert Bartley (who once said that in America "there aren't any poor people left, you know, just a few hermits or something like that")[35] even tried to blame the Enron scandal on "the societal collapse of standards and morality over the last three decades or so."[36] It must have been the '60s, with its long hair, free love, and phony Cayman Island–subsidiary tax-dodge schemes.

But though they may have devolved into self-parody with their indignation at the undeserved good fortune of the poor, the *Journal* was not alone. Reagan Attorney General Ed Meese picked up the line a few days later, saying on Fox's *Hannity and Colmes* on November 26, "Well, it's very unfortunate that we have the situation in our country now, where as I believe someone pointed out a short time ago on your program, that we now have a constituency [the poor] that pays no taxes whatsoever" (once again, a conservative charges that the poor pay "no taxes" when in fact they pay plenty of taxes, just not federal income taxes). The next stop was, of course, the Bush administration

---

[33] "The Non-Taxpaying Class," *Wall Street Journal*, November 20, 2002, p. A20.
[34] "Enron's Sins," *Wall Street Journal*, January 18, 2002.
[35] Blaine Harden, "The Editor Who Claims to Think Like a President," *Washington Post Magazine*, July 11, 1982, p. 12.
[36] Robert Bartley, "I'm OK, You're OK! Enron's OK?" *Wall Street Journal*, January 21, 2002.

itself. "The increasing reliance on taxing higher-income households and targeted social preferences at lower incomes stands in the way of moving to a simpler, flatter tax system," said Glenn Hubbard, the chairman of Bush's Council of Economic Advisers.[37]

Lowering the taxes paid by the wealthy has always been where Bush's heart was, but convincing Americans to go along requires a little creative argumentation. In arguing for the 2001 tax cut, he tried to claim that every small-business owner in America would benefit from lowering the top rate. On March 16, 2001 he gave a speech to small-business owners in which he stated that, "According to the Treasury Department, nationwide there are more than 17.4 million small-business owners and entrepreneurs who stand to benefit from dropping the top rate from 39.6 to 33 percent."[38] Here, Bush was telling a double lie. First, his Treasury Department lied: its press release issued just before said that "many" of the country's 17.4 million small-business owners paid the top rate; Bush then said that *all* of them pay the top rate. In fact, only *1.4 percent* of the country's small-business owners pay the top rate. According to the latest figures available at the time, only 691,000 Americans—business owners or not—paid the top rate. Only 180,000 small businesses—not 17.4 million—paid the top rate.[39] Bush repeated the lie in a speech a week later: "Most small businesses pay at the 39.6 percent rate. And by dropping the top rate to 33 percent, we stimulate small businesses in America."[40] Is 1.4 percent "most"? No more so than 1.4 percent is "all." Bush was simply lying.

During the 2000 campaign, Bush made this charge about Al Gore: "He's invented a new calculator. It's a calculator where you put real numbers in and it comes out with political numbers."[41] It must have sounded to Bush like a fine idea because every time a tax

[37] Jonathan Weisman, "New Tax Plan May Bring Shift in Burden," *Washington Post*, December 16, 2002, p. A3.
[38] Speech at the White House, March 16, 2001.
[39] Figures from the Center on Budget and Policy Priorities.
[40] Speech to the National Newspaper Association conference, March 22, 2001.
[41] Alison Mitchell, "Taking Up Where Debate Left Off, Bush Assails Gore on Spending," *New York Times*, October 5, 2000, p. A30.

question comes up, Bush devises a new way to twist the numbers and deceive Americans about the effects of his plans. When he set about to promote his 2003 tax-cut plan centering on the elimination of taxes on stock dividends, Bush said, "Ninety-two million Americans will keep an average of $1,083 more of their own money."[42] Here Bush was employing an old trick, the use of an "average" radically distorted by the outliers. For instance, if you put nine McDonald's workers in a room with Bill Gates, the "average" income of the group would be around a billion dollars a year, but that doesn't accurately describe the group. A more accurate description of the tax cut Bush was posing would have noted that the typical tax cut for those in the middle of the income scale would be $289, whereas the typical tax cut for those in the top 1 percent would be $30,127.[43] At Dick Cheney's 2001 level of income, the vice president would have gotten a much-needed stimulus of $326,555.[44]

To see how absurd Bush's "average" thousand-dollar tax break is, consider these figures on the 2003 tax bill, compiled by Citizens for Tax Justice:

- In 2003, 49 percent of taxpayers will get $100 or less from the tax bill. For these 65.7 million unlucky taxpayers, the average tax reduction will be only $19.
- In 2004, 47 percent of taxpayers will get $100 or less. The average tax cut for these 63.4 million taxpayers will be $19.
- In 2005, 74 percent of taxpayers will get $100 or less from the president's plan. The average tax reduction for these 97.9 million taxpayers will be $5.
- In 2006, 88 percent of taxpayers will get $100 or less from the tax bill. For these 118 million taxpayers, the average tax reduction will be $4.[45]

[42] Speech in Chicago, January 7, 2003.
[43] Figures from Citizens for Tax Justice.
[44] Based on analysis by Bloomberg News, reported in Elisabeth Bumiller, "Bush's Bold, and Risky, Economic Plan," New York Times, January 8, 2003, p. A1.
[45] "Most Taxpayers Get Little Help From Latest Bush Tax Plan," Citizens for Tax Justice, May 30, 2003.

Faced with data like these, conservatives often respond that the rich should get the biggest tax cuts because they pay a large share of federal income taxes. This is true—but the size of that share isn't because they're taxed so heavily, it's because they make so much money. Their share of income taxes keeps increasing because income inequality keeps increasing. In 1998 the wealthiest 1 percent of Americans garnered more of the country's total income than in any year since 1936, when the country was still mired in the Great Depression. Before Bush's tax cut was enacted, the median American family of four was paying a smaller percentage of its income in federal income taxes than in any year since 1966.[46]

In a rare moment of candor during the 2000 campaign, Bush admitted that he wished he could give an even bigger tax break to the wealthiest Americans but realized that it probably wouldn't sell. "I wanted to cut a little more at the top rate," he said, "but I wasn't able to justify it."[47]

DEATH AND TAXES

Of all the provisions in Bush's tax-cut plan, the repeal of the estate tax should have been the hardest to sell since it was such a blatant giveaway to the richest among us. So Bush and his allies decided that they would lie about it, banking on the fact that most people don't understand the details of the tax and thus could be easily deceived.

To begin, a few essential facts: when the debate over Bush's tax plan began in 2000, the estate tax (also called the inheritance tax) applied only to inheritances larger than $675,000. That number was scheduled to rise to $1 million by 2006. Since most ordinary people don't leave that kind of money behind, for most people the tax is irrelevant; in fact, 98 percent of estates paid no estate tax. No tax is paid on estates passed to a spouse. Half of the total revenue from the tax was paid by the largest 5 percent of taxable estates, those valued

---

[46] Figures from the Center on Budget and Policy Priorities.
[47] Dan Balz, "Bush Bets He Can Sell Tax Cut Where Others Have Failed," *Washington Post*, December 13, 1999, p. A2.

at more than $5 million. Repealing the estate tax will cost $740 billion in the decade after the repeal is complete.[48]

Republicans scored a significant victory with their repetition on this issue, as they have on a number of other points recently. By referring to the estate tax as the "death tax" over and over, Republicans eventually reached a point where the term pops up in any story about the tax. At first, journalists referred to it as "what Republicans refer to as the 'death tax.'" That soon became "what its opponents refer to as the 'death tax,'" and then "what some refer to as the 'death tax,'" then "the so-called 'death tax,'" and in some places "the 'death tax.'" This terminology is fundamentally dishonest, for it implies, as Republicans would like Americans to believe, that the tax is a tax on death and since everyone dies, everyone pays it. In actuality, of course, it is a tax on inheritance— and only on the inheritances of the wealthiest 2 percent.

Since there are few taxes that are as targeted so narrowly to the rich, the estate tax's opponents had to come up with a rationale that could make repeal sound reasonable without making them seem like they were carrying water for the wealthiest of the wealthy. So they came up with the second big lie, which they use nearly every time they discuss the issue: the estate tax forces the liquidation of family farms and small businesses. One hears this argument again and again—as President Bush has said on many occasions, "To keep farms in the family, we are going to get rid of the death tax."[49]

Sounds compassionate but, like many of the premises on which Bush bases his policies, it just isn't true. What are the facts? An Iowa State University economist who studied the issue was unable to find even *a single case* of a family farm being sold in order to pay estate taxes. The American Farm Bureau Federation, which advocates estate-tax repeal, was unable (not for lack of trying) to produce a single case either.[50] This is due in part to the fact that the exemption in the law for family farms and small businesses is twice the normal exemption; this means that a couple inheriting a farm could exempt

---

[48] Figures from the Center on Budget and Policy Priorities.
[49] David Cay Johnston, "Talk of Lost Farms Reflects Muddle of Estate Tax Debate," *New York Times*, April 8, 2001.
[50] David Cay Johnston, "Talk of Lost Farms Reflects Muddle of Estate Tax Debate," *New York Times*, April 8, 2001.

the first $2.6 million of its value from the tax, a figure that would have been $4 million by 2006. In addition, there were enough loopholes that after an afternoon with a tax lawyer, any farmer could easily arrange his or her estate to be completely exempt from taxes. As Bush was no doubt happy to learn, even in 2003 a poll by NPR, the Kaiser Family Foundation, and Harvard's Kennedy School of Government found that half of all Americans believed that most families have to pay the estate tax when someone dies.[51]

If as they say Republicans are only concerned about the tax's effect on small businesses and family farms, there's a simple solution: raise the exemption for small businesses and family farms. Put it at $10 million, or even higher, or eliminate the tax for family farms and small businesses altogether. Problem solved. Since so few farms and small businesses are subject to the tax to begin with, it wouldn't take that much of a bite out of the treasury. But then that's not really the point, and estate-tax opponents have actually fought against raising the exemptions for farms and businesses.

From the Republican perspective, giving benefits to the wealthy encourages "entrepreneurship" and bold, job-creating investment. Giving benefits to the poor and middle class, on the other hand, creates only sloth and dependence. To take just one small example, while he was promoting an elimination of the taxes on stock dividends, Bush proposed to raise the rents of people living in public housing, a move, the administration said, "intended to promote work,"[52] presumably because it will make these already poor people a little bit poorer. While it may sound like a caricature, many Republicans genuinely believe that the rich are just better people: only from this perspective could one argue, as some Republican members of Congress have, that a tax on large inheritances is "a tax on virtue."[53]

---

[51] Survey conducted for NPR, the Kaiser Family Foundation, and the Kennedy School of Government, April 2003.

[52] Robert Pear, "Renters Receiving U.S. Aid to Pay More Under Budget Proposal," New York Times, February 11, 2003.

[53] Christopher Cox, "The Death Tax, Ethics and Entrepreneurship," The Hill, April 25, 2001, p. 30; Rep. Jennifer Dunn (R-WA) was quoted saying the same thing, Charles Pope, "House Passes Estate Tax Phaseout," Seattle Post-Intelligencer, April 5, 2001, p. A3.

On the estate tax, Bush followed the same strategy he applies to taxes generally: take a huge benefit to the wealthy, devise terms and arguments that hide its true beneficiaries, then ·sell it as actually intended to help ordinary folks, throwing in a few outright lies in the process. Bush understands that tax policy—with its dollars, percentages, forecasts, and projections—can be complex and confusing. For Bush, this is an opportunity to deceive, to proclaim his support for the little guy while working as hard as he can for the big guy.

Other Republicans got on board Bush's effort to sell a plan whose greatest benefits go to the wealthiest as a boon for average people. In March 2001, the head of the National Association of Manufacturers, a business lobbying group, sent out a memo based on a strategy coordinated with Speaker of the House Dennis Hastert asking for people to come to a rally in support of Bush's tax-cut plan. But in order to make it appear that the participants were not corporate lobbyists but rather ordinary folks, they were instructed to come in disguise. "The theme involves working Americans," said the memo. "Visually, this will involve a sea of hard hats, which our construction and contractor and building groups are working very hard to provide. But the Speaker's office was very clear in saying that they do not need people in suits. If people want to participate—AND WE DO NEED BODIES—they must be DRESSED DOWN, appear to be REAL WORKER types, etc. We plan to have hard hats for people to wear."[54] Republicans regularly perform this masquerade; in 2003 White House aides instructed people standing behind Bush at an event promoting his tax cut to remove their ties, so they would appear to be ordinary folks.[55]

"This is a war," Karl Rove said, "and we need to make an ongoing commitment to winning the effort to repeal the death tax."[56] Republican allies like the National Association of Manufacturers lined up to do their part. Out in the country, they relied on deception as often as they

[54] Juliet Eilperin and Dan Morgan, "Something Borrowed, Something Blue; Memo Enlists Lobbyists to Trade White Collars for Hard Hats at GOP Tax Cut Rally," *Washington Post*, March 9, 2001, p. A16.
[55] Elisabeth Bumiller, "Keepers of Bush Image Lift Stagecraft to New Heights," *New York Times*, May 16, 2003, p. A1.
[56] Mike Allen, "Rove Urges 'War' for Permanent Repeal of Estate Tax," *Washington Post*, June 14, 2002, p. A5.

did in the capital. One group, Americans for Job Security, ran blatantly dishonest ads against Democratic senators criticizing them for voting to keep the inheritance tax. The ad featured "Ruth" and "Lloyd" fretting because they got a tax bill after Lloyd's father passed on. Here's an excerpt of the one targeted at Minnesota senator Paul Wellstone:

> **Ruth:** What's going to happen?
> **Lloyd:** We're going to have to sell the farm.
> **Ruth:** No, Lloyd, we're going to call Paul Wellstone and tell him our folks paid their fair share and to keep his money-grubbing hands off our farm!

Wellstone's actual position was that all farms and small businesses should be exempt from the estate tax, and it should only apply to other estates over $7 million. And just who is Americans for Job Security, you might ask? A group of Americans concerned about job security? Not exactly. It's a group bankrolled by large corporations and associations of large corporations (most notably the insurance industry) to lobby and advertise in support of low taxes and Republican candidates. In 2000, Trent Lott told lobbyists that if they wanted action on their bills, they ought to pony up some cash to Americans for Job Security.[57]

Bush added one more deception to his argument on the estate tax when he referred to the fact that his tax bill eliminated the estate tax, then revived it again in 2011—a dishonest gimmick his administration had come up with to hide the bill's true cost—as "a quirk in the law," as if it was some unintended consequence no one had known about. "It's hard for me to explain why they repealed it but didn't repeal it," he said, playing dumb.[58] Of course, he knew quite well why his Republican allies in Congress, in cooperation with his White House, constructed the bill that he signed that way. In arguing for speeding up the implementation of the top-rate tax cuts in 2003, Bush said, "If tax relief is good enough for Americans three

---

[57] Mike Allen, "GOP Pressures Tech Firms to Help Michigan Senator," *Washington Post*, May 16, 2000, p. A7.
[58] Sandra Sobieraj, "Bush Seeks Eradication of Estate Tax," Associated Press, June 7, 2002.

years from now, it is good enough for Americans today."[59] He must not have felt that way two years earlier, when hiding the cost of the tax cut for the wealthy was the immediate goal. But the use of "sunset" provisions—wherein a tax cut is enacted with an expiration date after which the *status quo ante* will return—has become a feature of every Bush tax proposal, a convenient way to make each bill seem smaller than it actually is, done with the understanding that Congress will eventually vote to make the tax permanent.

The estate-tax deception used by the Americans for Job Security is an example of a rhetorical tactic George W. Bush employs with regularity to deceive people about the effects of his policies. He comes up with a feel-good justification—in this case, keeping farms in the family—then posits it as the motivation for a policy it has little or nothing to do with. When in 2003 he proposed eliminating taxes on stock dividends, yet another handout for the wealthy, he tried to sell it as a way to help the elderly. "For the good of our senior citizens," Bush said, "I'm asking the United States Congress to abolish the double taxation of dividends."[60] His press secretary, Ari Fleischer, argued that Congress should pass the first wartime tax cut in American history—and one directed at the wealthiest Americans to boot—"so that when our men and women in the military return home, they'll have jobs to come home to."[61] But of course, being soldiers *is* their job, and those who serve in the reserves have their jobs protected by law. The strategy here is clear: to tie an otherwise unpalatable tax cut as a means of helping a sympathetic group, such as senior citizens, the family farm, small business, or our soldiers in a time of war. These are all people that Americans want to aid, so a plea on their behalf is half-won. But in truth, the tax cuts have little or nothing to do with them.

DOUBLE DECEPTION

The Bush administration's central claim when they argued in 2003 for ending taxes on corporate dividends was that since corporate profits are

---

[59] Speech in Chicago, January 7, 2003.
[60] Speech in Chicago, January 7, 2003.
[61] Dana Milbank, "Bush Administration Using War to Justify Its Tax Cut," *Washington Post*, March 26, 2003, p. A4.

taxed, then shareholders pay taxes on their dividends, dividend taxes constitute a terribly unjust "double taxation." The success of the "double taxation" claim proved beyond a shadow of a doubt that any argument no matter how absurd will, if repeated often enough, be treated with utmost seriousness by reporters, who would never have been so impolite as to point out its plain dishonesty. To paraphrase the great cartoonist Ruben Bolling, see if you can spot the "double taxation" in this story: Bob gets a paycheck and pays taxes on his income, then he uses some of his money to pay his plumber, Alice, who pays taxes on that income. Alice uses some of her money to buy a DVD player, and the shop owner, Joe, pays taxes on that income. Joe then uses some of his money to make a car payment, and the bank pays taxes on that income. The bank then pays a dividend to its stockholder, Winthrop, who pays taxes on that income. Winthrop then uses some of his money to tip his caddy, Skip, who pays taxes on that income. So where's the "double taxation"? You guessed it—it's only the tax paid by the rich guy (Winthrop) that is the morally abhorrent double taxation.[62]

In the Bush administration, any department can be enlisted to participate in a propaganda effort, particularly when the topic is taxes. Reversing their previous stance, Bush's Treasury Department helpfully released a set of distributional tables showing how his 2003 tax proposal would affect people at different income levels. The only problem was, they simply didn't count the proposal's largest feature, the elimination of the tax on stock dividends, just as Bush had discounted the estate-tax repeal when calculating the proportion of his 2001 tax cut that went to the richest 1 percent. Karl Rove then had a sit-down with reporters, in which he actually said that eliminating taxes on stock dividends was aimed at "the little guy" and that President Bush is really a populist who thinks only of the common folk. "Give him a choice between Wall Street and Main Street and he'll choose Main Street every time."[63] Others also commented; Bush's plan to give a new round of tax breaks to the wealthy "is very much

---

[62] Bolling's *Tom the Dancing Bug* comic, "Can You Spot the Double Taxation?" appeared on March 27, 2003. I took the liberty of giving the characters names.
[63] Richard Stevenson, "Top Strategist Terms Bush a Populist about Taxes," *New York Times*, January 23, 2003.

pro-poor," said Glenn Hubbard, the chief economic adviser. "That's what the president is all about."[64] Bush then claimed that a survey of economists by the Blue Chip Forecast predicted a higher rate of growth if his tax cut was passed, while the actual report said no such thing.[65]

Why would Bush be so interested in removing the tax on stock dividends, a move for which, to put it mildly, there was no public fervor? Writer and former Republican strategist Kevin Phillips suggested that the source might be the stock from which Bush himself sprung:

> Great-grandfather George H. Walker was the president of two major New York investment firms: G.H. Walker & Co. and W.A. Harriman and Co. Grandfather Prescott Bush was the managing partner of Brown Bros., Harriman & Co. Presidential uncles Jonathan and Prescott Jr. have been, respectively, the heads of small investment firms named J. Bush & Co. and Prescott Bush & Co. Prescott Bush Jr. has also been closely involved with Asset Management International Financing and Settlement Ltd. Presidential brother Marvin runs hedge funds at investment company Winston Partners. Presidential brother Neil started an investment deal in Austin, and both George H.W. and George W. Bush have been in the kind of oil business that is largely driven by tax shelters and financing from friends and relatives.[66]

This is the world from which Bush comes, a world of wealth, influence, and privilege, where the country's aristocrats accumulate huge fortunes on the sweat of ordinary people's brows, benefit mightily from the society their government creates, yet fight tooth and nail to avoid having to contribute anything to that society's upkeep.

A Passion for Wealth

What is so offensive about Bush's tax policies is not simply that

---

[64] Jonathan Weisman, "Bush Plan Keys on Growth to Solve Poverty Problem," *Washington Post*, February 9, 2003, p. A6.
[65] Bryan Keefer, "Bush's Blue Chip Deception," Spinsanity.org, March 2, 2003.
[66] Kevin Phillips, "A Tax Cut Rooted in the Bush Pedigree," *Los Angeles Times*, January 12, 2003.

they are so skewed toward helping the richest Americans, but that this goal seems to animate Bush and his administration to heights of passion unseen on any other issue. The mundane problems affecting ordinary Americans—struggles to pay the mortgage, feed the family, get decent health care—are met by Bush with a shrug. He'll proclaim his concern about problems like these, but when it comes time to do something about it, Bush's attention wanders. But the idea that millionaires and corporations might have to pay their fair share of taxes offends Bush to the bone. It makes him angry; it gets his blood boiling. There is no political capital he will not expend, no crisis too distracting, no priority too pressing to stay him from his mission of freeing the wealthiest from the burden of taxation.

The depths of his passion became evident in early 2002 when Senate Majority Leader Tom Daschle had the temerity to attempt to engage the administration in a debate about the effects of Bush's tax cuts on the federal budget and the economy. "Not only did the tax cut fail to prevent a recession, as its supporters said it would," Daschle said, "it probably made the recession worse."[67] In response, Bush decided he would simply lie about the argument Daschle had made. Just before, Republican pollster Frank Luntz distributed a memo to Republicans, saying, "It is time for someone, everyone, to start using the phrase 'Daschle Democrats' and the word 'obstructionist' in the same sentence. It's time for Congressional Republicans to personalize the individual that is standing directly in the way of economic security, and even national security. Remember what the Democrats did to Gingrich? We need to do exactly the same thing to Daschle."[68] They promptly took his advice, streaming to the Sunday talk shows to repeat the word "obstructionist" like a mantra. Senator Rick Santorum called the mild-mannered Daschle a "rabid dog."[69] The Family Research

[67] Alison Mitchell, "Democrat Assails Bush on Economy," *New York Times*, January 5, 2002, p. A1.
[68] Todd Purdum, "G.O.P. Pushes to Make Daschle Appear a National Villain," *New York Times*, December 21, 2001, p. A36.
[69] Stephen Dinan, "Bush's Faith-Based Initiative Stalled in Congress This Year," *Washington Times*, December 7, 2001, p. A15.

Council ran ads in South Dakota featuring side-by-side photos of Daschle and Saddam Hussein.

So when the surplus disappeared, and Daschle and other Democrats began to point to the logical explanation—not the few billion dollars that the government had spent in the wake of September 11 but the $1.35 trillion tax cut—Bush reacted by implying that criticizing the administration's fiscal policies was un-American. In a speech in Ontario, California, he said, "There are troubling signs that the old way is beginning to creep into the people's minds in Washington. After all, it's an election year." As always, if you disagree with Bush you are branded a partisan, clinging to the reviled "old way." "But America is better than that," Bush said. "We're better than that."

Bush then went on to respond to an argument no one had made, moving deftly from near-truth to outright lie:

- Step one—almost true statement: *"There's going to be people who say we can't have the tax cut go through."* This referred to the many provisions of the 2001 tax cut that were slated to take effect in later years. Democrats were in fact raising the possibility that portions of the tax cut (not all the tax cut as Bush said) that had yet to take effect—the ones benefiting the wealthiest Americans—should be repealed.
- Step two—deceptive statement: *"That's a tax raise."* Of course it isn't. No one would pay more than they had before if a tax cut that had not yet taken effect were repealed. By no reasonable definition could that be considered an increase in anyone's taxes. An increase in taxes is when you pay more taxes than you used to.
- Step three—outright lie: *"I challenge their economics when they say raising taxes will help the country recover."* No one said anything resembling "raising taxes will help the country recover." What they argued instead was that the tax cut was

responsible for the return to deficits, which endangered the long-term economic health of the country in a hundred different ways. Some were recommending repealing cuts slated to take effect in 2004 and later, when everyone agreed the 2002 recession would be over.

Finally, Bush gave the lectern-thumping statement of resolve. "Not over my dead body will they raise your taxes!" he said to cheers from the crowd.[70] This is the worst kind of demagoguery: lying about his opponents, then showing his strength and leadership by pledging to stand up to the straw man he has created.

As columnist Robert Scheer noted, Bush's manly challenge was troubling not only for its dishonesty but for the priorities it revealed. "Notice that he didn't say 'over my dead body' will the homeless—many of them actually employed in low-paying jobs—sleep in the snows of Minneapolis because the 'faith-based' as well as government shelters are short on funds," Scheer wrote. "Nor is it 'over my dead body' that Enron workers will be left holding the bag emptied by the President's good friend, Kenneth L. 'Kenny Boy' Lay. Nor is it 'over my dead body' that the Boeing company will be given a $22 billion Air Force contract as it fires thousands of its workers.[71] No, the one thing for which Bush is willing to lay down his life is the preservation of tax cuts for the wealthy.

What was the pundits' reaction to Bush's lie? In some corners, high praise. On *Hardball*, host Chris Matthews couldn't say enough about it. "The Democratic senator came out and said, 'We don't think it was a good idea to cut taxes.' And what the president did was spin it and said, 'Those damn Democrats are going to raise taxes'…That was a brilliant piece of spin. That was Reaganesque." Matthews's guest, Howard Fineman of *Newsweek*, agreed. "He did everything but say, 'Go ahead, make my day.'" "Right," Matthews responded. "Well, is it smart politics as well as

---

[70] Speech in Ontario, California, January 5, 2002.
[71] Robert Scheer, "Let Down His Rich Pals? Over His Dead Body," *Los Angeles Times*, January 8, 2002, Metro p. 11.

national leadership, or what do you make of it?" "Probably smart politics," Fineman said, "because there's no outcry in the country to raise taxes."[72]

As usual, the "objective" press refused to call a lie a lie, preferring to stick to the he-said–she-said style that treats all claims, no matter how false or outrageous, as having equal value. When Ted Kennedy proposed repealing some of the provisions of the tax cut most targeted to the wealthy, this is how the "liberal" *Washington Post* described the disagreement: "Bush contends that canceling a scheduled tax cut is equivalent to a tax increase. Democrats dispute that, but Bush levels the charge regularly and with relish. 'I think raising taxes in the midst of a recession is wrong economic policy—it would be a huge mistake.'"[73] Note again that Bush lied in two ways here: first by claiming that repealing part of the tax cut that had yet to take effect is an increase and then by characterizing it as "in the midst of a recession." In fact, the provisions Kennedy proposed repealing weren't slated to take effect until 2004. Bush wanted people to believe that if Kennedy had his way, they would have to pay more on their next tax bill than they did on their last, a contention that was doubly false.

Conservative commentators received their RNC talking points and fell into line, even at the price of stunning intellectual dishonesty. George Will, describing the dispute in the *Washington Post,* said, "So this is Daschleized arithmetic: Your taxes under current law are X. Your taxes would be X plus Y under a new law repealing the older law. But the new law does not raise your taxes."[74] But in truth, Will's taxes are X, and if part of the tax cut were repealed they would remain X. There is no X plus Y.

---

[72] *Hardball*, January 7, 2002. Here is an example of Fineman's hard-hitting analysis of Bush: "He's the Texas Ranger of the World, and wants everyone to know it. He's the guy with the silver badge, issuing warnings to the cattle rustlers. He will cut deals when necessary—his history shows that—but, as a matter of inclination and strategy, he's the toughest talker on his team. So far, in the aftermath of Sept. 11, that stance has served him, and the country, well." ("George Walker, Texas Ranger," msnbc.com, February 13, 2002. Thanks to Josh Marshall's Talking Points Memo for pointing out this nugget.)

[73] Mike Allen and Helen Dewar, "Kennedy Urges Deferral of Some Tax Cuts," *Washington Post*, January 17, 2002, p. A4.

[74] George Will, "The Daschle Democrats," *Washington Post*, January 13, 2002, p. B7.

Everyone on the Republican team got into the "not cutting taxes is raising taxes" act. Here's Bush spokesman Ari Fleischer, attempting the same deception: "When you tell the American people that we promise you, and it's the law of the land, that you are going to have more money in your next paycheck, and then the Democrats say, 'We're going to take that money out of your paycheck' to the American people, that is nothing but a tax hike."[75] Notice how Fleischer talks about "your next paycheck" to deceive people into believing he's talking about their next paycheck and not tax changes scheduled to take effect years hence.

While the Bush administration was undertaking this particular deception, Republican National Committee chair Marc Racicot had the misfortune of appearing in a forum in which he could be quizzed about it repeatedly. On *Meet the Press*, host Tim Russert observed, as others had, that Florida Governor Jeb Bush had recently decided to delay a scheduled tax cut in order to balance his state's budget. Under repeated questioning by Russert, Racicot finally admitted that under the administration's logic Jeb was raising taxes. But once he was clear of the studio, Racicot had his office issue a press release saying, "I do not believe Gov. Bush supports any sort of tax increase."[76] Later, Tom Brokaw asked President Bush the same question, which Bush dodged by using the time-honored technique of answering a different question altogether:

> **Brokaw:** Some of your advisers here in the White House are saying to the Democrats on Capitol Hill, "If you defer the tax cuts we'd like to have, that's the same as a tax increase."
>
> **Bush:** Yeah.
>
> **Brokaw:** Will you say to Jeb, "Hey, if you defer, you're raising taxes in Florida?"
>
> **Bush:** No, what I'm going to say to him is that we've got different circumstances. One, I'm not—there's not a balanced budget amendment that constrains the federal government, and in times of war or national emergency or recession, we might run a deficit, and we will.[77]

---

[75] Elisabeth Bumiller, "If the Math's a Bit Fuzzy, the Politics Are Clear," *New York Times*, January 21, 2002, p. A11.

[76] William March, "Republican Rhetoric Deals Sharp Blow to Governor," *Tampa Tribune*, January 24, 2002.

[77] *NBC Nightly News*, January 23, 2002.

Jeb Bush was no doubt relieved to hear that he would not be accused by his brother of being a tax raiser. In making this case, the goal of the administration and its allies in the conservative commentariat was not simply to argue against repeal of any portion of the tax cut, but to take a lie (not cutting taxes is raising taxes) and present it as a matter of partisan contestation. Reporters know how to discuss partisan arguments: Democrats say this, Republicans say that. Where's the truth? It depends who you ask. In this frame all arguments are given equal weight, even if one is plainly untrue.

It is this convention of journalism—combined with the fact that most reporters are not only not policy experts but usually lacking in the time or inclination to do the research necessary to identify the truth of competing claims—that makes deception on policy disputes possible. George W. Bush understands only too well that if he says his tax plans are aimed at helping the middle class, the reporter's response is to find a Democrat to dispute the claim, not to simply observe that the claim is utter nonsense. The result is news that makes it nearly impossible for ordinary citizens to divine who is telling the truth.

Just how far will the Republicans go to help the ruling class avoid taxation? Consider this story. When the economy went south in 2001, Bush's Republican allies had the solution: a huge tax break for the biggest of corporations. Republicans in the House pushed through a "stimulus" bill that repealed the corporate alternative minimum tax, which sets a floor of taxes so that corporations can't use fancy accounting and shelters to avoid paying taxes on their profits. The sole purpose of the repeal was to allow corporations to avoid paying taxes.

But repealing the corporate alternative minimum tax wasn't enough for the Republicans. They actually passed a bill in the House repealing the tax *retroactively,* which would mean giving refunds to corporations for the taxes they had paid over the previous fifteen years. For instance, IBM, which the year before made nearly $6 billion in profits on which their highly competent accountants managed to ensure they would pay taxes of only 3.4 percent, would now receive a rebate check from the American taxpayer in the amount of $1.4 billion. Enron, which paid no taxes in four of the previous five years, would now get a check for $254 million. The total cost of the corporate giveaway would have been well over $200 billion in the first three years alone, which means that you, your next-door neighbor, the cashier down at your local supermarket, and every other American adult would have had to fork over nearly $1,000 so that General Motors wouldn't be subject to the onerous 1.5 percent they paid in federal income taxes the previous year (their refund check would have been $833 million).[78] At the same time, the Republicans were fighting Democratic efforts to extend unemployment benefits. "The model of thought that says we need to go out and extend unemployment benefits and health-insurance benefits and so forth," said House Majority Leader Dick Armey, "is not I think one that is commensurate with the American spirit here."[79] Giving a $254 million check to Enron, on the other hand, was apparently commensurate with House Republicans' particular view of the American spirit.

One corporate lobbyist pushing for the bill after September 11 argued that patriotism demanded an enormous corporate giveaway. "I wouldn't be doing the job—not necessarily for my clients" who included IBM and GE "but for my country if I wasn't being helpful in terms of offering ideas that can be helpful in stimulating the economy," said lobbyist Kenneth Kies.[80] The House-passed stimulus plan's alternative minimum tax repeal was so unconscionable that when political consultants held focus groups to gauge reaction to the plan and told people about its provisions, the people literally refused to believe it was being described accurately to them.[81]

---

[78] "House GOP 'Stimulus' Bill Offers 16 Large, Low-Tax Corporations $7.4 Billion in Instant Tax Rebates," Citizens for Tax Justice, October 26, 2001.

[79] Lizette Alvarez, "House Republican Leaders Balk at Any Help for Laid-Off Workers," New York Times, September 26, 2001, p. C6.

[80] Glenn Kessler and John Lancaster, "The Lobbyists behind the Stimulus Bill," Washington Post Weekly Edition, November 19-25, p. 13.

[81] Paul Krugman, "A No-Win Outcome," New York Times, December 21, 2001, p. A39.

Even some conservatives acknowledge the degree to which George W. Bush and the Republican party have adopted an ideology that revolves around the interests of corporations and the wealthy with a notable absence of principle underlying it. David Brooks, writing in the conservative *Weekly Standard,* recounted, "As the economy appeared to be slipping into recession, Republicans came up with a stimulus package that contained almost no conservative ideas. Indeed, it contained practically no ideas of any sort. It was just a collection of corporate pork, self-serving subsidies, and narrowly focused favors." Brooks argued that contemporary conservatism had ceased to be about ideas. "If politics is overtaken by the corporate mentality," he wrote, "then government just becomes a grubby enterprise of redistributing federal dollars from their people to our people."[82]

The Republican stance on taxes, like that on many issues, has the rhetorical advantage of simple-mindedness. From "Read my lips!" to "It's your money!" its articulation is sure to generate applause. We should recall that when George Bush Sr. broke his pledge never to raise taxes, he did so because he was confronted with the deficit his predecessor bequeathed to him, and he decided that of all the alternatives a tax increase was the least unpalatable. While it was unpopular, it was also the right thing to do. But the approach his son takes—that tax cuts are the answer to good times, bad times, and any times in between—is all about avoiding the hard choices of which real governing is made.

The combination of his economic policies and his antigovernment rhetoric indicate that George W. Bush seems to believe that generating huge budget deficits will starve government, hamstringing it for future endeavors. But as law professors Stephen Holmes and Cass Sunstein argue persuasively in their book *The Cost of Rights: Why Liberty Depends on Taxes,* all the rights enjoyed by people in a free society—particularly those valued so much by

---

[82] David Brooks, "The Problem With K Street Conservatism," *Weekly Standard,* June 24, 2002.

libertarians—have practical meaning *only* because government is there to protect them. Taxes are therefore not an affront to freedom, but the means by which freedom is sustained.[83] Your right to own property, for instance, depends on the government's willingness and ability to put out the fire burning in a house down the block, enforce the contract under which you gave money to the previous owner in the exchange for your house (evicting him if he refuses to leave), pay for the police and courts who deter burglars from stealing your television or your neighbor from driving his car through your front window when your daughter's music gets too loud, and prevent foreign armies from bivouacking in your living room and cleaning out your refrigerator. Since the electrical wires installed in the home have to conform to safety standards set by the government, your house is unlikely to burst into flames when you turn on a lamp. The value of your property is further enhanced by the fact that you can drive to it on a road built by the government and obtain water and dispose of sewage through pipes laid by the government. We all share in the cost of providing these protections and services by paying taxes.

Although most Americans understand this basic fact of life, at the same time nobody likes paying taxes, another fact of life Bush understands and exploits. He knows it isn't too tough to fool people when it comes to taxes, since they are so ready to be told they pay too much. For instance, about two out of every five of us believes that Americans pay more in taxes than Western Europeans do, when in fact tax rates in Western Europe are significantly higher.[84] Among the thirty industrialized countries of the Organization for Economic Cooperation and Development, twenty-seven had taxes making up a larger proportion of GDP than the United States in 2001, *before* the Bush tax cut took effect. Only Korea, Japan, and Mexico had lower taxes than the United States.[85]

---

[83] Stephan Holmes and Cass Sunstein, *The Cost of Rights: Why Liberty Depends on Taxes*. New York: W.W. Norton, 1999.
[84] Data from periodic polls conducted by the Pew Research Center for the People and the Press.
[85] Figures from Citizens for Tax Justice.

It takes no courage to tell people their taxes are too high. When the president says he's for "tax relief," the typical citizen responds, "Sounds good to me." As long as it doesn't feel like a lie and she remains ignorant of the fact that the tax cuts Bush wants have nothing to do with her, Bush can maintain her support. Bush's passion for cutting taxes for the wealthy is impossible to state forthrightly, for it would validate the criticisms of Democrats and alienate the vast majority of Americans. But changing the proposals themselves is out of the question, so Bush lies about them. He lies about who gets what, he lies about what the costs are, he lies about why he proposes what he does, and the press plays along by playing dumb, reporting each lie as a matter of he-said–she-said.

As Jonathan Chait observed, "Conservatives like to think of lying as a reflection of personal character that, almost by definition, has no bearing on public policy. Thus, misstating the cost of your mother-in-law's dog's medicine is evidence of pathological mendacity, but lying about who gets your tax cut is of no consequence at all."[86] So often, Bush has assured us of what an honest guy he is. But on the issue that is in some ways the most important of his presidency, when you consider the long-term consequences of the return to federal deficits, Bush's dishonesty has been simply mind-boggling.

It's hard to avoid the conclusion that as we begin the twenty-first century, Republicans just don't know how to manage the economy. Their devotion to tax cuts for the wealthy and corporations can only be described as faith-based—empirical evidence shows such cuts don't create the promised explosions of economic growth, yet they return to them again and again. During the presidency of Bill Clinton—the man who raised taxes on the wealthy—around twenty-two million new jobs were created. As of this writing, there have been approximately three million jobs lost under George W. Bush.[87] According to one analysis, for every dollar Bush has given in tax cuts, he has added $3.60 to the national debt—money we'll all have

---

[86] Jonathan Chait, "True Lies," *New Republic Online*, May 14, 2001.
[87] Figures from the Bureau of Labor Statistics through July 2003.

to pay back.[88] Absent an unprecedented explosion of job creation in the last few months of his term, Bush's economy will have fewer jobs at the end of his term than at the beginning, a feat not accomplished since the administration of Herbert Hoover.

Yet George W. Bush proclaims that we should not pass on our problems to other generations. He tells us that his tax cuts benefit those at the bottom of the economic ladder, that taxes on stock dividends are immoral double taxation and eliminating them is only meant to help senior citizens, that abolishing the inheritance tax is only meant to save family farms, and that anyone who objects to tax giveaways for the wealthy wants to raise taxes on ordinary people, every contention a lie. There is no goal that engenders greater passion and greater deception from the Bush White House than cutting taxes. And in one of their greatest gifts to the president, reporters refuse to sort the false from the true, as the public waits in vain to be guided through complex arguments toward understanding. Each year brings a new tax cut proposal, sure to be marketed as a means of helping those Americans most want to help. But the truth is that these tax cuts are invariably constructed to benefit of the richest among us. And the watchdogs of the press throw up their hands, hide yet again behind a "He Said/She Said" neutrality, and allow the latest round of tax deception to proceed unhindered.

[88] David Cay Johnston, "Studies Say Tax Cuts Now Will Bring Bigger Bill Later," *New York Times*, September 23, 2003, p. C2.

8.

Bushocracy

The New Face of Democracy

"Freedom is the nonnegotiable demand of human dignity."
—*George W. Bush, talking about other countries.*[1]

"There ought to be limits to freedom."
—*George W. Bush, talking about a website
that had made fun of him.*[2]

L ike any American politician, George W. Bush proclaims his fealty
to democracy. He exalts freedom, praises the framers, and cites
liberty as a precious value to which his commitment is steadfast. The
rhetoric is grand, but Bush's record paints are far less inspiring picture.
In fact, one need not look far to find democratic principles that have
come under assault from the Bush administration and its allies. Due
process, citizens' access to information, one-person-one-vote elections, checks and balances, government openness, the importance of
dissent, each has been denied and undermined at one time or another.
After all, Bush took power despite having lost the 2000 election, only
through the intercession of friendly Republican judges. Once that was

---

[1] From Bush's National Security Strategy issued September 2002; it may be read
here: www.whitehouse.gov/nsc/nss.html.
[2] Wayne Slater, "Federal Panel Declines to Regulate Web Site Satirizing Bush,"
Dallas Morning News, April 19, 2000, p. 7A.

accomplished with barely a bleat of protest from the opposition and nods of approval from the press Bush felt free to ignore the inconvenient reality of democracy whenever it suited his goals. And so the most dangerous part of the fraud may be what its success has done to democracy in America and threatens to do in the future.

"I worry about a regime that is closed and not transparent," said George W. Bush in 2002.[3] When Bush spoke these words, he was actually talking about the government of North Korea, but he might well have been describing his own. Since it took power, the Bush administration has been quite open about the fact that they believe the powers and privileges of the executive branch have eroded over recent decades, and they intend to do all they can to restore them. But along with telling Congress and the judiciary to go away at every available opportunity, the administration has undertaken an attack on the very idea of openness in government. Bush understands well what James Madison warned, that, "Knowledge will forever govern ignorance; and a people who mean to be their own governors must arm themselves with the power which knowledge gives."[4] He has apparently decided that his work depends on keeping Americans ignorant. Though he proclaimed May 1, 2003 to be "Loyalty Day," urging Americans to pledge their blind allegiance to the government, when Americans ask what that government is up to, Bush's reply is, None of your business.

One way he has endeavored to hide the truth from Americans is by undermining our principal impediment to government secrecy, the Freedom of Information Act. FOIA was enacted in 1966 and then strengthened in 1975 in the wake of Watergate and the revelations of the myriad ways the Nixon administration abused its power and misused federal agencies. At the urging of his aides Dick Cheney and Donald Rumsfeld, Gerald Ford vetoed the bill, but Congress overrode the veto and the strengthened FOIA became law.[5]

Although there are many exemptions—information about national security issues, trade secrets, and law enforcement

[3] Elisabeth Bumiller, "Bush Says the U.S. Plans No Attack on North Korea," *New York Times*, February 20, 2002, p. A1.
[4] James Madison, letter to W.T. Barry, August 4, 1822.
[5] Bruce Shapiro, "Restoring the Imperial Presidency," Salon.com, June 17, 2002.

operations, to name a few—FOIA directs the federal government to produce information about its activities to any citizen who requests it. If you want a list of how much money was spent on each national park or which companies have been fined by the EPA or what the latest Transportation Department rules on highway construction are, all you have to do is ask.

To put it simply, there are few federal laws that go more to the heart of democracy than FOIA. It is based on a simple proposition: the people have a right to know what their government is up to. If any citizen—a journalist, a scholar, or just an ordinary person—asks the government for a report it produced or data it gathered, the government has to hand it over. If no one would be harmed by the release of the information—even if it proves embarrassing to the government—we the people have a right to see it.

In practice, government agencies have plenty of room to move under FOIA. The primary way they get away with withholding information is through delay. Anyone who has tried filing an FOIA request knows that even before the Bush administration came to town, prying information from the federal government could be a daunting task. Agencies would delay filling the requests for weeks, months, and even years. Often it took the threat of a lawsuit to get them to cough up information.

Nonetheless, previous administrations at least made some attempt to live up to the spirit of the law. The standard used by the Clinton administration was that documents would be withheld from the public only if disclosure would be harmful. That seems reasonable enough—it protects the public's right to know what the government is up to but allows the government to withhold information whose release would be dangerous.

But after September 11, Bush and his advisers saw an opportunity to take a buzzsaw to FOIA. In an October 12, 2001 memo distributed to all executive agencies, Attorney General John Ashcroft turned the Clinton-administration position on its head. Under the new rules, federal employees were instructed to stonewall any and all requests for information. "When you carefully consider FOIA requests and decide to withhold records, in whole or in part," Ashcroft wrote, "you can be assured that the Department of Justice will defend your decisions unless they lack a sound legal basis."[6] In other words, if you can find *any* reason that is legal to withhold any and all documents from the American people, Ashcroft said, the Justice Department will back you up.

But having his Attorney General instruct the entire executive branch to undermine the spirit of the Freedom of Information Act wasn't enough. Three weeks later, Bush decided to repeal the Presidential Records Act with an executive order. This law, passed in 1978, provides that all presidential records (excepting those involving national security) will become open for public inspection twelve years after a president leaves office. Why was Bush so concerned about gutting the act? For starters, the twelve years had expired on the Reagan presidency, meaning that records of the Reagan administration's actions—including those of Bush administration officials such as Colin Powell and budget director Mitch Daniels, as well as Bush's father—would have to be released to journalists and historians. Executive Order 13233 put a stop to that. It provided that in order for a presidential record to be released, the former president *and* the sitting president had to give their permission. The Executive Order also granted the same privilege to vice presidents, something Dick Cheney was no doubt pleased about. Among other things, the order would require a citizen (or journalist, or historian) who wanted to view the records to show a "compelling" need, an extraordinarily high legal standard that if accepted by the courts would make it virtually impossible to gain access to presidential records, regardless of their content. Like many of his predecessors, President Bush, who endlessly proclaimed "I trust the people" during his campaign for office, appears to believe that the people can simply not be trusted to know what the president does, even twelve years after he does it. While the move would be grossly undemocratic at any time,

[6] "Washington Dateline," Associated Press, November 15, 2001.

it was particularly insulting at a time when Americans were being told that they must wage war in the name of freedom.

Interestingly enough, the executive order was written by Brett Kavanaugh, a White House lawyer who, when he worked for Independent Counsel Kenneth Starr, fought an effort by Bill Clinton to keep his aide Bruce Lindsey from having to testify before Starr's grand jury. Starr and Kavanaugh argued that Clinton's effort to invoke a "deliberative process" privilege was nonsense. Now that a Republican was in the White House, Kavanaugh enshrined that privilege in an executive order.[7]

The administration's public-relations strategy in defending this assault on public knowledge could be termed the Full Orwell. Press secretary Ari Fleischer said that as a result of the executive order, "more information will be forthcoming."[8] White House counsel Alberto Gonzales wrote an op-ed saying, "This order ensures expeditious disclosure of documents to provide historians, scholars and the public valuable insights into the way our government works."[9] This was simply not true. Less information is not more information, and greater secrecy is not expeditious disclosure.

This was not the first time Bush tried to keep the public from accessing information about his activities. When Bush left the Texas governor's mansion, he undertook a similar effort to keep records from his governorship away from the light of day. He ordered his records sent to his father's presidential library at Texas A&M University, where they would be under the control of Bush loyalists and out of the reach of Texas's Public Information Act, which would allow the citizens of Texas to learn what Bush had done while in office. The administrators of the library at A&M promptly declared their belief that Texas law didn't apply to them, and so no one could see the records.[10] While he was still governor,

---

[7] Russ Baker, "What Are They Hiding?" *The Nation*, February 25, 2002, p. 11.
[8] Elisabeth Bumiller, "Bush Keeps a Grip on Presidential Papers," *New York Times*, November 2, 2001, p. A22.
[9] Alberto Gonzalez, "Freedom, Openness, and Presidential Papers," *Washington Post*, December 20, 2001, p. A43.
[10] Alison Leigh Cowan, "Battling Over Records of Bush's Governorship," *New York Times*, February 11, 2002.

Bush also tried to muzzle any Texas A&M professors who might consider criticizing him or his father. After one professor made a critical comment about his father's speaking ability, the university received calls from Bush's staff. The university promptly sent out an email threatening that anyone from the George Bush School of Government and Public Service who was quoted saying anything that could "cause embarrassment to the Bush family" could be terminated.[11]

SECRETS AND LIES

Bush's efforts to eviscerate the Freedom of Information Act and the Presidential Records Act demonstrate more than his Nixonian love of secrecy. They highlight the antidemocratic leitmotiv running through his presidency. Bush seems to view democracy as an annoyance, something to be circumvented, restrained, and avoided. The head of the nonpartisan General Accounting Office said in 2002 that the Bush administration was less forthcoming with information and responses to congressional inquiries than any he could recall.[12]

This feeling may have been in part a result of the administration's efforts to keep the GAO from learning exactly who met with Vice President Cheney as he was formulating the administration's energy policy. In this effort, Cheney sought the input of a wide variety of corporate executives, from the coal industry to the oil industry to the electricity industry, and took time out of his busy schedule to have a private meeting with three top officials from Enron.[13] It was little surprise; when Bush assembled an energy-advisory committee early in his term, sixty-two of the sixty-three members of the committee had ties to corporate energy interests.[14] The GAO eventually sued to get the list of Cheney's meetings—not

---

[11] John Kirsch, "Faculty Fears Family Control of Bush School," *Dallas Morning News*, August 22, 1999, p. 49A.

[12] Adam Clymer, "Justice Dept. Balks at Effort to Study Antiterror Powers," *New York Times*, August 15, 2002, p. A21.

[13] Judy Pasternak, "Bush's Energy Plan Bares Industry Clout," *Los Angeles Times*, August 26, 2001, p. A1.

[14] "The Bottom Line," *Mother Jones*, September/October 2003, p. 53.

notes of the meetings or anything about what was discussed but just a list of who got the vice president's ear. Cheney fought the GAO's request every step of the way, arguing that requiring him to tell the public whom he was meeting with would limit his ability to get "unvarnished advice."[15]

In other words, it would be impossible for the vice president to get unvarnished advice from oil-company executives if the public knew he was meeting with oil-company executives. If nothing else, this argument is an admission that there is something fishy going on. Think about it this way: if someone had a legitimate case to make to the administration on a matter of policy, why would they be afraid to have the public know they were talking to the administration? And if the administration had a good reason to listen to them, why would they be afraid to have the public know they were listening? If the Sierra Club, say, lobbies the government on the Arctic National Wildlife Refuge, they'll walk right up to the cameras afterward and say, We told the administration why we think it's a bad idea to drill for oil in ANWR. The question keeps coming up: just what was Dick Cheney trying so hard to hide?

Cheney was fortunate enough to have the GAO's case heard by U.S. District Judge John Bates, who had worked for Ken Starr's Whitewater inquiry and had given $1,000 to the 2000 Bush-Cheney campaign, then was rewarded with a lifetime appointment to the federal bench.[16] Bates, who had successfully argued that notes of conversations between Hillary Clinton and her attorneys should be turned over to a grand jury, ruled emphatically that Congress had no right to ask whom Cheney had met with and threw out the case. Under pressure from the White House and congressional Republicans (a number of whom attempted to blackmail the GAO by threatening to cut the agency's budget if it didn't drop the suit), the GAO eventually decided to drop its appeal.[17]

---

[15] *This Week*, ABC, January 27, 2002.
[16] "Closing the Door: Bush Acts to Restrict Information," *Seattle Times*, March 3, 2002, p. A3.
[17] Peter Brand and Alexander Bolton, "GOP Threats Halted GAO Cheney Suit," *The Hill*, February 19, 2003.

Given this record of secrecy over matters weighty and trivial, it should have been no surprise that one of the greatest tragedies in American history was greeted by the Bush administration with unceasing efforts to clamp down on information and keep anyone from asking questions that might yield discomforting answers. At every step, the Bush administration has acted to prevent investigating agencies from looking too deeply into the intelligence failures that allowed September 11 to occur, and failing that, to keep whatever is found from reaching the public. In January of 2002, both Bush and Dick Cheney strongly implied to Democratic Senate leader Tom Daschle that if Democrats pressed for public hearings on September 11, the administration would accuse them of hampering the war on terrorism.[18] When the congressional intelligence committees finally completed the results of their investigation, they found that the administration had "reclassified" testimony and information that had been public; even Porter Goss, the Republican chairman of the House Intelligence Committee, called dealing with the White House's efforts to hide information from the public "horrendously frustrating."[19]

The administration went so far as to expressly forbid congressional committees investigating intelligence failures related to September 11 from revealing who in the White House was briefed about matters relating to al-Qaeda by classifying the identities of those who had gotten the information—even the president. CIA director George Tenet told the committee that what the president knew and when he knew it could not be revealed, even if the information itself was public: "The president's knowledge of intelligence information relevant to this inquiry remains classified," Tenet said, "even when the substance of that intelligence information has been declassified."[20] Let's be clear about this: there is absolutely no

---

[18] Brian Montopoli, "Schlep to Judgment," *Washington Monthly*, September 2003, p. 38.

[19] Michael Isikoff and Mark Hosenball, "The Secrets of September 11," *Newsweek* Web exclusive, April 30, 2003.

[20] John Prados, "'Slow-Walked and Stonewalled,'" *Bulletin of the Atomic Scientists*, March 1, 2003, p. 28.

legitimate national-security reason for hiding the identities of administration officials who received certain information. The information itself might or might not reveal "sources and methods" of intelligence gathering, but once the information itself is public there is no reason to keep who got it a secret, particularly when we're talking about the president. Except, of course, the big reason: avoiding embarrassment. And this is a prime reason many documents are classified in the first place; no secret is guarded more closely by the government than the fact that terrible mistakes were made. The famous "Pentagon Papers" case, in which the Nixon administration tried to prevent the *New York Times* and *Washington Post* from publishing leaked documents, was over a history of the Vietnam War, revealing what a mess the government had made of things.

So what exactly is Bush trying to hide when it comes to September 11? The obvious answer is anything that might suggest that they should have done more to prevent the attacks. In addressing the question, National Security Adviser Condoleezza Rice told reporters a number of falsehoods to define the administration's ignorance as understandable. First, she said, "I don't think anybody could have predicted that these people would…try to use a hijacked airplane as a missile."[21] But the fact is, in 1994 French authorities foiled a plot by Islamic radicals to ram a hijacked plane into the Eiffel Tower, an incident Rice was surely aware of.[22] And Italian officials received information about the possibility of such an attack by al-Qaeda at the G8 economic summit in Genoa, which President Bush attended, which is why anti-aircraft batteries were placed at the Genoa airport and the airspace over the meeting site was closed.[23] (Rice is fond of this technique—dismiss your failures through professions of widespread ignorance. She recently argued that the reconstruction of Iraq was more complicated than the administration had predicted because they were fooled by nice pictures into thinking Saddam Hussein wasn't such a bad guy: "If there was

---

[21] *All Things Considered*, NPR, May 16, 2002.
[22] *NBC Nightly News*, September 30, 2001.
[23] "Italy Says It Closed Airspace During G-8 Because of Airborne Threat against Bush," Associated Press, September 26, 2001.

something that was really underestimated, it was how really awful
Saddam Hussein was to his own people," she said. "I know it's hard
to believe that you could underestimate that, but when you look at
an infrastructure that looked gleaming, if you looked at pictures of
Baghdad—but when you think about it, it was pictures of presidential palaces—and you look instead at the living conditions of people
in Basra or in Sadr City; if you look at the fact that the electrical
power grid was serving really only 50 percent of the country; if you
look at the fact that there were large parts of the country with no
sewage, yes, this is a hard task.")[24]

More to the point, a 1999 government study warned that Osama
Bin Laden might send "suicide bombers belonging to al-Qaeda's Martyrdom Brigade [to] crash-land an aircraft…into the Pentagon, the
headquarters of the Central Intelligence Agency (CIA) or the White
House."[25] So somebody predicted it—Bush's national-security team
just didn't pay attention. When the Bush team took office in January
2001, Clinton National Security Adviser Sandy Berger arranged a
series of ten briefings for his successor and her staff. He told Condoleezza Rice, "I believe that the Bush administration will spend more
time on terrorism generally, and on al-Qaeda specifically, than any
other subject." The Clinton team handed the Bush team a comprehensive plan years in the making to attack al-Qaeda. It included covert
actions in Afghanistan, going after their financial resources, working
with countries where the terrorist network was active—almost exactly
the steps the Bush administration would finally get around to taking
after September 11. The Bush team ignored the plan. Their aversion to
doing anything recommended by the Clinton administration would
prove disastrous. Instead of implementing the Clinton plan, Bush
assigned Dick Cheney to lead the administration's efforts on terrorism
and to start from scratch and come up with an entirely new strategy. It
came to nothing.[26]

---

[24] Al Kamen, "Faith-Based Initiative," *Washington Post*, September 10, 2003, p.
A17.
[25] Tony Allen-Mills, "Bush Hit by New Claim of Hijack Alert," *Sunday Times of
London*, May 19, 2002.
[26] Michael Elliot, "They Had a Plan," *Time*, August 12, 2002, p. 28.

When it was revealed that on August 6, 2001—one month before September 11—Bush had received an intelligence briefing in which he was told that Osama Bin Laden was planning to hijack airplanes, Condoleezza Rice told the press the briefing was only about attacks overseas. But it turned out that this, too, was a lie—the title of the briefing memo given to Bush was "Bin Laden Determined to Strike in U.S."[27] It was later reported that American Predator drone airplanes had spotted Osama Bin Laden on three separate occasions prior to September 11—but Bush never gave an order to go after the al-Qaeda leader.

The White House then fell back on charging that by raising questions, Democrats were doing Bin Laden's bidding. Communications Director Dan Bartlett said the Democrats' questions "are exactly what our opponents, our enemies, want us to do."[28] Bartlett's Freudian slip—conflating "opponents," i.e., the opposition party, with "enemies," i.e., terrorists, reveals the Bush you're-either-with-us-or-with-the-terrorists perspective.

Meanwhile, the National Republican Congressional Committee compiled and circulated a list of votes by Democrats opposing weapons systems, for use in bludgeoning them into silence.[29] On CNN, pundit Bob Novak followed orders, listing some of New York Congressman Jerrold Nadler's votes and then asking Nadler whether he had "disqualified [himself] to speak on national security."[30] In other words, only people who agree with the Republican position on the size of the military budget should be allowed to speak on national security.

For more than a year, Bush fought the creation of an independent commission to investigate the intelligence failures that led to September 11. At one point, members of the House and Senate intelligence committees thought they had worked out the details of the commission so it could be added to the intelligence authorization bill but found out

---

[27] Bob Woodward and Dan Eggen, "Aug. Memo Warned of Attacks within U.S." *Washington Post*, May 19, 2002, p. A1.
[28] Dan Balz, "Bush and GOP Defend White House Response," *Washington Post*, May 18, 2002, p. A1.
[29] Elisabeth Bumiller, "Bush and His Aides Accuse Democrats of Second-Guessing," *New York Times*, May 18, 2002, p. A1.
[30] CNN *Crossfire*, May 17, 2002.

that the White House had instructed the Republican House leadership to prevent the commission from coming to the floor, effectively killing it.[31] After families of the September 11 victims finally shamed him into it, Bush signed on to the creation of the commission but appointed Henry Kissinger—not exactly the first person one thinks of when the goal is to expose government mistakes and wrongdoing—to be its chair. When the commission's work finally got underway, investigators were stymied by the Justice Department's insistence that any interviews of government officials be watched over by a "minder," either the interviewee's boss or someone else from their agency.[32] If this sounds familiar, it's because the same technique was used by Saddam Hussein to intimidate scientists being interviewed by UN weapons inspectors. The commission investigating the intelligence failures leading up to the greatest crime in American history was initially funded with a pathetic $3 million—a fraction of the $7 million spent to investigate Whitewater, and less even than the $5 million Congress spent on studying the effects of casino gambling.[33]

Although Kissinger pulled out of the commission when it became apparent he would have to reveal which foreign governments he advises (who knows who was on that list), he was not the only character with a checkered past Bush appointed to an important post. Take Elliot Abrams, who spent much of his time in the Reagan administration defending the brutal human-rights record of the dictatorships Reagan's government was propping up in Central and South America. Abrams pleaded guilty to perjury before Congress but was pardoned by Bush's father. George W. hired him to work on the National Security Council, in charge of democracy and human-rights issues. Bush also brought in John Poindexter, who was convicted of lying to Congress over the Iran-Contra affair (his conviction was reversed because of his immunity agreement), to run the "Total Information Awareness" effort, an

[31] Helen Dewar, "House GOP Stops 9/11 Probe Plan," *Washington Post*, October 11, 2002, p. A14.

[32] Press conference with Tom Kean and Lee Hamilton, cochairs of the 9/11 commission, Washington, DC, July 8, 2003.

[33] The funding was later increased to a still inadequate $11 million. Brian Montopoli, "Schlep to Judgment," *Washington Monthly*, September 2003, pp. 38–43.

Orwellian initiative to spy on each and every American. As Poindexter's résumé (temporarily posted on a government website) says, he "brings a unique blend of experience to problems from the highest levels of government to the laboratory...Noted for creative solutions to difficult issues." You can't argue with his unique blend of experience and creativity—how many people can say they've sold arms to terrorists, then used the money to finance an illegal war in Central America while lying to Congress about it?

Although the fact that Bush gave Abrams and Poindexter positions of power was brazen, it shouldn't have been too surprising. It was only further demonstration of the Bush administration's contempt for the American people and their elected representatives. If the people cannot be trusted to assent to the government's every move, they must simply be lied to.[34]

There is, however, one exception to the Bush administration's principle of executive secrecy: records that could embarrass Bill Clinton. Though they defend to the death Dick Cheney's right to get frank advice from oil-company executives by keeping secret even the executives' identities, they quickly released to a congressional committee transcripts of a conversation between Clinton and Israeli Prime Minister Ehud Barak in which the two discussed the pardon of Marc Rich, after which the transcripts were promptly leaked to the press. According to congressional staffers and Clinton officials, as far as anyone knew it was the first time *in history* a transcript of a conversation between a president and a foreign leader had been released to the public. When former Clinton staffers realized that further transcripts of conversations between Clinton and Barak provided context that would place the leaked discussion in a more benign light, they petitioned for the release of those transcripts as well. Bush's White House refused—only the transcript that painted Clinton in the worst possible light would be released. The Bush administration also released thousands of email messages from senior Clinton administration officials.[35]

---

[34] David Greenberg made this point in "Back, But Not by Popular Demand," *Washington Post*, December 8, 2002, p. B1.
[35] Joshua Micah Marshall, "Bush's Executive Privilege Two-Step," Salon.com, February 7, 2002.

ONE PERSON, ONE VOTE...OR THEREABOUTS

It should not be surprising that a president so disdainful of the principle of open government would look on what most people regard as the basis of democracy—the principle of one person, one vote—with mixed feelings. As the 2000 election approached, many analysts began to predict the possibility that George W. Bush would win the popular vote but Al Gore would win the electoral vote. "The race remains neck and neck with the growing possibility that George W. Bush could win the popular vote but lose the electoral vote to Al Gore," said the *Boston Globe*.[36] The *Christian Science Monitor*'s analysis was the same: "This year, the presidential race is so quirkily close that it's possible one candidate, George W. Bush (R), could win the popular vote, and another, Al Gore (D), could win in the Electoral College."[37] "The scenario runs something like this," wrote the *Atlanta Constitution*. "Gore scores an electoral victory based on wins in a handful of states....Bush loses out in the Electoral College, but actually gets more votes nationally."[38] Naturally, Republicans asked about such a possibility considered it an injustice of the highest order. "I think there would be an outrage," said Republican Congressman Ray LaHood of Illinois,[39] whose own outrage was oddly muted when his party's candidate turned out to be the one who benefited.

Some reports said the Bush campaign was planning to fight it out in the court of public opinion if they lost the electoral vote while winning the popular vote. According to the *New York Daily News*, "A massive talk-radio operation would be encouraged...'We'd have ads, too,' says an anonymous Bush aide."[40] When asked about the article

---

[36] "Campaign 2000: The Daily Fix," *Boston Globe,* November 6, 2000, p. A23.
[37] "The Last, Frenzied Push for Votes," *Christian Science Monitor*, November 6, 2000, p. A1.
[38] Bob Deans, "Electoral Shock: Winning the Most Votes Doesn't Guarantee the White House," *Atlanta Journal and Constitution*, November 5, 2000, p. 1F.
[39] Bob Deans, "Electoral Shock: Winning the Most Votes Doesn't Guarantee the White House," *Atlanta Journal and Constitution*, November 5, 2000, p. 1F.
[40] Michael Kramer, "Bush Set to Fight an Electoral College Loss," *New York Daily News*, November 1, 2000, p. 6.

after the election, Karl Rove denied it, saying the possibility of a campaign to persuade electors to vote for Bush "was never discussed. It may have been discussed at a higher level of the campaign, like the interns and the mail room clerks, but I never heard it discussed until I read it in the newspaper."[41] But others dispute Rove's account. CNN analyst Jeff Greenfield reported that "at least two conservative commentators were specifically briefed by the Bush campaign shortly before taking to the airwaves about the line of attack to be taken in the event that Bush wound up losing the electoral count despite a popular vote lead." Kenneth Duberstein, who served as the elder George Bush's White House Chief of Staff, said, "It was part of the talking points."[42]

When election night ended with Al Gore winning the popular vote but George W. Bush poised to win the electoral vote, Republicans rediscovered their love of the Electoral College. A number actually argued that Bush's claim to legitimacy could be supported by the fact that the landmass covered by the counties Bush won comprised a greater total acreage than that of the counties Gore won, quite possibly the most bizarre argument offered on any detail of the 2000 election.[43]

One might have thought the fact that for the fourth time in American history a presidential candidate took the White House despite losing the popular vote would have initiated a lively debate on the wisdom of the Electoral College (the others were John Quincy Adams in 1824, Rutherford B. Hayes in 1876, and Benjamin Harrison in 1888). Unfortunately, that debate never took place. But in assessing the Bush presidency one can hardly avoid the topic, since Bush owes his ascension to this anachronism with no analogue in any of the world's democracies.

---

[41] Kathleen Hall Jamieson and Paul Waldman (eds.), *Electing the President 2000: The Insiders' View*. Philadelphia: University of Pennsylvania Press, 2001.

[42] Jeff Greenfield, *Oh Waiter! One Order of Crow!* New York: Putnam, 2001, p. 14.

[43] Senator Mitch McConnell made this ridiculous case in the introduction he wrote to *Securing Democracy: Why We Have an Electoral College* by Gary Gregg (Wilmington, DE: ISI Books, 2001), a book whose title, oddly enough, was not meant ironically.

The most common argument made in favor of the Electoral College is that it forces candidates to travel the country, seeking support from a variety of regions and people. If it were abolished, it is thought, candidates would ignore small states and spend all their time in California and New York, piling up votes where they are concentrated. Hardly a compelling argument, particularly when we saw how much time Bush and Gore spent stumping in North Dakota and Rhode Island (none). What the Electoral College actually forces candidates to do is visit only those states where the polls show a tight race. Other states—whether large or small—are ignored.

Although some happen to be blessed (or cursed, depending on your perspective) to live in a "battleground" state, most Americans were snubbed by the candidates in 2000. One out of four Americans lives in California, New York, or Texas, but they were largely disregarded because state polls showed one candidate with a clear lead. There were fifteen states—including most of the country's small states—where neither Bush, Gore, Cheney, nor Lieberman showed up even a single time during the general election. In contrast, between July 1 and election day the candidates and their running mates visited the states of Florida, Pennsylvania, and Michigan a combined total of 107 times (Pennsylvania was the champ, drawing 39 visits).[44] The election of 2004 will be no different—the same states will get attention, and the same states will be ignored.

When it was written, the American Constitution was an extraordinary document, yet one that was deeply flawed with a number of undemocratic provisions. Over time, the Constitution was amended to make democracy more real, yet the Electoral College managed to escape the corrective impulse. Even if the arguments in favor of the Electoral College were not based on false premises, it would still be incompatible with democracy. There is simply no more fundamental principle to democratic elections

---

[44] Based on records of candidate visits compiled by the Associated Press.

than the idea that the person who gets more votes wins. If you don't believe in that principle, you don't believe in democracy. Anyone would acknowledge that an election in which everyone had one vote but people who have red hair get two votes could not be called democratic. But in the American system, people who live in small states have their votes count for more than people who live in large states because the number of electoral votes is determined by the number of representatives and senators each state has. Wyoming's 500,000 people get two electoral votes from their two senators, but so do California's 35 million people. The Electoral College has no other purpose but to circumvent the will of the people. In 2000 it operated exactly as it was intended by the framers, as a failsafe by which wise men could overrule the unwashed masses if they elected the wrong person. When the Electoral College winner and the vote winner are the same candidate, it is irrelevant; only when the Electoral College overrules the will of the people has it done what it was designed to do.

Even if it had not made it possible for him to take power, it would be unsurprising that George W. Bush has no problem with the Electoral College, since the principle of one person–one vote—that every American has an equal right to elect their leaders—is not a value to which he seems particularly committed. One of Bush's first official acts was to have the "No Taxation without Representation" license plates removed from the presidential limousine, which Bill Clinton had installed in support of the District of Columbia's efforts to secure voting rights for its citizens.[45] This might seem like a trivial matter, but Bush's opposition to congressional voting rights for the residents of the District of Columbia—an opposition he shares with most Republicans who hold power—shows that his commitment to democracy is less than complete.

This is not a complicated issue. You cannot simultaneously oppose congressional representation for the 572,000 Americans

---

[45] Robert Pierre, "Bush Will Not Keep 'Taxation' Car Tags," *Washington Post*, January 20, 2001, p. B4.

who live in the District of Columbia and say that you favor democracy. The two positions are fundamentally incompatible. Unsurprisingly, the American public believes democracy demands representation for D.C. A 1999 poll found that three out of four Americans support congressional representation for D.C.[46] Many Republicans oppose it because if the residents of D.C. were allowed representation in Congress, they would likely elect Democrats. If you favor democracy only when you like the way people vote, then you don't favor democracy.

But preventing people from voting is a critical part of Republican election strategy. After the 2000 election, a group of Republican congressional staffers met to devise strategies to prevent African-Americans and people who belonged to labor unions from voting, the latest in a long line of Republican "ballot security" efforts. One McCain aide disgusted at the effort said sarcastically, "We could poll-tax them. And giving them shitty voting machines seems to be the latest tactic."[47] In 2002, as in years past, there were reports from all over the country of efforts by Republicans to prevent African-Americans from voting. In Baltimore, flyers turned up in black neighborhoods telling people that they couldn't vote if they had any unpaid parking tickets or overdue rent.[48] In Arkansas, Republican poll workers confronted African-American voters, demanding to see identification and photographing them.[49] In Tennessee, GOP poll-watchers were instructed to raise objections to any voter who had registered by motor-voter.[50] In the run-off election to determine the winner of Louisiana's Senate race, residents of predominately African-American public-housing projects found flyers on their doors reading, "Vote!!! Bad Weather? No problem!!! If the weather is uncomfortable on election day (Saturday December 7th) Remember

[46] Spencer Hsu, "Voting-Rights Lobbying Blitz Staged in DC," *Washington Post*, May 16, 2002, p. B7.

[47] Roger Simon, *Divided We Stand*. New York: Crown, 2001, pp. 301–2.

[48] Craig Whitlock and Martin Weil, "Plan to Hire Poll Workers Upsets GOP," *Washington Post*, November 4, 2002, p. B4.

[49] Gail Russell Chaddock, "As Vote Arrives, Lawyers Are Ready," *Christian Science Monitor*, November 4, 2002, p. 1.

[50] Chris Joyner, "Warning on Voter Harassment Issued," *Chattanooga Times/Free Press*, November 5, 2002.

you can wait and cast your ballot on Tuesday December 10th," which, of course, they couldn't. [51]

And of course, we should not forget that his brother Jeb and his campaign cochair Katherine Harris made George W. Bush's "victory" in Florida in 2000 possible by contracting with a corporation called Database Technologies to create a "scrub list" of alleged "ex-felons," 57,700 of whom were removed from Florida's voter rolls. The company made no effort to verify if the people on its scrub lists were actually the same people who had committed crimes: if the name, race, and birth date matched or even *nearly* matched someone on the list, they were tossed off the rolls. Database Technologies offered to conduct a more thorough check of things like address histories, but Harris's office told them it was unnecessary. [52] The vast majority of those "scrubbed" were perfectly eligible to vote—some had committed only misdemeanors; some had committed a felony in another state (and were thus still eligible to vote in Florida); and some had the misfortune of having a name, age, and race similar to someone who had once committed a crime. A disproportionate number of these wrongly disenfranchised voters were African-Americans, who arrived at the polls on November 7, 2000, to learn that they would not be allowed to vote. By 2002, Database Technologies admitted that all but 3,000 people on the scrub list (which actually held 94,000 names) should not have had their voting rights taken away. As a company official testified after the election, the Florida state government told them to scrub anyone whose name was a 90 percent match of a felon's name. When the company objected that such a standard would result in the mistaken elimination of many legitimate voters, the state responded by ordering them to go to an 80 percent match. [53] In response to a suit by the NAACP, the state of Florida finally agreed to fix the list—but held off doing so until after the 2002 election, when Jeb Bush was safely reelected. [54]

---

[51] Lee Hockstader and Adam Nossiter, "GOP Outmaneuvered in La. Runoff," *Washington Post*, December 9, 2002, p. A4.

[52] Greg Palast, "The Great Florida Ex-Con Game," *Harper's*, March 1, 2002, p. 48.

[53] Greg Palast, *The Best Democracy Money Can Buy*. New York: Plume, 2003, p. 58-59.

[54] Greg Palast, "Jeb Bush's Secret Weapon," Salon.com, November 1, 2002.

It is little exaggeration to say that Jeb Bush and Katherine Harris used the scrub list to steal the 2000 election for George W. Bush. The story was uncovered by investigative reporter Greg Palast, who found the American media profoundly uninterested in exploring one of the most consequential voter frauds in American history. When he gave information to CBS News in the hope they would do their own reporting on it, he was told by a producer, "I'm sorry, but your story didn't hold up." And how did CBS know? "We called Jeb Bush's office." And that was that.[55] "Given the outcome of our work in Florida," a spokesman for the company that conducted the scrub later said, "and with a new president in place, we think our services will expand across the country."[56]

GETTING DIRTY ABOUT RACE

To those familiar with the Republican party's complicated history on the topic of race, it was hardly surprising. That history came uncomfortably to the fore in late 2002, when Trent Lott was driven from the Senate leadership after proclaiming at Strom Thurmond's one hundredth birthday party, "I want to say this about my state: when Strom Thurmond ran for president we voted for him. We're proud of it. And if the rest of the country had of followed our lead we wouldn't have had all these problems over all these years, either." Thurmond's 1948 presidential campaign can be fairly well summed up in this statement: "There's not enough troops in the Army to force the Southern people to admit the nigra race into our theaters, into our swimming pools, into our homes and into our churches!"[57] Although Lott's remarks eventually became a major story once he received criticism from fellow conservatives, reactionary politics on the right tends to be greeted with a shrug.

---

[55] Greg Palast, "Silence of the Media Lambs," Tompaine.com, May 24, 2001.

[56] Greg Palast, *The Best Democracy Money Can Buy*. New York: Plume, 2003, p. 29. Archives of Palast's extraordinary reporting on this topic may be found at www.gregpalast.com.

[57] Most transcriptions of this speech politely use the word "negro," while many who have heard it insist the word Thurmond used was "nigger." Although he speaks the word quickly, based on my own hearing I believe that "nigra" is the most likely suspect. Readers who would like to hear Thurmond's speech for themselves can visit http://discover.npr.org/features/feature.jhtml?wfId=865900.

Lott himself had years before heaped praise on the Council of Conservative Citizens, a successor to the notorious White Citizens Councils, known colloquially as the "uptown Klan" (speaking at their national convention in 1992, Lott said, "The people in this room stand for the right principles and the right philosophy"[58]); that history presented no threat to his spot in the Republican leadership. The ever-growing dominance of the Republican party by ultra-conservative Southerners like Lott, Tom DeLay, and George W. Bush (who although he was born in Connecticut has the fervor of the converted when it comes to public displays of Southernness) has over time made this ideology appear to reporters to be mainstream, while liberal Democrats are characterized as extremists whose ideology places them outside "real" Americans. But when John Ashcroft lauds the magazine *Southern Partisan*—a neoconfederate journal that regularly defends slavery and praises the KKK—by saying it "helps set the record straight" about the old South, it is considered par for the course for a conservative.[59]

Despite his peculiarly Southern outlook, Trent Lott is never referred to as a "Mississippi conservative." If a liberal comes from a place that votes reliably Democratic, on the other hand, his home is used to portray him as an outsider. Consider the evaluations made of Senator John Kerry as he entered the 2004 presidential race. "He lends himself to caricature as the haughty Massachusetts liberal," said the *New York Times*.[60] On CNN, Kate O'Beirne said Kerry sounds "like a left-wing Massachusetts liberal."[61] Sean Hannity asked William Bennett, "Does he have a

[58] Lott spoke at the CCC's national conference in Greenwood, Mississippi, on April 11, 1992. When asked a few years later about his appearances before the CCC, Lott simply lied, saying he had "no firsthand knowledge" of the group. Days later, a copy of the CCC's newsletter, *Citizens Informer* (which regularly runs Lott's columns) turned up with a photo of Lott standing in front of the CCC banner, addressing the convention. Lott then issued a statement distancing himself from the group, of which his uncle is a member. Thomas Edsall, "Lott Renounces White 'Racialist' Group He Praised in 1992," *Washington Post*, December 18, 1998, p. A2.
[59] John Solomon, "Ashcroft Once Hailed Confederates," Associated Press, December 27, 2000.
[60] Adam Nagourney, "Antiwar Veteran Eager for Battle," *New York Times*, December 9, 2002, p. A24.
[61] *The Capital Gang*, December 7, 2002.

shot, a Massachusetts liberal?" Bennett responded, "The problem,
he is, and this isn't name calling now, he's a Massachusetts liberal."[62] CNN's Bill Schneider put his finger on the problem:
"Kerry is by any definition a liberal. Even worse, a Massachusetts
liberal."[63] Cokie Roberts summed it up: "But it is also true that if
John Kerry does win the nomination for the Democratic party,
that could be a problem for the party. He is a Massachusetts liberal."[64] The Scripps Howard news service put out a set of baseball-
card–like descriptions for eight Democrats considering runs for
the White House. Kerry's read, "Age: 58. Current job: Senator.
Political description: Massachusetts liberal."[65]

Nancy Pelosi, the Democratic leader in the House, found upon
her ascension that she had been rechristened "San Francisco Liberal
Nancy Pelosi." But what do the particular politics of Massachusetts
and San Francisco tell us about Kerry and Pelosi? While San Francisco is the nation's most liberal large city, Pelosi's issue positions are
squarely within her party—she supports gay rights, for instance,
but so does virtually the entire Democratic caucus. There is even
less about Massachusetts—a state that is now on its fourth Republican governor in a row—that makes it or John Kerry somehow
unusual.

In contrast, the fact that Trent Lott hails from Mississippi actually tells us something about him, putting his propensity to frater-
nize with neo-confederates and his occasional slips revealing a
nostalgia for segregation in context. In this Lott is far different
from a conservative from Idaho or Orange County, California.
That is not to say that all or even most Mississippians are racist,
but race is the central force in Southern political history. When a
Southern politician praises "states' rights" (or a Northern politician does so in front of a Southern audience), it has a distinct set
of connotations.

[62] *Hannity & Colmes*, December 3, 2002.
[63] *Inside Politics*, December 2, 2002.
[64] NPR *Morning Edition*, December 2, 2002.
[65] Bill Straub, "8 Democrats to Watch in Presidential Sweepstakes," Scripps
Howard, November 20, 2002.

Ever since Richard Nixon employed the "Southern strategy" in 1968—using code words like "law and order" to convince white Southerners that he was on their side when it came to racial issues—the Republican party has used racial appeals to gain the support of white voters. The most egregious example, of course, was George H.W. Bush's use of the William Horton story to imply that if Michael Dukakis were elected, hordes of dark-skinned convicts would rampage across the land, raping white women. Horton had skipped furlough from a Massachusetts prison and terrorized a white couple in Maryland. He was featured in Bush Sr.'s speeches and his menacing mug shot appeared in a number of ads aired by Republican groups. Although the Bush campaign is often referred to as having aired the "Willie Horton ad," none of the campaign's ads featured Horton. But the campaign did air an ad titled "Revolving Door" that showed convicts going in and out of a revolving door as a series of deceptive and false statistics about the alleged excesses of the Massachusetts furlough program appeared on screen.[66]

One appalling footnote to the 1988 campaign that has been largely lost to history is that before 1988, Horton was known as "William." Someone in the Bush campaign—perhaps Lee Atwater or Roger Ailes, although we will never know—apparently decided that "William" didn't sound quite black enough, so he was rechristened as "Willie" whenever the story was told. The press obliged by adopting the appellation. And what was Bush's response when Atwater and Ailes proposed centering the campaign on Willie Horton? He might have said, "No way. Not only is that line of attack a distortion of my opponent's record, it's a despicable attempt to play on racist fears. And it has absolutely nothing to do with what a president does." But Bush Sr. signed on with the Horton strategy, to his eternal shame.

These anecdotes don't indicate that the Republicans are the party of racism and Jim Crow, and the party as a whole is not responsible for the actions of every volunteer working for its candidates anywhere.

---

[66] For a detailed analysis of the deceptions used in this ad, see Kathleen Hall Jamieson, *Dirty Politics: Deception, Distraction, and Democracy.* New York: Oxford University Press, 1992.

But they do show the racist strain that continues to run through the GOP. And the Republican indulgence of those who pine for the glory of the antebellum South reaches all the way to the top. Let's recall what happened in the 2000 South Carolina primary, where one of the most pressing issues was whether the state would do away with the Confederate flag. The Stars and Bars had flown over the South Carolina statehouse since 1962 (Georgia put theirs up in 1956, Alabama in 1963), installed by segregationists in order to thumb their noses at the federal government and proclaim their fealty to Jim Crow. In South Carolina in 2000, the issue pitted conservatives arguing that the flag represented "Southern heritage" against pretty much everyone else in the world, who know what the flag really means. Unwilling to embrace the Confederate flag but frightened of alienating the white South Carolinians who supported it, both Bush and John McCain steadfastly refused to take a position on the issue. Both asserted that the decision should be left to the people of South Carolina—as though there was some question of a presidential directive on the flag—but wouldn't say what their own opinion was. In a debate in Columbia on January 7, moderator Brian Williams tried mightily to pin Bush down:

Williams: Gov. Bush, a few blocks from here on top of the state capitol building the Confederate flag flies with the state flag and the U.S. flag. It is, as you can hear from the reaction of tonight's crowd of 3,000 people from South Carolina, a hot-button issue here. The question is: Does the flag offend you personally?

Bush: The answer to your question is—and what you're trying to get me to do is to express the will of the people of South Carolina is what you're trying to get —

Williams: No, I'm asking you about your personal opinion—

Bush: The people of South Carolina. Brian, I believe the people of South Carolina can figure out what to do with this flag issue. It's the people of South Carolina—

Williams: If I may—

Bush: I don't believe it's the role of someone from outside South Carolina and someone running for president to come into this state and tell the people of South Carolina what to do with their business when it comes to the flag.

Williams: As an American citizen, do you have a visceral reaction to seeing the Confederate flag—

Bush: As an American citizen, I trust the people of South Carolina to make the decision for South Carolina.

Truly some heavy lifting in the evasion department. On February 15, Larry King moderated another debate in South Carolina and tried again to get Bush to reveal his feelings about the flag: "If your state of Texas then proposed the Confederate flag," King asked, "you would campaign against it?" Displaying his commitment to tackling the tough issues, Bush replied, "We've got the Lone Star flag flying over Texas. Let's talk about that issue." No one took him up on his offer.

In October of 2000, long after the primaries were over, McCain admitted that he had concealed his true feelings. "Clearly the thing that drove the decision not to get involved was polling, which I shouldn't have done," he said. "I think the right stance would have been from the beginning to say that it should come down." McCain went on to admit that he showed "a singular lack of courage."[67] This is a quality McCain knows something about; it takes courage to admit you were wrong, more so to admit you were cowardly.

For his part, Bush bobbed and weaved, keeping his actual opinion on the Confederate flag a secret from the voters. As a political strategy it worked, but on the question of moral and political leadership it was shameful. If Bush actually believed the flag should stay up but kept that belief a secret, then he finds common cause with bigots. If he actually believed it should come

---

[67] Schuyle Kropf, "McCain Regrets His Stance on Flag," *Charleston Post & Courier*, October 20, 2000, p. B5.

down but kept that belief a secret, he is an unprincipled opportunist. Either way, he's a moral coward. And reporters, ever mindful of being accused of being liberal northeastern elitists, let him get away with it.

But down in the Palmetto State, Bush knew his audience and knew how to push their buttons. When he was asked in the same debate why he had refused to meet with the Log Cabin Republicans, a gay GOP group, Bush took the opportunity to imply that McCain was a little too friendly with gays. "They had made a commitment to John McCain," he said by way of justification. It was a lie (the Log Cabin Republicans made no endorsement during the primaries) but no matter—it got the message across. Bush also told South Carolinians, "John McCain is a man who's called me an anti-Catholic bigot."[68] McCain never said any such thing, but it was another useful lie.

At one event in South Carolina, a supporter came up to Bush and complained, "Y'all haven't even hit his soft spots," urging Bush to get vicious with McCain. "I know, and we're going to," Bush responded, but noted that the smear campaign would be below the radar: "I'm not going to do it on TV."[69]

So while Bush was getting nasty, his allies were doing the real work. Richard Hines, who can best be termed a confederate activist, sent out mass mailings saying McCain wanted to bring down the confederate flag. Bush stood on a stage smiling as an unhinged veteran speaking in support of the Texas governor accused McCain of betraying his fellow veterans. And of course, he kicked off his campaign by giving a speech at Bob Jones University, whose founder denounced the Catholic Church as a satanic cult. Bush neglected to say anything about the university's policy prohibiting interracial dating. (Bob Jones U has long held a special place in the hearts of Republicans; Ronald Reagan tried unsuccessfully to force the IRS to grant the university tax-exempt status despite its racially discriminatory policies.)[70]

---

[68] Bush is shown making this statement in the film *Journeys with George*.

[69] CNN *Worldview*, February 12, 2000.

[70] Kevin Costelloe, "Supreme Court Asked to Decide Tax Exemption Issue," Associated Press, February 26, 1982.

Just as Bush intended, the vicious whisper campaign against McCain went largely unnoticed. Here is a polite description written in *Newsweek* after the election was over of the campaign waged on Bush's behalf:

> Voters were told that McCain was a liar, a hypocrite, a philanderer and a jerk. They were told he was not a hero at all but a Manchurian Candidate, brainwashed or broken in captivity and sent home to betray his comrades in arms. They were told that he had had sex with some of his jailers; that he had married a drug addict; that he had had extramarital affairs, one with the singer Connie Stevens; and that he had arranged a murder to cover his tracks. They were informed that the McCains had adopted a black child (an allusion to their dark-skinned 8-year-old Bridget, whom his wife, Cindy, had brought home from one of Mother Teresa's orphanages in Bangladesh). They were told that Bridget actually was not Bangladeshi at all but McCain's own love child, one of several he had sired with American black hookers. They were told that the McCains had to adopt because he had infected Cindy with a venereal disease that destroyed her uterus.[71]

One thing we know about the Bushes is that when the going gets tough, they get mean. They're well bred and they usually mind their manners, but faced with the specter of defeat they will consent to the most despicable actions being taken on their behalf. It happened with the father and William Horton; it happened with the son and John McCain in South Carolina. Never once did Bush stand up and tell his supporters to stop the vile phone calls and mailings; the only time he said anything about negative campaigning was when he feigned deep offense after a McCain ad accused him of "twist[ing] the truth, like Clinton." Later, before the New York primary, Bush's campaign aired ads saying that McCain opposed breast-cancer research because he voted against an enormous omnibus spending bill, despite the fact that McCain had supported breast-cancer

[71] "Pumping Iron, Digging Gold, Pressing Flesh," *Newsweek*, November 20, 2000, p. 50.

research on multiple occasions and his own sister was a breast-cancer survivor. When reporters asked if Bush really believed the assertion his ads were making, he said, "No, I don't believe that."[72] In other words, Bush knowingly approved an ad that lied about McCain. But those who run for office against men named Bush better be prepared to play hardball; outright lies and the exploitation of racism are little more than arrows in the quiver, to be fired when needed.

As ugly as the Republican party's recent history on the topic of race is, it doesn't prove that every Republican who uses the code words, the whisper campaigns, and the "ballot security" efforts has hatred in his heart. While Trent Lott may or may not be a racist, there is little evidence that George W. Bush is, at least on a personal basis. But the South Carolina primary showed that like others in his party, Bush was willing to enter a Faustian bargain, giving a wink and a nod to neo-confederates and bigots in order to win a few extra votes.

As the Republican party has become increasingly dependent on white Southerners, the party's leaders have understood that they need the votes of not only those who have put the South's ugly history behind them, but those for whom "issues" like the Confederate flag go to the heart of their identity. So come election time, they enlist the most retrograde elements of their party, assuring them that if you consider Jim Crow the good old days, the GOP is your home. To be sure, there are millions of white Southerners of goodwill who vote Republican for any number of reasons. But the GOP needs the bigot vote, too. This is not lost on George W. Bush.

When Trent Lott gave his tribute to Strom Thurmond, he forgot that he wasn't in Mississippi, but he also forgot that there is no middle ground on this issue. Saying that things would have been better had Strom Thurmond been elected president is only slightly less morally vile than saying that Europe would have been better off had the Nazis won World War II. To each succeeding generation, the

[72] Terry Neal and Edward Walsh, "Bush Begins N.Y. Swing Talking Breast Cancer," *Washington Post*, March 5, 2000, p. A6.

views of people like Thurmond and Jesse Helms seem more appalling and more distant. But the Republican party still clings to the vestiges of the Old South, mining it for votes, trotting out the Confederate flag and "states' rights" whenever an election gets close. History will record that, fortunately for our country, the conservatives lost the battle over civil rights. It will also record the moral failure of the Republican party of the late twentieth and early twenty-first centuries. George W. Bush can claim to be a "different kind of Republican," but that failure is his as well.

VAST CONSPIRACIES

When Hillary Clinton charged in 1998 that a "vast right-wing conspiracy" was out to get her husband, the Washington and media elites scoffed. "That is nonsense," said Ken Starr.[73] "Who's she talking about?" asked Trent Lott incredulously.[74] George Will accused the First Lady of "breathing fresh life into the paranoid style in American politics."[75] Mary McGrory called Hillary "belligerent."[76]

We have since learned, of course, that Hillary was right. Call it a conspiracy or simply a well-organized coalition; the fact is that Republicans have a tightly coordinated system that links conservative donors, lobbyists, media outlets, publishers, pundits, activists, lawyers, congressional staff, and the White House in a seamless web. The effectiveness of this system was most apparent during the Clinton impeachment. To trace just one thread, Richard Mellon Scaife, the ultra-right Pittsburgh multimillionaire, funded the "Arkansas Project" at the *American Spectator* magazine, overseen by Ted Olson (who would go on to become George W. Bush's Solicitor General) to dig up dirt on Bill Clinton. The *Spectator* published an article mentioning a woman named "Paula," who turned out to be Paula

---

[73] Charles Zehren, "Conspiracy Theorist," *New York Daily News*, January 28, 1998, p. A24.
[74] Katherine Roth, "'Vast Conspiracy: Hillary," *Chicago Sun-Times*, January 27, 1998, p. 1.
[75] George Will, "Conspiracy Theory to the Rescue," *Washington Post*, January 29, 1998, p. A19.
[76] Mary McGrory, "Wonk If You Believe," *Washington Post*, January 29, 1998, p. A2.

Jones; she then filed a harassment suit against Bill Clinton with the assistance of more conservative funders who paid her legal fees. A team of lawyers known as the "elves" acted as intermediaries between the Jones legal team and Ken Starr's independent-counsel office, passing information back and forth to set the perjury trap for Clinton when he was deposed in the Jones lawsuit and bringing Monica Lewinsky and Linda Tripp to Starr's attention; the ensuing investigation was then flogged endlessly on conservative talk radio and in conservative newspapers, who coordinated their message with the congressional Republicans pushing Clinton's impeachment forward.[77]

David Brock, who was the right-wing hit man who wrote that *American Spectator* article before his rejection of and by the right, told former journalist and Clinton adviser Sidney Blumenthal about a meeting he attended in 1997, well before the Lewinsky scandal broke:

> The assembled guests were from *The Washington Times*, the *Wall Street Journal* editorial board, Regnery Publishing…radio talk shows, and the *Spectator*. That evening's business was to develop ideas to help the featured speaker, Representative Bob Barr, Republican from Georgia, on his resolution for the impeachment of the President. Barr's proposal had no specificity, citing only "systematic abuse of office." Barr complained he was having "limited success" rounding up cosponsors. John Fund, a *Wall Street Journal* editorial writer, piped up. "When Congress shows spine, there will be indictments." He said impeachment was a question "not of law, but of political will." There were gestures of assent, according to Brock.[78]

While there is no space here to revisit the impeachment in any detail, it is no exaggeration to say that when Bill Clinton was elected, some on the right decided that if the democratic process did

---

[77] The coordination of the right on the Clinton impeachment has been documented in a number of books, most notably Jeffrey Toobin's *A Vast Conspiracy*, David Brock's *Blinded by the Right*, and Sidney Blumenthal's *The Clinton Wars*.
[78] Sidney Blumenthal, *The Clinton Wars*. New York: Farrar, Straus, and Giroux, 2003, pp. 334–5.

not produce the results they wanted, it would have to be hijacked. While this feeling may have started with a relatively small number of people before rapidly spreading throughout the Republican ranks, it is important to note that those who made the initial decision to wage war on democracy itself were not obscure characters, not lone nutcases yelling on a street corner. They were members of Congress, radio hosts, respected attorneys, and writers for some of America's most influential publications, all backed up with millions of dollars from the likes of Richard Mellon Scaife.

The coordination of conservative efforts began as a legitimate means of fighting the war of ideas. Beginning in the 1960s, conservatives painstakingly built a network of publications, think tanks, and political organizations to develop and advocate conservative ideas.[79] Out of this infrastructure grew a system of coordination, the clearest manifestation of which is the weekly meeting held every Wednesday in the offices of Grover Norquist's Americans for Tax Reform. Among the hundred or so people who attend are Capitol Hill staffers, reporters from the conservative press, Republican lobbyists, conservative activists, and GOP consultants. The meetings are an opportunity to share information, plot strategy, and coordinate the conservative message. George W. Bush started sending representatives to the Wednesday meetings before he even announced his candidacy for the presidency, and White House aides continue to attend. As Norquist said in early 2001, "There isn't an us and them with this administration. They is us. We is them."[80]

While many different kinds of conservatives attend Norquist's meetings (and similar ones run by Paul Weyrich), the effort is animated by a kind of warrior spirit that clearly demarcates between the righteous and the wicked. Democrats and liberals are the enemy, and they must be crushed without mercy. As Newt Gingrich told the conservative Heritage Foundation back in 1988, "This war [between liberals and conservatives] has to be fought with the scale

---

[79] This effort is discussed in detail in Sidney Blumenthal, *The Rise of the Counter-Establishment*. New York: Times Books, 1986.

[80] Robin Toner, "Conservatives Savor Their Role as Insiders at the White House," *New York Times*, March 19, 2001, p. A1.

and duration and savagery that is only true of civil wars."[81] After George W. Bush took office in 2001, Norquist told the crowd at a Republican fundraiser, "The Democrats are the Lefties, the takers, the coercive utopians....They are not stupid, they are evil. Evil!"[82]

Though they succeeded in impeaching Clinton, the right didn't have sufficient support among the American people for their campaign to achieve his removal from office. So when his term came to an end, they turned their wrath on Al Gore. That Gore got more votes than George W. Bush only fueled their rage, but they were saved when it turned out that the willingness to abandon democracy in the quest for power went all the way to the Supreme Court, and that body's conservative majority cut off the counting of votes in Florida.

Back on Capitol Hill, Republicans have worked since they took over Congress in 1994 to make K Street a Democrat-free zone; in 1996, Haley Barbour, then chairman of the Republican National Committee, gathered a group of corporate CEOs and instructed them to purge their lobbying offices of Democrats. Senator Rick Santorum now holds a weekly meeting where a group of conservatives pores over every job opening among Washington's lobbying firms; the firms are then instructed that only Republicans may be hired.[83] Meanwhile, House Majority Leader Tom DeLay engineered a re-redistricting in Texas to change the congressional map to better favor Republicans; unlike in Colorado, where a similar re-redistricting was successful months before, Democratic legislators temporarily foiled the plan by fleeing the state. In California, Republicans financed a recall drive to oust Governor Gray Davis, who had been reelected just months before. There were no allegations of corruption or illegality; Republicans merely alleged that Davis had mishandled the state budget at a time when nearly every state in the Union was facing a budget crisis similar to California's.

---

[81] Newt Gingrich, "Building the Conservative Movement after Ronald Reagan," Heritage Foundation Reports, April 21, 1988.

[82] Tom Baxter, "Speech Hints at Agenda," *Atlanta Journal and Constitution*, January 21, 2001, p. 2B.

[83] Nicholas Confessore, "Welcome to the Machine," *Washington Monthly*, July/August 2003.

These episodes demonstrate that the American right has to a great extent abandoned democratic processes as the means by which power can be achieved and sustained. Their certainty in the rightness of their cause has convinced them that if they can't win by the ordinary rules, then the rules must be changed. If they can't get more votes, then the ballots must simply not be counted. If they can't get their people elected, then district lines must be drawn and redrawn, elections must be done over until a more satisfactory result is obtained. In 2004, should George W. Bush fail once again to gain as many votes as his opponent, we can be sure they will not go quietly.

Bush's Compatriots

When the Bush administration and its congressional allies produced the law-enforcement wish list known as the USA PATRIOT Act in the wake of September 11, the Senate Judiciary Committee asked Attorney General John Ashcroft to come and discuss the bill.[84] During his testimony, Ashcroft talked out of both sides of his mouth—in one breath arguing that constitutional protections would remain in place and in the next saying that bad people don't deserve them. He invoked the terrifying specter of Johnnie Cochran, arguing that secret military tribunals were necessary lest a suspect obtain a "flamboyant lawyer." He dismissed the Fourth and Sixth amendments to the Constitution as inconveniences to be discarded in a time of crisis, but showed his unswerving devotion to the Second amendment, claiming that though he could detain people without charges and spy on them without warrants, he couldn't possibly check whether they had purchased guns. But the most notable thing Ashcroft said during his testimony was this:

> To those who scare peace-loving people with phantoms of lost liberty, my message is this: your tactics only aid terrorists, for they erode our national unity and diminish our resolve. They give ammunition to

---

[84] The name of the act stands for "Uniting and Strengthening America by Providing Appropriate Tools Required to Intercept and Obstruct Terrorism Act of 2001."

America's enemies and pause to America's friends. They encourage people of goodwill to remain silent in the face of evil.[85]

Note carefully what Ashcroft said. He did not say that his critics
were mistaken in their analysis of the effects of the Bush administration's moves to combat terrorism. He did not argue against the
substance of their critique. Instead, he accused them of aiding terrorists and giving ammunition to America's enemies. While he
stopped just short of using the word, for all intents and purposes he
called the administration's critics traitors.

Ask yourself whether you can recall in your lifetime a statement
from an administration official that was a clearer repudiation of
American values. Unfortunately, the members of the committee
were either too stunned or too afraid to respond. None shouted,
"How dare you?" None called for Ashcroft's resignation. And few in
the media took up the flag.

Critical moments demand strong words, so we should be clear:
if anyone is guilty of treason, it's John Ashcroft. Ashcroft is a traitor to liberty, a traitor to justice, and a traitor to the noble ideals
on which America was founded. Despite what he may think,
Ashcroft is not a true American patriot. You can't claim to love
America and work every day to undermine American values. John
Ashcroft has more in common with the Taliban than with Jefferson, Madison, and Washington. If George W. Bush believed in
democracy, he would have fired Ashcroft the second he walked out
of that hearing room.

As abhorrent as Ashcroft's charge that anyone who criticized
the administration aids terrorists was, it was sadly nothing new for
his party. "National unity" is a value Republicans seem oddly
unconcerned about when there happens to be a Democrat in the
White House. At those times, criticism of the government is perfectly compatible with patriotism, and national divisions are an
ordinary and expected feature of democracy. But once the White

[85] Testimony before the Senate Judiciary Committee, December 7, 2001.

House is inhabited by a Republican, dissent is a danger and unity is a value greater than freedom. Republican commentator William Bennett even argued that holding opinions other than those of the majority is unpatriotic because it creates divisions between Americans, and "insofar as these divisions prevent the forging of a single people, they also prevent the building of a true and thoughtful patriotism."[86] So the only "thoughtful patriotism" is a blind adherence to the will of the majority. This is the patriotism of tyrants. It is the patriotism demanded by Stalin, Mao, Castro, and Saddam Hussein.

But the lines had been drawn, and no one wanted to be on the wrong side. During his post–September 11 address to Congress, Bush said, "Either you are with us, or you are with the terrorists." Apparently, most Americans misunderstood who "us" is. "Us" turned out to be not America but the Bush administration. If you criticize the president or the attorney general, if you raise questions about their decisions, if you display too much devotion to the Constitution, you apparently are with the terrorists.

Other Republicans picked up the charge as well. When Tom Daschle said six months after September 11 that the outcome of the war on terrorism was "still somewhat in doubt" and that it couldn't be considered a success unless Osama Bin Laden and Mullah Omar were captured, Republicans reacted with outrage. Trent Lott said, "How dare Senator Daschle criticize President Bush while we are fighting our war on terrorism, especially when we have troops in the field." Rep. Tom Davis, the chair of the National Republican Congressional Committee, said Daschle's "divisive comments have the effect of giving aid and comfort to our enemies by allowing them to exploit divisions in our country."[87] Recall that giving "aid and comfort to the enemy" is the definition of treason.

In the 2002 election, as they had so many times before, Republicans succeeded in part by branding their Democratic opponents as

---

[86] William Bennett, *Why We Fight*, quoted in Dick Polman, "A Clash over Who Is a Patriot," *Philadelphia Inquirer*, March 23, 2003, p. C1.

[87] Helen Dewar, "Lott Calls Daschle Divisive," *Washington Post*, March 1, 2002, p. A6.

unpatriotic. Bush himself got into the act when he asserted that because Democratic senators were unwilling to go along with Bush's plan to use the Department of Homeland Security to continue his war on unions, instead favoring a different version of the bill establishing the Department, "The Senate is more interested in special interests in Washington, and not interested in the security of the American people."[88]

Republicans all over the country saw their opening: if a Democrat favored a different version of the Homeland Security Department, they would be charged with being in league with terrorists. The most despicable example was the campaign of Georgia's Saxby Chambliss, who ran ads accusing incumbent Senator Max Cleland—a war hero who lost three limbs in Vietnam, a conflict Chambliss managed to avoid with a bum knee—of not caring about the security of his country. One notable ad featured three photos alongside one another: Saddam Hussein, Osama Bin Laden, and Max Cleland.[89] (As he was making his speech celebrating his election to his first six-year Senate term, Chambliss's supporters began a rousing chant of "Four more years! Four more years!)"[90] So after the election, President Bush naturally claimed that Republicans won because of their squeaky-clean campaigns. "Their accent was on the positive," he said. "If you want to succeed in American politics, change the tone."[91] The tone has certainly changed.

These episodes provide ample demonstration of a number of salient features of partisan conflict in contemporary America and of Republican tactics in particular. First, congressional Republicans, especially the Republican leadership, are never shy about getting nasty. The mere suggestion that maybe, perhaps, it could be, that possibly something a Republican administration did was less than perfect can generate the charge of treason. Second, there is an

[88] "Bush and Daschle Comments on Security and Politics" *New York Times*, September 26, 2002, p. A17.
[89] "Bin Laden Debuts in Chambliss TV Spot," *Roll Call*, October 14, 2002.
[90] Jim Tharpe, "Chambliss Topples Cleland," *Atlanta Journal and Constitution*, November 6, 2002, p. 1C.
[91] Mike Allen, "Bush Rhetoric Irks Democrats," msnbc.com, November 8, 2002.

antidemocratic strain running through the Republican party, ready to rear its ugly head when people like Lott and Davis see advantage in it. Notice that they didn't address the substance of anything Daschle said. They didn't argue that the future of the war is certain where Daschle said it was uncertain; they didn't claim that the war could be won if Bin Laden and Omar were still at large. Instead, they argued that debate itself was improper. One may, it is assumed, discuss the war as long as one praises the president and his administration. If one takes a different position, however, one has stepped out of bounds and inched toward treason. One can have no doubt that Ashcroft, Lott, and Davis love their country; what they plainly despise is democracy. As Theodore Roosevelt said, "To announce that there must be no criticism of the president, or that we are to stand by the president, right or wrong, is not only unpatriotic and servile, but is morally treasonable to the American public."[92]

When Lott and Davis's statements drew a chorus of criticism from Democrats, the *Washington Times* responded with an editorial saying, "The reality is that these modern-day McGovernites want to silence anyone who questions their carping criticism of the president's efforts to run the war."[93] This is another clear example of the Orwellian Misdirection in action. Daschle questioned the future success of the war. Lott and Davis took issue not with the substance of Daschle's questions, but with the fact that he was being critical of Bush. Daschle and many others replied that they had every right in a democracy to debate the critical issue of the moment. They replied to the substance of Lott's critique: Lott said, You're not allowed to criticize the president, and the Democrats responded, Yes we are. But the *Times* said that it was not Lott but Daschle and other Democrats who were attempting to "silence anyone who question[ed]" them.

Only later did we discover just how far Attorney General Ashcroft wanted to go. Immediately after September 11, the Attorney General

---

[92] *Kansas City Star*, May 7, 1918.
[93] "Whiners and Losers," *Washington Times*, March 5, 2002, p. A20.

proposed an indefinite suspension of habeas corpus, allowing the government to lock up anyone it wanted without charges—an idea even the White House found appalling. Later, the Justice Department prepared in secret a follow-up to the USA PATRIOT Act. Among other expansions of police power, the legislation would for the first time in American history grant the government the power to make secret arrests of American citizens. The draft legislation waited in a few well-chosen hands, presumably to be rammed through Congress during the war with Iraq, when the nation's attention would be otherwise occupied. Fortunately for America, the invaluable Center for Public Integrity exposed the plan, making it fade away, at least temporarily.[94]

While on a visit to Russia, nine months after his performance before the Judiciary Committee, Ashcroft arranged a satellite hookup to announce the arrest in a Chicago airport of one Jose Padilla, who, it was suspected, had plotted to construct a "dirty bomb," a conventional device laced with nuclear material. It was later revealed that Padilla had been arrested a month before in Chicago, and his "plotting" consisted of doing some Internet searches.[95]

But it was fitting that Ashcroft made the announcement from Moscow, because the Bush administration's approach to the Padilla case would have made Josef Stalin proud. They declared that Padilla, an American citizen, was an "enemy combatant." He was put in jail and not allowed to speak to a lawyer. President Bush decided Padilla would not be charged with or tried for any crime; instead, he would simply be held in jail indefinitely. By way of explanation, Bush said, "This guy Padilla is a bad guy."[96]

Bush may well have been right, and many Americans frightened of future terrorist attacks no doubt found that argument persuasive.

---

[94] David Savage, "Justice Dept. May Pursue Wider Power to Arrest Terror Suspects," *Los Angeles Times*, February 8, 2003, p. A24. Full disclosure: as a graduate student in the mid-1990s I spent a summer working at the Center for Public Integrity.
[95] Lydia Adetunji, "US Makes Fresh Arrest in 'Dirty Bomb' Inquiry," *Financial Times*, June 13, 2002, p. 10.
[96] Michael Hedges, "Bush Says Military Jail Appropriate; Bomb Suspect a 'Bad Guy,'" *Houston Chronicle*, June 12, 2002, p. A1.

But this question gets to the heart of what a democracy is. In a democracy, the president does not get to decide that someone is a "bad guy" and lock him up for the rest of his life. We have a court system to preserve fairness and justice; it does not exist only for those the government decides are nice people. Whether Padilla was actually conspiring with terrorists is absolutely irrelevant to whether he should have been given due process. In a democracy, the president does not get to decide that the Constitution applies to some Americans but not to others. As the Padilla case wound its way through the courts, the Bush administration's position was that the judgment on whether to keep Padilla in jail was theirs and theirs alone, and no court had the jurisdiction to say otherwise.

By their logic, Bush could have me locked up for life for writing this chapter; after all, according to the Attorney General, people who criticize the administration "only aid terrorists." You might say, well, he'd never do that. But a free society does not rely on the goodwill of its leaders as they decide that some parts of the Constitution are inconvenient for them at a particular moment. The power to lock people up lying in the hands of the president and not subject to any oversight or due process is the very definition of despotism.

As George W. Bush has said a number of times, "If this were a dictatorship, it would be a heck of a lot easier, just so long as I'm the dictator."[97] Bush understands that there is an inverse relationship between government secrecy and democratic outcomes. When policy is formulated and implemented with no public scrutiny, it need not reflect the public will. This is critical for Bush because there is so little public support for so much of what he wants to accomplish.

September 11 gave the Bush administration permission to unleash its wildest fantasies, from the police state desired by Ashcroft to the world domination envisioned by the civilian hawks in the Pentagon. As required by law, the administration released its "National Security Strategy" in September 2002. Although the document had in the past been a dry restatement of current policy, in Bush's hands it became a

---

[97] CNN, December 18, 2000.

breathtaking blueprint for permanent American hegemony, laying out a plan for global domination that included preemptive strikes on any potential enemy. There was a paranoid strain running through it, positing America as Gulliver, hemmed in on all sides by hostile Lilliputians. The strategy describes the mighty roar America will make as it breaks a hundred restraints, followed inevitably by the fury as we crush one tiny foe after another under our angry boot.

Decades-old alliances be damned, the document proclaims that the Bush administration "will not hesitate to act alone" and describes itself "convincing or compelling states to accept their sovereign responsibilities." Herein lies the extension of "you are with us or with the terrorists"—if the Bush administration decides a nation is being insufficiently helpful, they may be compelled to accept their responsibilities with a persuasive bombing campaign. The United States, the Strategy states, must "be strong enough to dissuade potential adversaries from pursuing a military build-up in hopes of surpassing, or equaling, the power of the United States."[98] The idea that any country might do so any time soon is rather absurd, given that we spend nearly as much on our military as the rest of the world combined. But an administration official told reporters, "It's not a statement that says the United States wants to alone be militarily so superior to everyone," but that "we will not allow an adversarial military power to rise."[99] So we don't want to be superior to everyone as long as we're superior to everyone.

Amazingly, according to the *New York Times*, "A senior White House official said Mr. Bush had edited the document heavily 'because he thought there were sections where we sounded overbearing or arrogant.'"[100] If the final version is toned down, one can only imagine what might have appeared in the original. In any case, reporters dutifully praised the new strategy, describing it over and over as "muscular."[101]

---

[98] The National Security Strategy may be read here: www.whitehouse.gov/nsc/nss.html.
[99] Karen DeYoung and Mike Allen, "Bush Shifts Strategy from Deterrence to Dominance," *Washington Post*, September 21, 2002, p. A1.
[100] David Sanger, "Bush to Outline Doctrine of Striking Foes First," *New York Times*, September 20, 2002, p. A1.
[101] For some examples, see the fourth footnote in Chapter 4.

Bush's strategy is indeed muscular, and therein lies the problem for those who are alarmed at the vision of the United States engaging in one war after another to impose its will on the world. It is difficult for Democrats to argue against without sounding like wimps. Those who counsel caution, who favor diplomacy over airstrikes, who believe war should be only a last resort, are easy for the right to caricature as insufficiently willing to defend their country. But of course, Bush's Iraq war had little to do with defending anything, as we discovered when Saddam's fearsome arsenal of weapons turned out to be a fantasy. But ever since Michael Dukakis took a ride in a tank in an ill-considered attempt to show he cared about defense, Democrats have lived in fear of looking small and weak. Republicans can be counted on to frame any debate about the use of force as toughness versus timidity, the manly against the milquetoasts. In such a debate, considerations like the suffering of civilians or the unintended consequences of military action get swept away, and liberals get steamrolled.

Though they wield the tragedy of September 11 like a bludgeon, the Bush administration won't tell Americans what they knew and what they did (or more properly, didn't do) in the days leading up to the attacks. They undermine key laws like the Freedom of Information Act and Presidential Records Act, they hide even the records of whom they meet with under claims of executive privilege, they bring back criminals from the government scandals of the past, they attack the very principles of due process, checks and balances, and government openness. And all the while, their party does everything it can to prevent those who disagree with it from voting.

The Bush administration's practical and rhetorical moves after September 11 were appalling but not surprising. Most security crises are accompanied by attempts by the government to seize new powers for itself and attack the patriotism of any who raise questions. Many said that at a time like this we should be rallying behind our president, not examining his every action and word with a critical eye. I contend that the truth is just the opposite: it is in a time of

crisis, when the American people are angry and our government pre-
pares to unleash its extraordinary machinery of violence, that we
should be the most critical. We should question everything our government does, demand the truth with a clear voice, and insist that
America earn with its actions the moral superiority Bush so often
claims. When we do so there are those who will call us unpatriotic,
even imply that we are aiding the enemy. These are accusations
patriots have endured before and will again. But citizens in a free
society have not only the right but the obligation to question their
government. That is in large part what makes us free—and thus
what makes us American.

Epilogue

Fool Me Twice...

When Democrats complained in 1969 that Richard Nixon's Supreme Court nominee G. Harrold Carswell was not smart or accomplished enough to sit on the highest court in the land, Nebraska Republican Senator Roman Hruska famously said, "Even if he is mediocre, there are a lot of mediocre judges and people and lawyers. They are entitled to a little representation, aren't they, and a little chance? We can't have all Brandeises, Cardozos, and Frankfurters and stuff like that there." True enough, and we can't expect that every president will be Thomas Jefferson. But the problem with George W. Bush is not a mediocre intellect; in fact, while he may be no intellectual, he is quite shrewd. Rather, the problem is his willingness to lie, deceive, and dissemble in the service of his goals.

Since he moved to the national stage, Bush has done a fine job suppressing his well-known smirk, which communicates in a single facial expression a lifetime of unearned rewards. Like many aspects of Bush's personality and history, it has been carefully tucked away, hidden behind a complex and scrupulously maintained persona.

The Bush persona and the Bush agenda are inextricably intertwined, each dependent on the other. Without the popular vision of a president brimming over with honesty, integrity, and caring, sprung forth from the heartland and the bosom of the common people, "compassionate conservatism" would be seen for what it is, a cruel joke. The tax giveaways to the wealthy sold as a favor to the middle and lower classes would be greeted with scorn; the contempt for work and the people who do it would be noted and understood; the assaults on the environment and public health would be realized and opposed.

It may seem odd to those who value their intelligence that anyone in public life would actually encourage people to believe he isn't particularly bright. But when George W. Bush realized that his alleged lack of intelligence in the eyes of the press gave him the opportunity to lie without consequence, he knew he had struck political gold. Bush's opponents should have learned by now that the man they derided as a simpleton is anything but. Even granted the skill of those who labor in his service, were he not a politician of considerable talents Bush would never have been able to pull off the multiple feats of deception that have marked his presidency and bedeviled his opponents. As one commentator pointed out, Bill Clinton didn't destroy his enemies; he drove them insane, and they destroyed themselves.[1] George W. Bush is certainly maddening, particularly in the extraordinary luck that has followed him throughout his life, easing his path and saving him from his own inadequacies. The challenge for those who oppose him is to not let Bush drive them insane.

It has become apparent that those at the highest levels of leadership in today's Republican party, not least President Bush himself, are utterly ruthless when it comes to seeking and holding power. While they wield their institutional power deftly, they also benefit from the opposition's frequent inability to put up much resistance, whether in elections, policy disputes, or the day-to-day contest of politics.

If Democrats want to reverse the turn of events that finds them holding none of the three branches of government and faced with a White House occupied by a man they find unendingly infuriating,

---

[1] Garrett Epps, "The Court Justifier," *American Prospect*, December 16, 2002, p. 37.

the first step is to get up off their knees, stiffen their spines, and prepare to fight. This does not mean embracing the tactics of the right—neither refusing to accept the outcome of elections, nor embracing the politics of deception, nor becoming consumed by paranoid fantasies of your opponents' evil intents. But it does mean refusing to be cowed.

Bush and his supporters have a habit of arguing, sometimes implicitly and sometimes explicitly, that only they are the true Americans, and those who would oppose Bush must not love their country. Conservatives can always be relied on to charge liberals with insufficient patriotism, particularly in times of crisis, but a glance at our history shows that liberals have been the truest of patriots. America was founded with a dramatic statement proclaiming the fundamental dignity of human beings and equality before the law as a primary organizing principle of government. Nonetheless, this statement was made in a context in which most Americans— women, slaves, those who didn't own property—were given fewer rights than those who held power. American political history is in significant part the story of gradual movement toward the path laid out by the Declaration of Independence and the Constitution, the slow widening of freedom to encompass more and more Americans.

At every step of the way, the conservatives of the day—whichever party they happened to inhabit at the time—aggressively fought the widening of freedom, whether it was the elimination of slavery, the enfranchisement of women, the passage of workers' rights laws and the elimination of child labor, or the dismantling of Jim Crow segregation in the South. Contemporary Republicans like to describe the GOP as "the party of Lincoln," but we should remember that the Republican and Democratic parties were very different one hundred and forty years ago than they are today. Ask yourself this: if George W. Bush, Dick Cheney, John Ashcroft, Tom Delay, Rush Limbaugh, and the rest of the Republican leaders of today had been alive in 1863, which side would they have been on?

But Bush would have us believe otherwise. He offers tributes to the liberal progress of the past, just as he tries to undermine it. He assures us that his heart is pure, though his actions tell a far different story. He claims that he is one of us, when in reality he is anything but. He weaves a web of pleasant-sounding words meant to descend over our eyes, rendering the truth out of focus. In short, George W. Bush has perpetrated on the American people a complex and ingenious fraud, fooling Americans about who he is, what he believes, what he has done, and what he intends to do.

In January 2002, Bush visited a federally funded job-training center in Portland, Oregon, lauding the fine work being done there to help people who had lost their jobs in the recession. When Bush released his 2003 budget a few weeks later, in the fine print was a provision cutting job-training programs by $545 million. The program that funds the Portland center was slated for an 80 percent cut. "I was like, 'How could you come visit here if you're going to do that?'" said a once-homeless young man who credited the program with turning his life around.[2]

This small episode offers a portrait of the Bush presidency in miniature and a case study in the true meaning of "compassionate conservatism." In person, George W. Bush is a friendly guy, all smiles and hugs. He'll show you how compassionate he is by telling you he's your friend, he shares your values, and he wants what you want. But when the cameras turn off and it comes time for Bush to actually *do* something to help people, the compassion you heard so much about disappears.

Conservatives reading this book may conclude that well, Bush may be a liar, but he's our liar. But as Lars-Erik Nelson said, "The enemy isn't conservatism. The enemy isn't liberalism. The enemy is bullshit."[3] While liberals may find George W. Bush's presidency distressing because they disagree with the policies he pursues, there is much more to despise than just his ideology. Each of us in our lifetimes

---

[2] Jeff Mapes, "Proposal Stings after Bush Visit," *Portland Oregonian*, February 2, 2002, p. E1.
[3] Paul Baumann, "Confessions of a Book Review Editor," *Columbia Journalism Review*, May/June 2001, p. 83.

will live under presidents both Democrat and Republican, liberal and conservative. What is so pernicious about the Bush presidency is not its hard-right agenda but the fact that it is built on and maintained by an endless procession of lies, each more brazen and sweeping than the last. American citizens have been lied to before by their presidents, and those lies have inspired everything from utter indifference to constructive outrage. But long ago, George W. Bush moved well past the amount of deceit we can reasonably be expected to bear.

And through it all, the American press has stood by while Bush perpetrated his fraud on the American public. Acting like theater critics, they praise the dexterity with which the fraud is staged—the Marlboro Man brush-clearing; the flyboy carrier landing; the innumerable photo-ops crafted with the singular purpose of hiding Bush's past, present, and future and replacing them with a pleasing facsimile more resistant to critical examination. Journalists have a job that is both extremely difficult and absolutely critical to the operation of democracy, and in their attempts to do that job as best they can they are subject to unceasing criticism. But the ultimate measure of their success is whether truth or falsehood has ruled the day. As we look back over recent American history, there is little doubt which has prevailed.

As the country came together to mourn those who died and sought hope and reassurance from their leaders after September 11, George W. Bush quickly understood that the aftermath of the terrorist attacks bestowed upon him political advantages he could never have imagined he would have. And he has never hesitated to exploit the mix of anger, grief, and fear the tragedy evokes in order to accomplish his partisan goals. It gave him justification for an explosion of military spending, as he proposed spending $379 billion in 2003 on the military, then $466 billion in 2004[4]—approximately $1,640 for

[4] This figure includes the $400 billion in Bush's budget, plus the $66 billion of the $87 billion supplemental request he made to Congress in September 2003 to cover costs in Iraq and Afghanistan (the other $21 billion was for civil reconstruction). Fred Kaplan, "The Military's Bloated Budget," Slate.com, September 12, 2003.

every man, woman, and child in America, and about as much as the military budgets of the rest of the entire world combined.[5] It offered a rationale for the issuance of a strategic doctrine that was quite literally a blueprint for eternal world hegemony, a document that in any other time would have been viewed as the product of a megalomaniacal imagination. It gave him the pretense to launch the invasion of Iraq that many on the right had sought for years. It allowed him to dismiss the enormous budget deficit he had created with his tax cut directed at the wealthiest Americans and deflect blame for his abysmal economic record. Above all, it distracted Americans from Bush's string of failures, leaving him assured that all he needed to do was invoke a new threat, offer unsubstantiated assurances of its connections to terrorism, and Americans could be frightened into ignoring the true nature of his presidency. Unsurprisingly, he and his advisers scheduled his 2004 convention to take place in New York and later than it had ever been held before—as close to the September 11 anniversary as possible—to milk every last ounce of political gain they could from the deaths of three thousand Americans, an act of political opportunism so cynical that it defies description.

Things could have been different. In the wake of September 11, America enjoyed the sympathy and goodwill of most of the world; a headline in the French newspaper *Le Monde* on September 12 read, "We Are All Americans Now." It was a unique moment in history, one which with any measure of vision and skill could have been used to create a world order in which America moved with other nations to address global problems while protecting its own interests.

But secure in his conviction that American interests could only be protected if the world cowed before us in fear and servility, George W. Bush systematically squandered every ounce of goodwill that arose out of the rubble of the World Trade Center in a remarkably short amount of time.

Even in the war on Iraq, a mission he believes God set him out upon, Bush never had sufficient faith in the American people to tell

---

[5] Data on global military expenditures are available from the Center for Defense Information, www.cdi.org.

them the truth.   As on so many other topics, George W. Bush lied again and again, yet through a combination of political skill, sheer bravado, and a pliant press corps, managed to maintain the illusion that he is a man of integrity who shares the values and hopes of ordinary people. As Bush famously said, "Fool me once, shame on— shame on you. Fool me—you can't get fooled again." Of course, we can get fooled again, just as we've been fooled before, and that is exactly what George W. Bush is counting on.

But in truth, neither Bush nor any other politician can fool us without our cooperation. If we shrug our shoulders and accommodate ourselves to official deception, if we focus only on whether our side wins and ignore how that victory is achieved, if we let cynicism or apathy or fear keep us from standing up for the truth, then we have failed to live up to the citizenship true democracy demands. And we will have no one to blame but ourselves.

Appendix
The Elements of Fraud

A Guide to Key Lies and Misdirections

Introduction
xv "The President's actions and his words are supported by all but the most partisan Americans." —Ari Fleischer

Chapter 1
2 "I've never lived in Washington in my life." —George W. Bush, 1999. In 1987 Bush moved his family to Washington, D.C. for a year and a half so he could work on his father's campaign.

6 "I heard he was angry about it, and it began to weigh heavy on my mind. I would have done it earlier had I realized I had offended him." —George W. Bush, explaining why he waited thirteen years to apologize to columnist Al Hunt for calling him a "no good fucking son of a bitch" in front of Hunt's wife and four-year-old son.

11 "He went to Greenwich Country Day and I went to San Jacinto Junior High School in Midland." —George W. Bush, explaining the difference between him and his father. In fact, Bush attended San Jacinto Junior High for just one year, then went to an elite private school in Houston, followed by spending his high school years at Andover.

Chapter 2

25 "I don't remember debates. I don't think we spent a lot of time debating it." —George W. Bush, explaining that he never gave much thought to the most contentious issue of his generation, whether the Vietnam war was right or not.

27 "I heard from contemporaries that there were openings in the Texas Air National Guard." —George W. Bush, explaining the accidental happenstance that led to his obtaining a coveted spot in the "Champagne Unit" of the Texas Air Guard.

27 "I don't know if Ben Barnes did or not, but he was not asked by me or my dad. I can just tell you, from my perspective, I never asked for, I don't believe I received special treatment." —George W. Bush, professing ignorance about the means by which he obtained his spot in the Texas Air Guard. Ben Barnes was the Speaker of the Texas House of Representatives at the time; he arranged for Bush's spot in the Guard.

29 "Some recollection." —Bush's memory of his alleged National Guard service while he lived in Alabama. There are no records of his having showed up for a single day; after an exhaustive search, his campaign was unable to produce anyone who could remember serving with him.

30 "The responsibility to show up and do your job." —George W. Bush, telling the *National Guard Review* what his time in the Guard taught him.

32 "Well, that's obviously not true, and the Governor has talked about that, as have people in Alabama who were with the Governor during that period of time." —Karl Rove, responding on *Meet the Press* to the charge that Bush never showed up for his service in Alabama. No one recalls serving there with Bush.

35 "No. I admitted I was wrong." —George W. Bush, when asked if he had been given a sobriety test during his arrest for drunk driving. As he acknowledged the next day, he had in fact been given a sobriety test.

36 "No." —George W. Bush, to *Dallas Morning News* reporter Wayne Slater when Slater asked him whether he had ever been arrested after 1968. When Slater began to ask for details, Karen Hughes jumped in and declared the interview over.

36 An "occasional beer." —George W. Bush, in a hearing pursuant to his drunk driving arrest, when asked how much he drank.

37 "For too long, our culture has sent the message, if it feels good, do it and if you've got a problem, just go ahead and blame somebody else. Each of us must understand that's not right. Each of us must understand that we are responsible for the decisions and choices we make in life." —George W. Bush, just before trying to blame the Democrats for revealing his drunk driving arrest.

43 "He was a supporter of Ann Richards in my run in 1994. And she named him the head of the Governor's Business Council. And I decided to leave him in place, just for the sake of continuity. And that's when I first got to know Ken, and worked with Ken, and he supported my candidacy." —George W. Bush, on Enron chairman Ken Lay. In fact, Lay and his wife gave a small donation to Richards's campaign, but gave Bush three times as much. Bush and Lay knew each other long before Bush became governor.

47 "I absolutely had no idea [that Harken was about to report a $23 million loss] and would not have sold it had I known." —George W. Bush, on the accounting shenanigans that led the SEC to sanction the Harken corporation, and whether he knew about them before he dumped almost a million dollars worth of Harken stock. As a member

of Harken's board of directors and its audit committee, Bush received memos revealing that the company was about to report a huge loss and would have trouble refinancing its debt.

47 "I thought the captain was supposed to be the last one off the sinking ship, not the first....This stinks." —George W. Bush, responding to the revelation that some of Enron's top executives dumped their stock just before the company's true condition was revealed—just as Bush had done at Harken.

48 "I was exonerated." —Bush, describing the outcome of the SEC's investigation of his Harken stock dump. A letter from the SEC said the fact that they were not pursuing a case against Bush "must in no way be construed as indicating that [Bush] has been exonerated or that no action may ultimately result from the staff's investigation."

48 "The president is concerned about corporations in America who take advantage, set up operations outside of America, in an effort to lower their taxes." —Ari Fleischer, in July 2002. The next day, it was revealed that Harken set up a subsidiary in the Cayman Islands in an effort to lower their taxes while Bush was there, just as Halliburton did when Dick Cheney was its CEO.

49 "I challenge compensation committees to put an end to all company loans to corporate officers." At Harken, Bush received $180,000 in sub–prime rate loans from the company.

49 "Corporate leaders should be required to tell the public promptly whenever they buy or sell company stock for personal gain." On four occasions when he was a corporate board member, Bush failed to inform the SEC of his stock sales by the legal deadline.

50 "An honest disagreement about accounting procedures." —George W. Bush, describing what happened when the SEC caught Harken fraudulently inflating its profits.

Chapter 3

55 "I will repair the broken bonds of trust between Americans and their government." —George W. Bush, March 7, 2000.

59 "This man has outspent me, the special interests are outspending me." —George W. Bush, talking about Al Gore. Bush spent more than $185 million in 2000, more than any other candidate in the history of planet Earth.

67 "While Washington deadlocked, he delivered a patient's bill of rights that's a model for America." —A 2000 primary ad for George W. Bush. Bush vetoed one version of a patient's bill of rights in Texas, fought against another version, then allowed it to become law without his signature when it garnered a veto-proof majority.

69 "He's the biggest spender we've ever had in the history of politics." —George W. Bush, on Al Gore. The biggest government spender was of course Franklin Roosevelt; during the height of World War II government spending accounted for over 40 percent of GDP. The postwar champ remains Ronald Reagan, that noted advocate of limited government; at the height of his military buildup government spending accounted for 23.6 percent of GDP.

69 Gore's prescription drug plan "forces seniors into one HMO, selected by the federal government." —Bush campaign ad, 2000. Gore's plan didn't force seniors to do anything; the alleged HMO to which the ad referred was Medicare itself, which is not an HMO at all.

69 "If I'm not mistaken." —George W. Bush, alleging that Gore had been a member of the National Rifle Association. In fact, Gore had never been a member of the NRA.

69 "A little birdie." —George W. Bush, when asked where he got the idea that Al Gore had been a member of the NRA.

77 "We found the weapons of mass destruction." —George W. Bush, speaking to Polish television in May of 2003. No weapons of mass destruction have been found in Iraq.

81 "I think a way to put it would be it's unconfirmed at this point." —Dick Cheney, peddling a thoroughly discredited story about September 11 hijacker Mohammed Atta meeting Iraqi intelligence officials in Prague. Atta was in the United States at the time the alleged meeting took place.

82 "We now know that Saddam has resumed his efforts to acquire nuclear weapons. Among other sources, we've gotten this from the firsthand testimony of defectors—including Saddam's own son-in-law." Saddam had his son-in-law killed in 1996. What the son-in-law, Hussein Kamel, had told American intelligence officials in 1995 was that Saddam had a nuclear program before the 1991 Gulf War, but that it had not been restarted after the war.

83 Saddam Hussein "has, in fact, reconstituted nuclear weapons." —Dick Cheney, speaking on *Meet the Press*. No one actually believed Saddam had nuclear weapons.

84 "A very senior al-Qaeda leader received medical treatment in Baghdad this year." —George W. Bush, trying to make the case of connections between Iraq and al-Qaeda. As American intelligence officials knew quite well, the man in question, Abu Mussab Zarqawi, was not a member of Al-Qaeda but of an entirely different terrorist group.

94 "I've been to war. I've raised twins. If I had a choice, I'd rather go to war." —George W. Bush, describing his fictional war record.

94 "I want to remind you what I told the American people, that if I'm the president—when I was campaigning, if I were to become the president, we would have deficits only in the case of war, a recession or a national emergency." —George W. Bush, claiming that he had prepared America for his budget deficits. He never said any such thing.

95 "I was sitting outside the classroom waiting to go in, and I saw an airplane hit the tower—the TV was obviously on, and I use to fly myself, and I said, 'There's one terrible pilot.' And I said, 'It must have been a horrible accident.'" —George W. Bush, describing his reaction to the attacks on the World Trade Center to a child. Bush did not see the first plane hit the tower and mistakenly believed it was a "terrible pilot," because the impact of the first plane was not shown on television. By the time Bush saw any video, he had been informed of both impacts and knew quite well it was a terrorist attack.

Chapter 4

111 "Mr. Gore is a far more seasoned debater than Mr. Bush." —The *New York Times*, reporting on the 2000 presidential election debates. In fact, Gore's previous performance in debates was competent at best, while Bush had performed very well in previous debates, even besting Ross Perot.

112 "[I] brought Republicans and Democrats together…to get a patient's bill of rights through." —George W. Bush in a 2000 debate with Al Gore, describing his efforts with the Texas Patients' Bill of Rights. In fact, he vetoed the first version of the bill and never signed it into law after his veto was overturned.

113 "Fuzzy math." —George W. Bush, in the first debate, alleging that Gore's criticisms of his plans were untrue. In fact, every one of Gore's criticisms to which Bush referred were accurate.

114 "Look at the way Clinton goes out, they trash the plash." —Sean Hannity, describing the supposed vandalism of the White House by Clinton's staff. The GAO investigation uncovered that only $20,000 in damage had been done, an amount equivalent to $50 per office for eight years of use.

126 "A yearlong study by a consortium of news organizations has concluded...The winner is, and was, George W. Bush." —Matt Lauer, reporting as others in the media did on the results of an independent study of the Florida votes. The study actually found that in forty-four different counting scenarios, Gore and Bush would each win twenty-two of them.

133 "I truly am not that concerned about him." —George W. Bush, speaking about Osama Bin Laden. His communications director added, "I don't know if finding Bin Laden is one of our objectives."

Chapter 5

143 "There is some strategy to it." —Rich Bond, describing the conservative effort to spread the "liberal media" charge to intimidate the mainstream press and thereby influence coverage.

146 "Their constant attacks on conservative principles reveal just how much they hate the idea of traditional American values." —J.C. Watts, describing liberals in a fundraising letter. Rhetoric such as this is often used by the right to build contempt for liberals.

148 "The Democratic party and its leadership is dominated by elitists..." —Ed Gillespie, responding to a Democratic argument that America should use less energy.

153 "Only through a movement-wide effort and constant repetition can our voices unite in perfect harmony." —Frank Luntz. The widespread use of repetitive language is one of the most effective tools of the right to promote reactionary policies.

Chapter 6

159 "First and foremost, we got to make sure we fully fund LIHEAP, which is a way to help low-income folks, particularly here in the East, to pay for their high fuel bills." —George W. Bush, during a debate with Al Gore. Bush's first budget cut LIHEAP by 24.4 percent. The next year, he proposed cutting the program a further 21.4 percent.

170 "These historic reforms will improve our public schools by creating an environment where every child can learn through real accountability, unprecedented flexibility for states and school districts, greater local control, more options for parents, and more funding for what works." —George W. Bush, talking about the No Child Left Behind Act. Regardless of the merit of federally imposed testing requirements, they certainly represent the very opposite of "unprecedented flexibility" and "greater local control."

179 "I read the report put out by the bureaucracy." —George W. Bush, speaking about an EPA report on global warming. The next day, press secretary Ari Fleischer admitted that Bush had not actually read the 268-page report, saying, "Whenever presidents say they read it, you can read that to be he was briefed."

186 "It will allow farmers and ranchers to plan and operate based on market realities, not government dictates." —George W. Bush, upon signing the most pork-laden farm bill in history, a $180 billion behemoth by which government shields farmers from the cruel realities of the market by larding subsidies and setting prices.

193 "I value you as a person and I value you as a human being, and I want you to know, Glen, that what I say publicly about gay people doesn't

pertain to you." —George W. Bush, to Texas state representative Glen Maxey, who is gay.

Chapter 7

202 "We've got a deficit because we went through a recession....We've got a recession because we went to war and I said to our troops, 'If we're going to commit you into harm's way you deserve the best equipment, the best training, the best possible pay.'" —George W. Bush, engaging in a bit of time-traveling argumentation. Though the recession started in March 2001, it was apparently caused by a war that began two years later.

210 "Those in the greatest need should receive the greatest help." —George W. Bush, in his convention speech. According to Bush's tax plan, "those in the greatest need" turn out to be people with incomes over $300,000.

214 "According to the Treasury Department, nationwide there are more than 17.4 million small business owners and entrepreneurs who stand to benefit from dropping the top rate from 39.6 to 33 percent." —George W. Bush, arguing for his tax plan in March 2001. In fact, only 1.4% of the country's small business owners pay the top rate. According to the latest figures available at the time, only 691,000 Americans—business owners or not—paid the top rate. Only 180,000 small businesses—not 17.4 million—paid the top rate.

215 "Ninety-two million Americans will keep an average of $1,083 more of their own money." —George W. Bush, arguing for eliminating the tax on stock dividends. In fact, the typical tax cut for those in the middle of the income scale would be $289, whereas the typical tax cut for those in the top 1 percent would be $30,127. At Dick Cheney's 2001 level of income, the vice president would have gotten a much-needed stimulus of $326,555.

215 "To keep farms in the family, we are going to get rid of the death tax."
—George W. Bush, arguing for the repeal of the estate tax, which
applies only to the largest inheritances. There has not been a single
recorded case of a family farm having to be sold to pay the estate tax.

220 "It's hard for me to explain why they repealed it but didn't repeal it,"
—George W. Bush, playing dumb about the sunset provisions his
administration and its allies in Congress inserted into his tax bill to
hide its true cost.

222 "Give him a choice between Wall Street and Main Street and he'll
choose Main Street every time." —Karl Rove, testifying to Bush's
populist bona fides. Bush's plan to give tax breaks to the wealthy "is
very much pro-poor," said Glenn Hubbard, his chief economic
adviser. "That's what the president is all about."

225 "There's going to be people who say we can't have the tax cut go
through. That's a tax raise. I challenge their economics when they say
raising taxes will help the country recover." —George W. Bush, arguing against some Democrats who proposed repealing portions of
Bush's 2001 tax cut, mostly benefiting the wealthy, that had yet to
take effect. Equating not cutting taxes with raising taxes is simply
false. And no one said "raising taxes will help the country recover"—
the tax cuts in question were scheduled to take effect years later.

Chapter 8

238 "I trust the people." —George W. Bush, a statement he made hundreds of times.

239 "This order ensures expeditious disclosure of documents to provide
historians, scholars and the public valuable insights into the way our
government works." —White House counsel Alberto Gonzales, on
Bush's gutting of the Presidential Records Act, making it virtually

impossible for historians, scholars, and the public to get presidential records. Press secretary Ari Fleischer said that as a result of their restriction on information, "more information will be forthcoming."

243 "I don't think anybody could have predicted that these people would...try to use a hijacked airplane as a missile." —Condoleezza Rice, explaining the Bush administration's failure to foresee the September 11 attacks. In fact, that very possibility had been considered by security officials earlier in the year at the G8 economic summit in Genoa, which President Bush attended, which is why anti-aircraft batteries were placed at the Genoa airport and the airspace over the meeting site was closed. More to the point, a 1999 government study warned that Osama Bin Laden might send "suicide bombers belonging to Al-Qaeda's Martyrdom Brigade [to] crash-land an aircraft...into the Pentagon, the headquarters of the Central Intelligence Agency (CIA) or the White House."

260 "They had made a commitment to John McCain." —George W. Bush, explaining why he refused to meet with the Log Cabin Republicans, a gay GOP group. In fact, the group had made no endorsement.

260 "John McCain is a man who's called me an anti-Catholic bigot." —George W. Bush, slandering John McCain. McCain never said any such thing.

262 "No, I don't believe that." —George W. Bush, admitting that he didn't believe his own television ads, which charged that John McCain opposed breast cancer research.

Index

Johnson, Lyndon, xix, 3, 21, 163
Johnson, Tim, 63
Joint Committee on Taxation, 203
Jones, Paula, 88–89, 264

K

Kaiser Family Foundation, 218
Kalb, Marvin, 99
Kamel, Hussein, 83
Kasich, John, 140, 203
Kaus, Mickey, 108
Kavanaugh, Brett, 239
Keeter, Scott, 159
Kennedy School of Government, 218
Kennedy, John F., 3, 5
Kerry, John, 255–56
Keyes, Alan, 140
Kies, Kenneth, 230
King, Larry, 259
King, Martin Luther, Jr., xviii
Kinsley, Michael, 57
Kissinger, Henry, 246–47
Knight-Ridder News Service, 84
Kondracke, Mort, 140
Krauthammer, Charles, 140
Kristof, Nicholas, 56
Kristol, Bill, 26
Krugman, Paul, 56, 203
Kudlow, Larry, 140

L

Labash, Matt, 151
labor issues, 182–83
LaHood, Ray, 248
Landrieu, Mary, 149
Lauer, Matt, 126
Lay, Ken, 42–45
    contributions to Bush campaigns,
        42, 44
layoffs, 188–89
Leahy, Patrick, 62
Lehrer, Jim, 89
Lemann, Nicholas, xi
Leo, John, 140
Letterman, David, 104

Lewinsky, Monica, 264
Lewis, Anthony, 121
Lewis, Terry, 127
"liberal" press bias charge, 24, 54,
        137, 139
    "hostile media" effect and, 149–50
    accuracy of, 140–41
    as political tactic, 139
    class warfare and, 147–50
    conservatives and, 142–43, 145,
        153–54
    fundraising uses, 146
    election coverage and, 141–42
    Fox News and, 150–53
    semantic arguments, 153
"liberal elite" strategy, 12–16
Lichtman, Alan, 122
Liddy, G. Gordon, 140
Lieberman, Joe, 187, 250
Limbaugh, David, 140
Limbaugh, Rush, 25, 143
Lincoln, Abraham, 21
Lindh, John Walker, 155
Lindsey, Bruce, 239
Log Cabin Republicans, 260
Los Angeles Times, 53, 100, 125, 197
Lott, Trent, 25, 61, 164, 197, 220,
        254–56, 262–63
Low Income Home Energy Assistance
        Program (LIHEAP), 159–60
Lowry, Rich, 140
Luntz, Frank, 153, 175, 224
Lyons, Gene, 52

M

Malkin, Michelle, 140
Marshall, John, 101
Matalin, Mary, 45
Matthews, Chris, 116, 226
Maxey, Glen, 193
McCain, John, 59, 108
    Bush, George W. and, 260–62
    Confederate flag and, 259–60
McCain-Feingold campaign-finance-
        reform bill, 67

Acknowledgments

I was aided in writing this book by the wisdom and advice of a great many people. Early drafts were critiqued by Tim Bartlett, Chris Carrick, James Devitt, Todd Robins, and Ayelet Waldman. My agent, Bridget Kinsella, was an insightful reader and a tireless advocate on my behalf. Dominique Raccah, the president of Sourcebooks, had the vision to see the book's potential; my editor, Peter Lynch, enabled that potential to be realized. Finally, the book would have never been written had not my extraordinary wife convinced me that other people might be interested in what I had to say.

About the Author

Paul Waldman is a rising star in the world of political commentary. Formerly the associate director of the Annenberg Public Policy Center, he is currently the executive editor of *The Gadflyer*, an Internet magazine about politics launched in January 2004.

In late 2002, Waldman published *The Press Effect: Politicians, Journalists, and the Stories That Shape the Political World*, coauthored with Kathleen Hall Jamieson. *Publishers Weekly* called *The Press Effect* "fascinating, well documented and entertaining...Intelligent and timely, this is an important addition to the literature on media and current events."

Waldman's writing has appeared in the *American Prospect*, the *Washington Post*, *Newsday*, and a wide variety of scholarly journals and edited volumes. He has appeared on *The O'Reilly Factor* and been quoted in outlets such as the Associated Press, *Newsday*, and *USA Today* as an expert on media coverage of politics, and has been interviewed on numerous radio programs, including the *Diane Rehm Show*, *On the Media*, and the *Leonard Lopate Show*.

Waldman holds a Ph.D. in communication from the University of Pennsylvania's renowned Annenberg School and has been analyzing the interplay of media and politics for the last decade.